Urban Governance, Voice and Poverty in the Developing World

Nick Devas

with
Philip Amis,
Jo Beall,
Ursula Grant,
Diana Mitlin,
Fiona Nunan
and
Carole Rakodi

London • Sterling, VA

First published in the UK and USA in 2004
by Earthscan Publications Ltd

ISBN: 1-85383-993-0 paperback
    1-85383-992-2 hardback

Typesetting by MapSet Ltd, Gateshead, UK
Printed and bound in the UK by CPI Bath
Cover design by Danny Gillespie
Cover photograph © Nick Devas (demonstration by street traders at
City Hall, Cebu, Philippines)

For a full list of publications please contact:

Earthscan
8–12 Camden High Street
London, NW1 0JH, UK
Tel: +44 (0)20 7387 8558
Fax: +44 (0)20 7387 8998
Email: earthinfo@earthscan.co.uk
Web: **www.earthscan.co.uk**

22883 Quicksilver Drive, Sterling, VA 20166-2012, USA

Earthscan publishes in association with WWF-UK and the International Institute for
Environment and Development

A catalogue record for this book is available from the British Library

Library of Congress Cataloging-in-Publication Data

Devas, Nick.
    Urban governance, voice, and poverty in the developing world / Nick Devas with
Philip Amis ... [et al.].
        p. cm.
    Includes bibliographical references and index.
    ISBN 1-85383-993-0 (pbk.) — ISBN 1-85383-992-2 (hardback)
    1. Urban poor—Developing countries. 2. Poverty—Developing countries. 3.
Municipal government—Developing countries. I. Amis, Philip. II. Title.

HV4173.U725 2004
339.4'6'091724—dc22

                                                                2004004915

This book is printed on elemental chlorine-free paper

Contents

List of Photographs

List of Figures, Tables and Boxes

Figures

Tables

Boxes

The Research Team

UK Team

International Development Department, School of Public Policy, University of Birmingham:
Nick Devas, Philip Amis, Richard Batley, Ursula Grant, Fiona Nunan, Ben Richards, Elizabeth Vidler

International Institute for Environment and Development, London:
Diana Mitlin, David Satterthwaite, Cecilia Tacoli

Department of Social Policy, London School of Economics:
Jo Beall, Nazneen Kanji

Department of City and Regional Planning, Cardiff University:
Carole Rakodi

City Research Teams

Ahmedabad:	Shyam Dutta
Bangalore:	Solomon Benjamin, R Bhuvaneswari
Cebu:	Felisa Etemadi
Colombo:	Austin Fernando, Steve Russell, Anoushka Wilson
Johannesburg:	Owen Crankshaw, Susan Parnell
Kumasi:	David Korboe, Kofi Diaw, Rudith King, D Inkoom, K M Abrampah
Mombasa:	Rose Gatabaki-Kamau
Recife:	Marcus Melo, Flávio Rezende, Cátia Lubambo
Santiago:	Alfredo Rodríguez, Lucy Winchester
Visakhapatnam:	Sashi Kumar

Additional Study: Agence d'Exécution des Travaux Urbains (AGETUR) Benin: Blandine Fanou
Additional Study: Participatory Budgeting: Brazil: Celina Souza

The research team would like to pay a special tribute to the memory of the late Dr Rose Gatabaki-Kamau, whose untimely death in December 2000 deprived us of a most valued colleague and friend.

About the Authors

Philip Amis is a Senior Lecturer in the International Development Department, University of Birmingham, specializing in urban poverty and urban policy, decentralization and aid management. He has worked as a consultant and researcher primarily in sub-Saharan Africa and south Asia. He has recently been involved in preparing an OECD (Organisation for Economic Co-operation and Development) publication on *Harmonising Donor Practices for Effective Aid Delivery*.

Jo Beall is a Reader in Development Studies at the Development Studies Institute (DESTIN) at the London School of Economics (LSE). She is a specialist on urban social development and urban governance and has researched these issues in south Asia and South Africa. She is co-author of *Uniting a Divided City: Governance and Social Exclusion in Johannesburg* (Earthscan, 2002) and editor of *A City for All: Valuing Difference and Working with Diversity* (Zed Books, 1997).

Nick Devas is a Senior Lecturer and Director of the International Development Department, University of Birmingham, specializing in issues of decentralized governance, urban management and public finance. He has worked as a consultant and researcher in a number of countries in Africa, Asia and Europe. Together with Carole Rakodi he edited *Managing Fast Growing Cities: New Approaches to Urban Planning and Management in the Developing World* (Longman, 1993), and is co-author with Ian Blore and Richard Slater of *Municipalities and Finance: A Sourcebook for Capacity Building* (Earthscan, 2004).

Ursula Grant is a researcher at the Overseas Development Institute, London, specializing in chronic poverty, local governance and participatory approaches. She has worked in east and west Africa, and Jamaica.

Diana Mitlin is an economist and social development specialist working at the International Institute for Environment and Development (IIED) in London and the Institute for Development Policy and Management, University of Manchester. She has a particular interest in urban poverty and grassroots civil society, participation and effective poverty reduction programmes.

Fiona Nunan is the Institutional and Social Development Advisor for the Integrated Lake Management project, Uganda. She worked as a lecturer with the International Development Department, University of Birmingham, from 1994 to 2002, specializing in environmental policy and management, the linkages between environment and poverty, urban environmental issues and peri-urban natural resource management, in Africa and south Asia.

Carole Rakodi, formerly with the Department of City and Regional Planning, Cardiff University, is now Professor of International Urban Development in the International Development Department, University of Birmingham. She is a geographer and urban planner specializing in urban land and housing policy, urban management and governance, and urban poverty and livelihoods. She has worked and carried out research mainly in Africa and also in India. She co-edited, with Tony Lloyd-Jones, *Urban Livelihoods: A People-centred Approach to Reducing Poverty* (Earthscan, 2002) and, with Sam Romaya, *Building Sustainable Urban Settlements: Approaches and Case Studies in the Developing World* (ITDG, 2002).

Preface

Poverty and governance are both issues high on the agenda of international agencies as well as of many governments in the South. The interconnections between poverty and governance are also receiving increased attention. But, so far, little research has been done on these issues at the sub-national level, and specifically in relation to urban areas. With the rapid growth of cities in the South, it is clear that poverty can no longer be regarded as predominantly a rural phenomenon. Urban areas account for a steadily growing share of the world's poor people. Thus it is timely to look at how the governance of the cities in the South affects the prospects and livelihoods of the poor of those cities, and how poor people can use their voice to influence the decisions of city government that affect them.

This book is based on a three-year research project examining the relationship between urban governance and poverty in ten cities in Asia, Africa and Latin America. The research was carried out between 1998 and 2001 by a team of researchers from the UK working with local researchers in each city. The team members are listed on page ix. The research was funded by the Economic and Social Research programme (ESCOR) of the UK Government's Department for International Development (DFID).

Field research involved reviewing existing studies; interviewing key actors from city governments and civil society; holding focus group discussions with groups of the urban poor, community organizations and non-governmental organizations (NGOs); and analysing data on poverty, service provision and finance. In five of the cities (Bangalore, Cebu, Johannesburg, Kumasi and Recife), more detailed case studies were prepared on the ways in which particular groups of the urban poor had sought to achieve improvements in their situation. Annex 1 gives further details about the research process. Annex 2 lists the 31 working papers from this research and indicates how they may be obtained.

Acknowledgements

The authors of this book gratefully acknowledge the enormous contribution of the other members of the team, both in the UK and in the cities concerned. Their contribution was not just in the carrying out of the research in the cities but also in the development of the ideas and approaches used in this research, as well as in the comparative analysis of the findings.

Particular appreciation is due to Carole Rakodi for her detailed comments on the draft chapters of this book, and to Annabel Devas for her proof-reading of the drafts and preparation of the text.

The funding for this research from DFID's ESCOR programme is also gratefully acknowledged.

Finally, we would like to express our appreciation for all those in the cities concerned who provided the raw material for this book: the residents, officials, elected representatives, activists and others who participated through interviews, group discussions and provision of information. In particular, we salute those who wrestle daily with grinding poverty and who demonstrate how it is possible to survive and even prosper against overwhelming odds. We salute, too, all those who struggle to improve the governance of cities for the benefit of all and particularly for the poor.

Disclaimer

List of Acronyms and Abbreviations

AGETUR	Agence d'Exécution des Travaux Urbains (Benin)
AMC	Ahmedabad Municipal Corporation
ANC	African National Congress
ASAG	Ahmedabad Study Action Group
BCC	Bangalore City Corporation
BDA	Bangalore Development Authority
CBD	central business district
CBO	community-based organization
CCUP	City Commission for Urban Poor (Cebu)
CDC	Community Development Council (Colombo)
CDF	Community Development Forum (Johannesburg)
CMC	Colombo Municipal Council
CMP	Community Mortgage Program (Philippines)
COMUL	Local Commissions for Tenure Regularization and Urbanization (Recife)
CPATODA	Cebu Port Authority Trisikad Drivers' Association
CSO	civil society organization
CWA	Communal Water Association (Cebu)
DACF	District Assemblies Common Fund (Kumasi)
DESTIN	Development Studies Institute
DFID	Department for International Development
DWUP	Division for the Welfare of the Urban Poor (Cebu)
ESCOR	Economic and Social Research programme
GJMC	Greater Johannesburg Metropolitan Council
GNP	gross national product
GONGO	Government sponsored NGO
GRO	grassroots organization
IDP	Integrated Development Plan (Johannesburg)
IIED	International Institute for Environment and Development
ILO	International Labour Organization
KCM	Kumasi Central Market
KMA	Kumasi Metropolitan Assembly
LDO	Land Development Objective (Johannesburg)
MCE	Metropolitan Chief Executive (Kumasi)
MLC	Metropolitan Local Council (Johannesburg)
MMC	Mombasa Municipal Council
NGO	non-governmental organization
ODA	Overseas Development Agency (now DFID)
OECD	Organisation for Economic Co-operation and Development
PB	participatory budgeting

PO	people's organization
PPP	purchasing power parity
PR	proportional representation
PREZEIS	Programme for the Regularization of Zones of Special Social Interest
PRSP	Poverty Reduction Strategy Paper
PT	Worker's Party (Brazil)
RDP	Reconstruction and Development Programme (South Africa)
ROSCA	Rotating Savings and Credit Association
Rs	rupees
SANCO	South African National Civics Organization
SC/ST	Scheduled Castes and Tribes (India)
SEWA	Self-Employed Women's Association (India)
SME	small and medium enterprise
SNP	Slum Networking Project (Ahmedabad)
SPEED	Squatter Prevention Encroachment Elimination Division (Cebu)
SSE	small-scale enterprise
UBSP	Urban Basic Services Programme
UNCHS	United Nations Centre for Human Settlements (*now* UN-Habitat)
UNDP	United Nations Development Programme
UN-Habitat	United Nations Human Settlements Programme (*formerly* UNCHS)
UNICEF	United Nations Children's Fund
ZEIS	Zones of Special Social Interest

Chapter 1

Introduction

Nick Devas

City governance matters for the poor. It can make the difference between maintaining a fragile foothold in the city and being swept away into ever deepening poverty. City governance is not just about the formal structures of city government, important as these may be. The position of the poor depends on a host of economic and social forces, institutions and relationships: the markets for labour, goods and services; household, kin and social relationships; and the availability of – or lack of – basic infrastructure, land, services and public safety.

The actions of city government can make matters worse for the poor, through inappropriate and repressive policies and interventions, or they can be supportive, for example, by ensuring access to essential infrastructure and services. But much of what affects the life-chances of the poor lies outside the control of city government, determined by the market and private businesses, by agencies of the central state, or by the collective voluntary action of civil society. The ways in which these elements interact, and the power relationships involved, are critical for the urban poor as they seek to establish and improve their position.

It is these interactions and relationships – informal as much as formal – that we refer to as city governance. Our concern in this volume is how the processes and relationships of city governance affect the poor, and how far those in poverty are able to use what influence they have to achieve a better outcome.

International attention is increasingly focused on issues of poverty. The World Bank's *World Development Report* for 2000/01, *Attacking Poverty* (World Bank, 2001a) is but one example. Poverty Reduction Strategy Papers (PRSPs) have replaced national development plans as the basis for negotiations between governments in the South and donor agencies. But until recently, poverty in the developing world has been seen mainly as a rural problem. Cities have been perceived as the locations of prosperity and manifestations of 'uneven development', while 'urban bias' in resource allocation has been blamed for slowing development and perpetuating rural poverty (Lipton, 1977). It is true that the majority of the world's poorest still live in rural areas, but the rapid growth of cities is changing the balance. Already, almost half of the world's population is urban, and three-quarters of the world's population growth now occurs in the urban areas of the developing world (UN-Habitat, 2001a, p3). Urban areas account for an increasing share of the world's poor (Haddad et al, 1999), and one estimate is that by 2035, half of the world's poor will be living in urban areas.[1]

Many of those living in the cities of Africa, Asia and Latin America do so in conditions of severe poverty, without access to adequate shelter or basic services. Some 30 million urban dwellers do not have access to safe drinking water (UN-Habitat, 2001a, p14) and 100 million have no permanent home (World Bank, 2000, p48). Statistics of urban poverty are, of course, bedevilled by questions of comparability, such as how poverty should be defined, where poverty lines should be drawn and to what extent these lines should reflect differences in living costs between rural and urban areas. These are issues that will be addressed further in Chapter 2. But it is clear that urban poverty can no longer be regarded as either an insignificant problem or simply a matter of transitional adjustment.

Traditionally, economic growth has been seen as the key to reducing poverty, and there are plenty of examples where sustained economic growth has dramatically reduced absolute levels of poverty. But, as is well known, economic growth alone is not sufficient to eradicate poverty. Indeed, economic growth tends to widen the gap between rich and poor, thereby increasing relative poverty, and even in some cases worsening the position of the poorest in absolute terms. How the benefits of economic growth are distributed is critical. Governments, both national and local, play a significant role in determining the distributional aspect of growth, whether for better or for worse. Democratization and the growth of civil society offer some possibilities for the poor to influence what happens.

While economic liberalization and globalization may have improved economic growth prospects in some countries, they have generally led to increased inequality, and in many cases conditions for the most vulnerable have worsened. Structural adjustment policies, privatization and deregulation have reduced the scope for government intervention on behalf of the poor, or made that intervention more indirect.[2] Yet what governments – national, regional and local – do or do not do still has a crucial impact on urban economic growth and on poverty, inequality and exclusion. While the 'room for manoeuvre' for city governments may be quite constrained, how they use it can have a significant impact on the poor.

This research and its key message

This book is based on a study of the relationship between urban governance and poverty in ten cities in Asia, Africa and Latin America. While there has been much interest in the relationship between issues of governance and poverty at the national level, little work has been done on this at the local or urban level. Although there is a growing literature (briefly reviewed in the next section) on various aspects of the urban condition such as the livelihoods of the poor, urban development, governance, management, and so on, little work has been done on the interconnections between these elements. The main questions addressed in this research were:

- What accounts for whether and how the poor benefit from urban economic growth (or change)?
- How can the poor bring their influence (their 'voice') to bear on the agenda of the various institutions of city governance?
- What political and institutional systems, processes and mechanisms, both formal and informal, result in inclusive and pro-poor decisions and outcomes?

The key message from the study is that the well-being of the urban poor can be improved by access to economic opportunities, supportive social networks, and greater access to assets (notably land), infrastructure and services. Whether and how these critical elements are available to the poor depends to a significant extent on how city governance functions: local political processes, informal as well as formal; the influence of the various civil society organizations (CSOs) representing the poor; and the capacity of city government to respond. Thus, city governance – embracing all those involved in making decisions that affect the livelihoods of the poor – is central. Voice matters: there are places where the urban poor are getting their voice heard, but the outcomes depend on a number of factors, including the nature of the particular local democratic institutions and processes, the resources available, and the ability of the poor to organize and articulate their demands. These are all aspects which will be explored further in this book.

How have urban governance and poverty been considered in previous work?

The growing international concern with poverty, along with international commitments to reducing global poverty, has spawned numerous studies and reports (eg World Bank, 2001a; UNDP, 2000a; DFID, 1997), including many linked to national poverty reduction strategy programmes (eg World Bank, 2002b). In the past, most attention has been focused on rural poverty, but the connections between rural and urban livelihoods are increasingly being recognized (eg Tacoli, 1998; Chant, 1998; Jerve, 2001; Volbeda, 2002). Those writing about poverty are also paying greater attention to issues of governance (Shepherd, 2000; Johnson and Start, 2001; Osmani, 2001; Craig and Porter, 2003). However, as already noted, the relationship between poverty and governance at the local or urban level is a relatively new area for research.

The 'urban' literature to date could be crudely categorized into five broad but overlapping groups. First, there are the wide-ranging treatments of urbanization internationally, dealing with the general problems of urban growth and its impact on urban society, for example, Gilbert and Gugler, 1992; Smith, 1996; Potter and Lloyd-Evans, 1998; Drakakis-Smith, 2000. Within this broad group are writings on urban sociology, including urban social movements (eg Castells, 1983, 2002; Fainstein and Hirst, 1995; Walton, 1998), and the wider political context, including the impact of the current neo-liberal agenda (Burgess et al, 1997). This urbanization and urban sociology literature has on the whole treated both urban poverty and governance in fairly general and theoretical terms.

Second, there is the literature on urban poverty, livelihood systems of the poor and social capital, including the output from location-specific research on these issues, for example, Amis and Rakodi, 1995 and other papers in the same issue of *Habitat International*; Wratten, 1995; Kanji, 1995; Beall, 1995; Brown and Ashman, 1996; Moser, 1996, 1998. We may also include under this broad category earlier works on the urban informal sector and informal settlements, such as Bromley and Gerry, 1973; Perlman, 1976; Moser, 1978; Moser and Peake, 1987, to name but a few. With the focus in this literature being on how those in poverty survive, less attention has been paid to governance issues, although more recent work (eg Jones and Nelson, 1999; Rakodi and Lloyd-Jones, 2002) begins to address this aspect, as does some of the literature on social capital (eg Evans, 1996; Harriss and de Renzio, 1997; Putzel, 1997).

Third, and closely related, is the literature on civil society and the role of community organizations and non-governmental organizations (NGOs) in relation to urban poverty, for example (among many): Hulme and Edwards, 1996; Douglass and Friedmann, 1998; Mitlin, 2001b. Some of this literature addresses the interactions between civil society and the state at the local level, based on specific city experience, for example, Klaarhamer, 1989; Peattie, 1990; van der Linden, 1997.

The fourth group is the literature on urban planning and management, including analyses of housing, land, services and the environment: Sivaramkrishnan and Green, 1986; Stren and White, 1989; van der Hoff and

Steinberg, 1992; Devas and Rakodi, 1993; Davey et al, 1996; Rüland 1996; UNCHS, 1996; Vanderschueren et al, 1999 (and other papers produced under the UN-Habitat/World Bank Urban Management Programme); Werna, 2000; Freire and Stren, 2001; Hardoy et al, 2001; Plummer, 2002. These have tended to treat issues in a rather more technocratic way, in some cases with a limited conceptualization of either the livelihood systems of the poor or the political processes of city governance.

The last group is literature on urban politics and specific political processes at the city level. Much has been written about urban politics and government in western industrialized countries, (eg Wolman and Goldsmith, 1992; Judge et al, 1995), including analyses of pluralism (Judge, 1995), regime theory (Stoker, 1995; Kantor et al, 1997), policy networks (Rhodes, 1997), partnerships (Peters, 1998; Pierre, 1998), and current issues of city government (Hambleton, 1990; Sharpe, 1995). There have also been many detailed studies on government and politics in particular North American cities, including the seminal work by Dahl (1961) and more recent material from Savitch and Thomas (1991) and Imbroscio (1997), as well as some studies on European cities.

Political and policy analysis in the developing world has tended to focus on the national level rather than the city level (Grindle, 1980; Grindle and Thomas, 1990; Hyden and Bratton, 1992; Hyden et al, 2000; Bangura, 2000) and more generally on state–society relations (Chazan et al, 1992; Migdal, 2001). One stream of literature that has been growing is that on decentralization and its impact on the poor: Crook and Manor, 1998; Blair, 2000; Crook and Sverrisson, 2001; and on parallel issues concerning citizen voice and local government accountability (eg Goetz and Gaventa, 2001; Devas and Grant, 2003). But, with the exception of Latin America, writings on urban governance and politics in the developing world have been comparatively rare, certainly until recently. Significant contributions in this general area include: Stren, 1978; Rüland 1992; Mabogunje, 1995; Stren with Kjellberg Bell, 1995; McCarney, 1996; Onibokun, 1997; Halfani, 1996a; Porrio, 1997; and Swilling, 1997. However, much of this writing remains at a fairly general level, often in the form of literature reviews with limited conceptual or empirical basis.[3]

The research on which this book is based seeks to build on all of these strands of writing on urban issues in the developing world, and to provide some empirical basis for a better understanding of how the processes of city governance affect those living in poverty.

The city case studies

Generalizing across cities on three continents is fraught with danger. Every city has its own unique history, setting, culture, economy and politics. Context is everything, or nearly everything. Nevertheless, there are understandings that can be gained from comparisons, although the absence of cross-country data compiled on a consistent basis prevents rigorous comparative analysis.

We cannot claim that the ten cities on which this book is based are representative of urban conditions around the world. For one thing, they are all large cities – between 0.5 million and 4 million. There is another whole research project (or several!) to be done on small cities and towns. But our city studies can be considered as representative in the sense that they each provide rich descriptions of the critical processes, together with explanations that enable a more generalized understanding of the issues to be formed.

We selected the cities with a view to providing some interesting contrasts:

- those cities where economic growth appeared to have reduced absolute poverty (eg Santiago) and those where there had been little economic growth (eg Mombasa);
- those where there had been at least some significant pro-poor initiatives (eg Cebu, Colombo, Recife) and those where there had been minimal attempts to address poverty (eg Kumasi, Mombasa);
- those where there had been radical political change (eg Johannesburg) and those where traditional arrangements had continued largely unchanged (eg Bangalore, Ahmedabad);
- those where decentralization had given greater scope to city government (eg Cebu, Recife) and those where there had been no real decentralization (Mombasa);
- those where there was evidence of an active civil society (Cebu, Johannesburg, Ahmedabad) and those where civil society appeared weak (Kumasi, Visakhapatnam);
- those where donor agencies had played a major role in urban improvement (Visakhapatnam) and those where they had not (Santiago, Mombasa).

Initial studies were undertaken in nine cities (see Box 1.1), from which four were selected for more detailed analysis (Bangalore, Cebu, Johannesburg, Kumasi), with an additional city (Recife) being selected for a detailed study of the participatory budgeting system. In addition, a small study was conducted on the arrangement (known as Agence d'Exécution des Travaux Urbains (AGETUR)) for labour-intensive urban public works in Benin, as an example of a specific poverty-reduction initiative.

The following provides snapshots of the situation in our ten cities. Further details on poverty levels and trends are given in Box 2.1 in Chapter 2.[4]

Ahmedabad, capital of the state of Gujarat, is an ancient city and the seventh largest in India. Its main industry, textiles, at one time accounted for 80 per cent of the city's employment, but the decline of the sector, together with major restructuring, has greatly reduced this. There has been a significant informalization of the economy in recent years. Despite this, the proportion of the population living in poverty fell substantially between the mid-1980s and the mid-1990s (see Box 2.1). However, polarization along social, economic and ethnic lines has increased in recent years, with regular outbreaks of communal violence. The literacy rate is 69 per cent. According to official statistics, 96 per cent of houses have either individual or shared water supplies, and 86 per cent have either individual or shared toilets. However, these figures exclude slum

---

BOX 1.1 THE CASE STUDY CITIES WITH
APPROXIMATE POPULATIONS

Ahmedabad, India: state capital, 3 million ($450 / $2149)

Bangalore, India: state capital, 6 million ($450 / $2149)

Cebu City, Philippines: provincial capital, 700,000 ($1020 / $3815)

Colombo, Sri Lanka: national capital, 700,000 ($820 / $3056)

Johannesburg, South Africa: largest city, 3.2 million ($3160 / $8318)

Kumasi, Ghana: regional capital, 800,000 ($390 / $1793)

Mombasa, Kenya: second largest city, 700,000 ($360 / $975)

Recife, Brazil: state capital, 1.3 million ($4420 / $6317)

Santiago, Chile: national capital, 5.5 million ($4740 / $8370)

Visakhapatnam, India: port/industrial centre, 1.2 million ($450 / $2149)

Notes: Figures in brackets: national per capita GNP 1999 in absolute terms and in purchasing power parity terms (PPP). Population figures for Cebu and Recife relate to the city/municipal government jurisdiction within a much larger metropolitan area; in some other cases – notably Johannesburg, Ahmedabad and Bangalore – the city government jurisdiction does not cover the entire metropolitan area.
Source: GNP per capita data from World Bank, 2001a.

---

settlements and so significantly overstate the true situation. In addition, the quality of these services is quite variable.

The Municipal Corporation, which covers most of the urban area, has a council elected on a ward basis, with some reserved seats for women and scheduled castes and tribes. The mayor, who is elected annually from among the councillors, has a largely ceremonial role. Executive power resides with the Municipal Commissioner, a state-appointed official, and the eight deputy Municipal Commissioners. There is a great range of non-governmental organizations (NGOs) and civil society organizations (CSOs) operating in the city, including the internationally renowned Self-Employed Women's Association (SEWA), and more than 1200 community-based organizations (CBOs).

Bangalore, the state capital of Karnataka, is India's sixth largest city and among the fastest growing of the country's large cities. In recent years, its economy has been centred on high-tech industries and it has become known as India's 'Silicon Valley', sharing in the sector's global boom of the early 1990s and the stagnation at the end of that decade. But the city's economy is also based on a mass of small enterprises, many of them unregistered and dependent on fragile networks of relationships. The economic boom has widened the gap between rich and poor, with prestigious developments alongside slum settlements – with the former often forcing out the latter. Nevertheless, available estimates suggest that the proportion of households living in poverty fell significantly during the decade up to the mid-1990s, although not by as much as in Ahmedabad. However, as with any statistics on poverty, these figures are widely contested. A quarter of the city's population live in defined slum areas. More than half the population depend for water on public taps that are often located far away and may deliver contaminated water. Many houses and even whole communities are without latrines.

Bangalore Municipal Corporation was established long ago, and its boundaries do not include large areas where some of the city's poorest live. Councillors are elected on a ward basis, with the mayor being elected indirectly. The externally appointed Municipal Commissioner wields considerable power. There has been significant fragmentation of responsibilities to unelected, state-controlled bodies, such as the Bangalore Urban Development Authority. Whilst there are many NGOs operating in the city, these are often viewed with some suspicion by the poor.

Cebu City is the core part of Metro Cebu (which includes nine other municipalities) and is the capital of the Central Visayas region of the Philippines. It is a major port and industrial centre. During the late 1980s/early 1990s it experienced an economic boom, but this was followed by a downturn in the late 1990s. Unemployment is now around 15 per cent, and a large proportion of the population are employed in the informal sector. Statistics on poverty vary widely, depending on the source and definitions, classifying anywhere between 19 per cent and 77 per cent of the population as poor (Etemadi, 2001, p19 and Table A3.1). Literacy is high (98 per cent) but less than 60 per cent of the city's population has access to piped water in their house or on their plot, and more than a third of the population do not have access to proper sanitation.

Cebu has a directly elected executive mayor and a legislature elected by proportional representation (PR). Below the city government there are 80 elected *barangays*. Decentralization in the early 1990s gave the city greater responsibilities and resources. NGOs enjoy something of a privileged position in governance at all levels in the Philippines, and many are actively engaged in issues of urban poverty. There are also a great many active CSOs and CBOs in Cebu.

Colombo is the commercial as well as the political capital of Sri Lanka. Its port handles virtually all the country's trade. Despite the civil war in the northeast of the country, the national economy has performed well, with an average annual growth rate of over 5 per cent a year during the 1990s. This has been mirrored in Colombo which has benefited from economic liberalization and the establishment of export processing zones. Sri Lanka has a reputation for relatively good human development indicators and has a range of welfare programmes for the poor. Nevertheless there is significant poverty: in 1990/91, 18 per cent of Colombo's population were below the official poverty line (World Bank, 1995, p7), and this has probably increased since then as a result of ethnic violence. Around 10 per cent of the city's population live in 'under-served settlements' and a quarter live in sub-standard housing. Although almost all households have access to piped water, supplies are intermittent, pressure is low and many people have to share public taps.

Colombo Municipal Council (CMC) is elected on a party-list proportional representation system, with a centrally appointed Municipal Commissioner playing a key role. Despite donor assistance with institutional development, CMC is beset by management and financial problems. This has not been helped by political disputes with central and provincial government. Service and development responsibilities are fragmented between a number of agencies, notably the Urban Development Authority. There are some 50 NGOs, many of them engaged in programmes for the urban poor. In terms of CBOs, Community Development Councils (CDCs) played a significant role in enabling residents to participate in decisions affecting them under the Million Houses Programme during the 1980s, but most of these have become dormant in recent years.

Johannesburg is the most important city in the South African economy, based originally on mining but now highly diversified. Under apartheid, the city was divided into 13 racially segregated local authorities. In the early 1990s these were reorganized into four Metropolitan Local Councils (MLCs), elected partly on a ward basis and partly by proportional representation, under the umbrella of the Greater Johannesburg Metropolitan Council (GJMC). This arrangement proved unsatisfactory and the MLCs were abolished in 2000, leaving the city with one, very large, single tier city government for over 3 million people.[5]

The legacy of the past is one of huge inequality, and an urban structure that seriously disadvantages the poor. Slow economic growth over the past decade, combined with rapid population growth, has led to growing unemployment (between 17 and 30 per cent, depending on definitions) and increased informalization of the economy. Urban poverty may well have increased, partly because the city is absorbing more of the rural poor, although accurate data are not available. Basic service levels are comparatively high, with 98 per cent of households having a tap in the house or on the plot, and 93 per cent having a flush toilet. However, there are marked differences in service levels between areas, with some squatter settlements still having minimal facilities, and the poor encounter severe problems in paying for these relatively high levels of services.

Kumasi, Ghana's second city, has a proud history as the centre of the Asante kingdom. Traditional authorities still exercise a degree of power, notably in relation to the allocation of land. The local economy is quite dynamic, with numerous small-scale manufacturers and workshops, many of which are informal. Structural adjustment and liberalization have had some positive impact on the national economy, but they have widened the gap between rich and poor. Data on urban poverty do not exist for Kumasi, but the national figures for urban areas excluding Accra suggest a modest reduction in poverty during the late 1980s and early 1990s, although the level appears to have increased again since then. While piped water is available in most areas, the pressure is low and the supply intermittent, and most people have to purchase water from private vendors at high prices. Only 30 per cent of households have satisfactory sanitation, with 40 per cent depending on a limited number of public toilets and many defecating in the open.

Kumasi Metropolitan Assembly (KMA) is elected on a ward basis but without political parties (officially, at least). Decentralization in Ghana gave the KMA additional powers and resources but the process is incomplete: KMA's revenue base is weak; voter turnout is low; most services are still effectively controlled by central ministries or agencies; and the Metropolitan Chief Executive (MCE) is appointed by the centre. The MCE at the time of the study behaved in an unpredictable and autocratic manner, dominating the KMA and preventing the establishment of the sub-city levels of government specified in the law. There are NGOs operating in the city but many exist only on paper and none has sought to engage with city government on behalf of the poor. There is also little in the way of sustained grassroots organization (GRO) in poor communities.

Mombasa is Kenya's second city and its major port and trading centre, serving much of eastern and central Africa. It has an ethnically diverse population with commercial life dominated by Arabs and coastal Kenyans. Failure to invest in modernizing the port and surrounding infrastructure has meant that the port's throughput has increased only slowly. The local economy, like that of Kenya as a whole, has been stagnant. The important tourist industry declined due to perceived insecurity and political unrest in the late 1990s. Formal sector employment has not kept pace with population growth and the economy has become increasingly informal. In 1994, one-quarter of households and one-third of individuals fell below the poverty line (Rakodi et al, 2000, p156), and there is a widespread perception that the position of the poor has worsened since then.

Mombasa Municipal Council (MMC) is elected on a ward basis with the mayor being elected by the councillors. It has had a reputation for patronage politics, poor management, weak service delivery and the application of regulations that disadvantage the poor. In recent years, the Council has tried to engage more with civil society organizations and to be more responsive to citizens, but its parlous financial situation means that it has no resources to improve services. Although over 80 per cent of residents are said to have access to water, the service is erratic or non-existent. Only 30 per cent of households have water-borne sanitation, two-thirds use pit latrines, many of which pollute the ground water, and the rest defecate in the bush. There has been a considerable growth in the activities and confidence of NGOs and CBOs representing the poor, although the concrete results of their endeavours have been limited. There has been little external donor support to the city in recent years.

Recife municipality, with a population of 1.3 million, is the core of the Greater Recife metropolitan area, made up of 14 municipalities with a total population of 3.1 million. It is the fourth largest urban centre in Brazil, and is located in the northeast, the poorest region of the country. Economic stagnation in the early 1990s resulted in increased unemployment: officially, 7 per cent of the population is unemployed, but the real level is more like 30 per cent. There is considerable poverty – in 1991, 30 per cent of households had incomes below one single minimum wage (Melo et al, 2001, p23) – as well as a high degree of inequality. Illiteracy is estimated at 14 per cent. Although 80 per cent of the population have piped water in their homes, only 48 per cent have access to sewerage.

Recife has a directly elected executive mayor and a legislature elected by proportional representation. Democratization and decentralization in Brazil have increased the importance of municipal government as well as its resources. One of the most significant innovations has been participatory budgeting, adopted in Recife, as in many other Brazilian cities, in the mid-1990s, but building on earlier local, participatory initiatives such as the *Prefitura nos Bairros* and *Prezeis* programmes started in the 1980s.

Santiago is by far the largest city in Chile, accounting for around half of the country's gross national product (GNP). The city, like the country, experienced rapid economic growth during the 1990s, averaging around 8 per cent per year. As a result, absolute poverty levels fell dramatically during the 1990s. However, these figures disguise huge inequalities and increasing problems of social exclusion. Unemployment was around 7 per cent in the late 1990s.There is almost 100 per cent provision of piped water, and 94 per cent for sewerage, with charges related to ability to pay (in principle, at least).

The city has expanded rapidly over the years, but there is no government for the city as a whole. Instead, the city is divided into 34 *comunas*, each with its own council elected on a proportional representation basis, and an executive mayor elected from among the councillors. There are big variations between *comunas* in terms of resources and service levels. Prior to the restoration of democracy in Chile, there was a highly active civil society engaging in issues concerning urban poverty, but in recent years there has been a retreat into 'private space' and civil society has become almost silent.

Visakhapatnam in Andra Pradesh is reputed to be the fastest growing urban area in India, its population having grown ten-fold in the 40 years from 1951. It has the largest and fastest growing port in India and a substantial industrial base. However, inadequate infrastructure is constraining further growth. Employment levels and wage rates are comparatively high, although there are uncertainties over the future of some of the traditional industries. No data on poverty were available for the city, but for the state of Andra Pradesh, urban poverty was estimated to be around 30 per cent in 1999 (Amis and Kumar, 2000, p19). One-quarter of Visakhapatnam's population live in areas designated as slums. Official figures of 90 per cent of households having access to piped water are disputed; nearly half of those depend on public taps which provide water for only limited periods. A large proportion of households depend on public toilet facilities which are often not maintained properly. In the 1990s, a slum upgrading project funded by the UK Government provided basic infrastructure and services in more than 80 per cent of slum areas, bringing considerable benefits to residents.

The Municipal Corporation, which was only established in 1978, is elected on a ward basis. It is perceived by many to be relatively well managed, and has succeeded in maintaining a budget surplus for a number of years. Compared to some other cities in India, political life is somewhat subdued. The business community plays a dominant role, although 'backward castes' have certain privileged positions. Similarly, there seems to be a low level of civil society activity, with no NGOs having any direct involvement in urban poverty issues and most CBOs being caste-based organizations pursuing their own interests.

Outline of the book

In the next chapter, Nick Devas reviews the key concepts used in this book, urban poverty and urban governance, and considers how the characteristics of urban poverty and governance have been affected by the processes of globalization, democratization and decentralization. The chapter provides a discussion of the definitions and measurement of urban poverty, and the problems of making comparisons between cities. It considers the range and nature of relationships involved in urban governance, and the ways in which democratization and decentralization have altered these relationships.

In Chapter 3, Ursula Grant looks at how urban economic change affects urban poverty. The particular question addressed here is whether and how the poor benefit from urban economic growth. The nature of labour markets and informal economic activity are critical factors in this. She then looks at what city governments can do to influence both city economic growth and the impact of that growth (or change) on the poor.

Jo Beall, in Chapter 4, develops further the analysis of the differentiated nature of urban poverty and of the livelihoods of the urban poor, based on the material from the city case studies. The survival of the poor depends on complex strategies and networks of relationships which contribute to social capital for the poor. These are highly vulnerable to external intervention, however well intended, so that a proper understanding of the livelihoods of the poor is a prerequisite for good urban governance. Beall also considers the problems of access and exclusion, and the limits to the social resources of the poor.

In Chapter 5, Carole Rakodi analyses urban political processes, as revealed in the city case studies. She considers the changing political context in the cities, the forms of urban democracy, including structures and processes, and mechanisms for extending citizen participation. She then goes on to analyse the various actors, their power relationships, strategies and political practices, in order to identify the ways in which the voices of the poor may be heard. She concludes by presenting a possible typology of urban political systems, differentiated on the basis of the relationships between citizens, civil society and the local state. These may be characterized by ad hoc personal favours, clientelistic relationships with those in power or more open negotiation and political bargaining, depending on how deeply democratic rights are entrenched in political culture, structures and practices.

Chapter 6 focuses on city government itself, and Nick Devas analyses the extent to which city governments in the case cities have both the capacity and the willingness to respond to the needs of the urban poor. City governments face serious constraints in terms of their jurisdictions, their mandate, their staff and particularly their finances. But there are examples amongst the case studies where city governments have been able to improve their financial position, overcome some of the constraints and adopt a more responsive and participatory approach to the urban poor.

In Chapter 7, Diana Mitlin looks at the role of civil society in relation to urban poverty. It is fashionable to see civil society as the counterweight to government in representing the interests of the poor. Yet grassroots organizations (GROs)[6] have many limitations, and may be far from representative of the urban poor. NGOs, too, are often viewed with suspicion by those they claim to serve. Nevertheless, there are examples from the case cities where GROs and NGOs have played a role in influencing city policies and practices in favour of the poor. These cases are critically analysed, as well as those where NGOs and CBOs have been less successful.

Philip Amis looks at the particular issue of city governments' approach to the informal sector in Chapter 8. All too often, city governments adopt a repressive policy towards informal sector trading, and even where they officially claim to favour the poor, interventions often have damaging effects on the fragile and location-specific income opportunities of the poor. Amis reviews examples from the city studies where the voice of the urban poor has had an influence in redirecting the policies and practices of city authorities in relation to the informal sector. He argues that, in the end, democratic accountability is the strongest bulwark against 'bad governance'.

Chapter 9 focuses on the issue of access to land, infrastructure and services. Fiona Nunan and Nick Devas examine the inadequacies of basic infrastructure and services in the case cities, and the impact of these on the poor. Access to land is crucial, not just for housing but also for the scope that it provides for economic activities. Access to basic infrastructure and services probably has a greater positive impact on the poor than most welfare programmes. Nunan and Devas review alternative approaches for improving access for the poor to land and basic services, and report on the ways in which city governments in the case cities have or have not sought to address the needs of the poor.

In the final chapter, Nick Devas presents a summary comparison between the ten cities in terms of a number of indicators considered in this study. He then reviews the main conclusions from the study, based on the original research questions, and identifies key policy implications – for elected representatives, city officials, community organizations, NGOs and donor agencies. He concludes with some suggested priorities for future research.

Notes

1   From Ravaillon, 2001. Measuring urban poverty is fraught with difficulties, as will be discussed in Chapter 2, and forecasting urban poverty depends on a host of assumptions. Nevertheless, it is clear that the number of urban dwellers living in poverty is increasing rapidly, as is the urban share of world poverty.
2   There is evidence that structural adjustment programmes have been accompanied by increased urban poverty (Moser et al, 1993) and have exerted a greater downward pressure on urban incomes than rural incomes, at least in Africa (Becker et al, 1994).

3   A couple of exceptions are Stren's detailed study of city government and politics in
     Mombasa in the 1960s (Stren, 1978), and Rüland's studies of cities in southeast
     Asia (Rüland, 1992).
4   Unless otherwise stated, data in this section (and elsewhere in this book) are taken
     from the city case studies.
5   Since then, 11 regional structures have been introduced within the metropolitan
     area.
6   Mitlin mainly uses the term grassroots organization, while other authors tend to use
     the term community-based organization.

Chapter 2

Urban Poverty and Governance in an Era of Globalization, Decentralization and Democratization

Nick Devas

This chapter unpacks two of the key concepts in this research: urban poverty and urban governance. It looks at how these concepts have been treated in the literature, and considers how the characteristics of urban poverty and urban governance have been affected by the current processes of globalization, decentralization and democratization.

Urban poverty

Defining and measuring urban poverty

A fundamental difficulty for research of this sort is the inadequacy of statistics on poverty at city level. While some cities have data about the numbers of people falling below a given 'poverty line' at a particular point in time, few have consistent data over time, let alone data on the more sophisticated indicators of the extent and nature of poverty. Nor are the available statistics in a form that is readily comparable across cities.

The first issue is how poverty is defined. Conventionally, a distinction is drawn between absolute poverty and relative poverty. The former relates to those who do not have sufficient income to afford a minimum level of nutrition and basic needs, while the latter is concerned with the position of the poor in relation to the rest of society, and so is an indicator of the degree of inequality. The conventional measure of absolute poverty is the headcount index, which indicates the numbers falling below a specified poverty line. This has the merit of simplicity and so is easily understood, but there are always debates about where the line should be set for a particular country or city. Using the international standard poverty line of $1 per day permits some comparison between countries, albeit very crude. Such measures of poverty suffer from a number of serious problems:

- the question of how, and by whom, the basket of basic needs is defined on which the poverty line is set, and the extent to which this reflects the perceptions of the poor themselves about what constitutes minimum needs;
- national poverty lines are, to a certain extent, politically determined, to show either a high or low level of poverty (depending on the purpose), and either an improving or worsening situation;
- a poverty line is inevitably arbitrary, and there may be a large proportion of the population falling just above the line but highly vulnerable to slipping back into poverty; some countries adopt more than one line in order to try to capture this;
- the international line is particularly arbitrary, even where attempts are made to adjust for differences between countries in relative purchasing power;
- a single figure for poverty says nothing about the depth of poverty – that is, how far the poor fall below the poverty line; one approach to this is to compute a figure for the 'poverty gap' which measures the additional income needed by the poor to rise above the poverty line;
- headcount and poverty gap indexes measure only income poverty and take no account of other aspects of deprivation, such as inadequate access to basic services, social exclusion and lack of voice that may be just as important to the poor as inadequate income;
- even as a measure of the economic position of the poor, monetary income is problematic, since not all incomes are in monetary form and the incomes of the poor are generally highly erratic; those who have an 'adequate' income one month may find themselves destitute the next as a result of ill health, loss of a family member or collapse of income earning activity.

In relation to data on urban poverty, two further issues arise:

- whether an adequate adjustment is made for the considerably greater costs of living for those in urban areas compared to rural areas, for example, for housing, water, sanitation, waste disposal, transport, etc; Satterthwaite (1997) concludes that international figures massively underestimate the extent of urban poverty;[1]

- how 'urban' is defined, since many of the poorest urban residents live outside the official municipal boundaries, and the distinction between urban and rural is often somewhat arbitrary.

In order to address the inadequacies of income measures of poverty, other indicators of quality of life can be used, such as infant mortality, life expectancy, illiteracy and access to water and sanitation. Such indicators can be a useful counterweight to crude measures of income, but they are rarely available below the national level. Nor are they unproblematic. For example, published statistics on the availability of water tend to overstate the position by recording all those who have access to a tap even though water may flow only intermittently – or not at all – through those taps. Average figures also tell us little about the position of the poor.

Relative poverty, by contrast, is concerned with the distribution of income, and with the share of national income received by the poor – usually the poorest 10–30 per cent of the population. By definition, there will always be some degree of relative poverty, since there will always be a poorest 10 per cent of the population, whether or not those concerned live in absolute poverty. Nevertheless, people's perceptions of their own poverty have as much to do with how their situation compares with the general standard of living as it does with achieving a minimum level of nutrition. Thus both measures can help to illuminate the position of the poor. Absolute and relative poverty can move in opposite directions – and often do, as economic growth lifts some out of absolute poverty but widens the gap between rich and poor.

The conventional ways of presenting relative poverty information are through a Lorenz curve (which plots the share of income received by each segment of the population) and a Gini index of income distribution. A Gini index of zero represents perfect equality, while an index of one represents complete inequality. It is notable that national level Gini indexes tend to be much higher – that is, indicating greater inequality – in Latin America (typically 0.50–0.65) and Africa (typically 0.40–0.60) than in Asia (typically 0.35–0.45) and OECD (Organisation for Economic Co-operation and Development) countries (typically 0.25–0.40). For our case study countries, Gini indexes range from 0.59 for South Africa and Brazil to 0.38 for India and 0.34 for Sri Lanka (World Bank, 2001b, Table 2.7). Such data are rarely available at city level, but if they were, it is likely that Gini indexes would be considerably higher in urban areas than for nations as a whole, reflecting the greater range of incomes in urban areas compared to rural areas.

The next problem is measuring poverty. This covers several of the issues already referred to, such as how poverty lines are defined and what is included. There are considerable difficulties in conducting surveys to measure poverty, both in relation to the poor, whose incomes may be extremely variable, and in relation to the rich who are generally adept at disguising their incomes. For the sake of comparability over time, methods and measures need to be applied consistently, but adjustments also have to be made to reflect changed patterns of expenditure needs and purchasing power of currency. Some countries, such as India, have well established methods for measuring poverty, but even so there are many questions about the reliability of the data produced. A particular problem in relation to urban level statistics is that they are often based on sample surveys from a number of urban centres, with the result that there is insufficient data about any one city for a city level analysis.

Writers such as Chambers (1995) and Satterthwaite (1995), have criticized conventional approaches to measuring poverty as reductionist, not only for measuring only what is measurable, thereby establishing the measurable as being what is important, but also for ignoring the perceptions of the poor themselves about what constitutes poverty. As a result of focusing on narrow measures of income poverty, professional policy prescriptions tend to emphasize formal income generation, ignoring the livelihood systems of the poor. In recent years, participatory poverty assessments have gained acceptance as a way of obtaining a more informed view about the nature, extent and causes of poverty, taking greater account of the perceptions of the poor themselves.

The problems of defining and measuring poverty over a period of time are well illustrated in Cebu. There have been a number of assessments of urban poverty in that city over the past decade. The official statistics show both a relatively low level of urban poverty and a decline in the level of poverty. Meanwhile, other assessments by independent researchers using multiple dimensions of poverty, including participatory assessments by the urban poor, show not only much higher levels of poverty but also that urban poverty is increasing. While differences in the incidence of poverty can be explained in terms of where the poverty line is drawn, differences in the trend are more difficult to explain. Thus, data on poverty always have to be treated with great caution.

What has been happening to urban poverty?

Whatever the limitations of headcount poverty measures, they do provide at least some indication of the scale of the problem. Figures produced by the World Bank suggest that the proportion of the world's population living in poverty (defined as having less than $1 per day) declined from 28.3 per cent in 1987 to 24.0 per cent in 1998, although the reduction was much smaller if China were excluded (World Bank, 2001b, Table 1.1). However, the actual number living in poverty was virtually unchanged at 1.2 billion, as a result of population growth (and the number increased if China were excluded). Improvements in east Asia were offset by worsening situations in south Asia, central Asia and sub-Saharan Africa.

Unfortunately, even such crude statistics are not available for urban poverty. The United Nations Human Settlements Programme (UN-Habitat) (UNCHS, 1996) suggests, based on country studies, that between a third and a half of the urban population could be regarded as living in poverty. That would suggest a figure of between 700 million and 1 billion in 2000.[2] In terms of trends, there is some evidence to suggest that the proportion of the urban population in poverty declined during the 1970s and 1980s, at least in Asia (Pernia, 1994),

Table 2.1 *Urban poverty in case study countries*

Country	Year	Urban population below poverty line	
		Percentage	Number (millions)
India	1972/3	41	47.3
India	1994	31	74.9
Sri Lanka	1978/9	19	0.6
Sri Lanka	1995/6	15	0.6
Philippines	1971	41	4.9
Philippines	1997	22	8.9
Kenya	1992	29	2.9
Ghana	1992	27	2.1
Brazil	1998	14	18.9

Source: 1990s data from World Bank, 2001b, Table 2.6, using urban population data from UN-Habitat, 2001a, to calculate the last column; 1970s data from Pernia (1994, p24)

although the absolute numbers living in poverty did not decrease (and in many cases went up) as a result of urban population growth. More recently, the proportion of the urban population living in poverty has probably been increasing, with the absolute numbers in poverty increasing substantially, as a result of structural adjustment and the economic downturn in Asia.

Table 2.1 presents basic headcount data for urban poverty in the case study countries (except Chile). This shows between 14 and 30 per cent of the urban population being below the nationally defined poverty line in the 1990s. In the light of the comments made in the previous section about the limitations of urban poverty data, it seems likely that these figures underestimate the extent of urban poverty. Table 2.1 also shows, for the three countries for which comparable data are available from the 1970s, that even where the percentage of the urban population below the poverty line has fallen significantly, the numbers in poverty can increase – and increase substantially. This encapsulates the problem for city governments: even where they are successful in promoting economic growth and implementing policies which enable the poor to escape poverty, in-migration of the rural poor continues to add to the numbers of the poor in cities. Indeed, the greater the success of the city in dealing with poverty, the more attractive it becomes for the rural poor.

City-level data on urban poverty, as already noted, are in most cases incomplete and out of date. For some cities, like Kumasi, Johannesburg and Visakhapatnam, even the most basic data on levels of urban poverty are unavailable, let alone data on trends or any more sophisticated measures. Box 2.1 summarizes the available data from the city case studies.

The differentiated nature of urban poverty

The discussion thus far has referred to the urban poor in statistical terms, as an undifferentiated mass. This is a far from adequate depiction of a complex issue. We have noted that deprivation involves far more than income poverty and includes vulnerability to economic and social shocks, insecurity, inadequate

BOX 2.1 CITY LEVEL DATA ON URBAN POVERTY

Ahmedabad. The proportion of the urban population living in poverty in India as a whole declined significantly over the 20 years up to the mid-1990s, but the numbers living in poverty increased substantially. Data for the state of Gujarat as a whole show a figure of 28 per cent of the urban population falling below the poverty line in 1993/4 (Dutta with Batley, 1999, Table 5.1, quoting Malhotra, 1997). In Ahmedabad itself, poverty has reduced substantially: the proportion of households in the lowest income category (less than Rs 25,000 per household per year at constant 1995/6 prices) fell from 35 per cent in 1985/6 to 11 per cent a decade later (Rao and Natrajan, 1996 and Natrajan, 1998, quoted in Dutta, 2000, p17).

Bangalore. For the state of Karnataka as a whole, estimates for 1993/4 placed 40 per cent of the urban population below the poverty line (Dutta with Batley, 1999, Table 5.1). In Bangalore, the proportion of households in the lowest income category (less than Rs 25,000 per year at constant 1995/6 prices) fell from 37 per cent in 1985/6 to 22 per cent in 1995/6 (Rao and Natrajan, 1996 and Natrajan, 1998, quoted in Dutta, 2000, p17).

Cebu. There is much debate among researchers about what has been happening to poverty in Cebu. Official statistics show the proportion of families below the poverty line in Cebu City to have declined from 34 per cent in 1985 to 19 per cent in 1997 (Etemadi, 2001, Table A3.1). Alternative statistics from research organizations and the city's own Department for the Welfare of the Urban Poor estimate the proportion of those in poverty to be around 65 to 70 per cent in 1995 (Etemadi, 1999, p29). The difference is mainly about where the poverty line is drawn. However, there are also differences of view about whether poverty is increasing or reducing. The National Statistical Office's Family Income and Expenditure Survey classified around 60 per cent of Cebu's population as being 'poor' or 'very poor' in 1991 (below the threshold of 60,000 pesos per year for a family of four). Using the same threshold, adjusted using the consumer price index, shows the proportion to have fallen to around 40 per cent, but according to the survey's categories more than 67 per cent were classified as 'poor' or 'very poor' in 1997 (Etemadi, 2001, Tables A3.3 and A3.5). In addition, the proportion of total income received by the poorest 30 per cent of the population has declined from 10.6 per cent to 10.1 per cent over that six-year period.

Colombo. The proportion of the population living below the poverty line in Colombo is estimated to have increased from 16 per cent in 1985/6 to 18 per cent in 1990/91, with the poverty gap also increasing during that period (World Bank, 1995, p7, quoted in Fernando et al, 1999, Table 3). This is despite a significant reduction in urban poverty in Sri Lanka generally between the late 1970s and the mid-1980s (Mills and Pernia, 1994, p24).

Johannesburg. No data were available from the Johannesburg study. Various estimates at the national level put between 39 and 49 per cent of the population below the poverty line in the early to mid-1990s, and indicate a slight decline in poverty since the 1970s (Beall et al, 1999, p22). Urban poverty is usually quoted as being less than half the national rate, but the basis for that is disputed (ibid, p15). South Africa has one of the most unequal income distributions in the world, with a Gini index of 0.59. Although overall inequality has reduced slightly in recent years, unemployment has increased, particularly for the unskilled, and there has been greater polarization of incomes within racial groups.

Kumasi. Again, no data are available on poverty in Kumasi. National level data for urban poverty (excluding the capital city) show a slight decline in those below the poverty line from 33 per cent in 1988 to 28 per cent in 1992 (Korboe et al, 1999, p187). However, the impact of continuing structural adjustment, together with economic mismanagement, is likely to have worsened urban poverty in the last ten years.

Mombasa. The 1994 Welfare Monitoring Survey identified 24 per cent of households and 32 per cent of individuals as falling below the poverty line in Mombasa. Evidence from the Kenyan Participatory Poverty Assessment suggests that poverty has been getting worse (Gatabaki-Kamau et al, 1999, pp25–26).

Recife. Brazil is another country with a highly unequal distribution of income. For the country as a whole, the proportion of the urban population falling below the poverty line increased from 23 per cent in 1990 to 25 per cent in 1996 (Melo et al, 2001, Table 4). Over the same period, the share of national income received by the poorest 50 per cent of urban residents fell marginally from 12.8 per cent to 12.3 per cent. For Recife itself, 44 per cent of the population were defined as poor in 1991, while 30 per cent of household heads received less than the official minimum salary (ibid, Tables 11 and 12).

Santiago. Among our case countries, Chile shows the greatest reduction in urban poverty, from 45 per cent below the poverty line in 1987 to 23 per cent in 1996 (the poverty line being defined as twice the cost of a basic basket of food sufficient to meet minimum nutritional requirements, Rodríguez and Winchester, 1999, pp33–34). During that period, economic growth in Chile was sustained at over 6.5 per cent per year. However, the good performance during that decade has to be placed against the massive increase in poverty that took place in the 1980s, and the slowdown in poverty reduction that has happened since the mid-1990s. Overall, income distribution has slightly worsened during the 1990s. There are also large numbers who are just above the poverty threshold who are extremely vulnerable to any increase in unemployment. For Santiago itself, the proportion living below the poverty line fell from 33 per cent in 1990 to 15 per cent in 1998 (Dockemdorff et al, 2000, p171). But citywide statistics mask considerable intra-city variations: the proportion below twice the poverty line varies between municipalities from under 2 per cent to nearly 30 per cent.

Visakhapatnam. Specific data are not available for Visakhapatnam, but figures for the state of Andra Pradesh indicate that the proportion of the urban population below the poverty line fell from 39 per cent in 1987 to 33 per cent in 1992 (Amis and Kumar, 2000, p190). In 1999, the State Government of Andra Pradesh indicated that 29.5 per cent of the state's urban population should be regarded as being below the urban poverty line (Kumar and Amis, 1999, p19).

access to essential services, social exclusion and powerlessness. The impact of these aspects of deprivation, and the ways in which individuals in poverty experience them, vary according to gender, ethnicity, age and family circumstances. Some forms of deprivation are location-specific (eg access to services); others are particular to certain groups (the homeless, the elderly). Even within households the experience of poverty can vary: there is ample evidence of intra-household differences in poverty, particularly in terms of gender and age (eg Kyomuhendo, 1999).

It is important to recognize the differentiated nature of poverty, deprivation and vulnerability. It cannot be assumed that the poor all have the same needs and interests just because they are poor. Attempts to address poverty in a generalized way are likely to fail to address the particular needs of specific groups of the poor. For example, general pro-poor policies that help some may have no impact on the poorest. The fact that the poor have differing, and often competing, interests makes it difficult to build effective civil society organizations of the poor. Rivalries and conflicting interests undermine the solidarity that is needed to bring about political change. This is illustrated in a number of the city case studies.

It is also important to recognize and understand the livelihood systems of the poor – and of the various groups of the poor. Poverty interventions by city governments, non-governmental organizations (NGOs) and donors need to be built on this understanding (Jones, 1999). Considerable progress has been made in this area, but not much of this understanding has yet filtered through to those who make decisions in national or city government. Research among the urban poor has demonstrated the complex arrangements and networks which those in poverty use in order to survive. These networks often cross the urban–rural divide. A useful analytical approach here is the assets–vulnerability framework (Moser, 1998; Rakodi, 1999a). This identifies the various forms of 'capital' – natural, physical, financial and social – which the poor make use of in maintaining their livelihoods, and the ways in which these forms of capital are vulnerable to risks and shocks. The framework enables an analysis to be made of how assets can be increased and vulnerability reduced. We will return to these issues particularly in Chapters 4 and 8.

Countering 'poverty pessimism'

In many cities the position of the poor is getting worse rather than better. Nevertheless, we need to challenge some of the more dire prognostications of the 'poverty pessimists' who claim that whatever happens, the poor always end up worse off. This is a form of economic and political determinism which argues that, because the poor are vulnerable, lacking resources and voice, virtually any change and any intervention renders them worse off. It is true that many changes and many interventions increase rather than reduce poverty, but this is not inevitable. Certainly, economic growth may increase relative poverty even while lifting some out of absolute poverty, since economic growth is often accompanied by a widening gap between rich and poor. But sustained economic growth can reduce absolute poverty over time, especially when combined with redistributive measures. The evidence is that economic growth has a greater impact on poverty where the distribution of income and wealth is relatively even, as in much of Asia, than where it is highly unequal, as in much of Latin America (World Bank, 2001a).

The debate over structural adjustment continues to rage (Sahn et al, 1997; Dijkstra and Donge, 2001). Its proponents argue that economic liberalization and institutional reform are necessary in order to create the conditions for longer-term growth from which all can benefit, including the poor. But economic liberalization can upset the fragile livelihoods of many of the poor and so lead to increased poverty in the short and even medium-term, unless countervailing measures are taken. Poorly designed interventions, even where they are intended to help the poor, may adversely affect some by destabilizing their fragile livelihood systems. Nevertheless, there are plenty of examples of interventions, by national governments, city governments or NGOs, that have enabled many of the poor to access new income opportunities and improve their situation.

Another version of 'poverty pessimism' argues that economic and political élites always obstruct reforms that might benefit the poor. It is true that the rich will be quick to defend their interests against attempts to redistribute resources. But there are also enlightened voices among the élite, whether out of genuine concern, self-interest, or the need to demonstrate responsiveness to the poor majority in order to achieve election to office. As Moore (1999) argues, experience demonstrates that economic and political reforms can be achieved by strategic alliances between the poor and sections of the élite. There are examples from our case studies of the urban poor organizing themselves, sometimes with the support of NGOs, making their voice heard, building alliances, and thereby succeeding in making small but perceptible gains. The question explored throughout this research is how the urban poor have been able to take advantage of the opportunities open to them and use whatever avenues of influence they have to assert their claims. There are enough examples from the cities concerned to show that it is not inevitable that the position of the poor always worsens.

Urban governance

The term governance has been widely adopted in the discourse of international development in recent years, but with varying connotations. It is often associated with normative values, as in the term 'good governance' which features so heavily in the discourse of donor agencies (Leftwich, 2000; World Bank, 1997; DFID, 1997). UN-Habitat (2001b), in its Global Campaign for Urban Governance, identifies a number of norms and principles:

- participation;
- decentralization;
- equity;
- inclusion;
- accountability;
- responsiveness to civil society;
- efficiency of service delivery;
- sustainability;
- security.

While there is widespread agreement on these principles (eg United Nations Development Programme (UNDP), 1997a, 2000b; Friedmann, 1998), the aim of the present research has been to identify what *is* rather than to prescribe what *ought to be*.

In this volume, we use the term 'governance' in a neutral sense to refer to the range of relationships between civil society and the state (McCarney et al, 1995; Swilling, 1997). According to Halfani (1997, p147), 'Governance provides the institutional framework within which the civic public realm is managed'.

The United Nations Development Programme (UNDP) defines governance as:

> '*the exercise of political, economic and administrative authority to manage a nation's affairs. It is the complex mechanisms, processes, relationships and institutions through which citizens and groups articulate their interests, exercise their rights and obligations and mediate their differences.*' (UNDP, 1997b, p9)

According to Stoker, governance is:

> '*the action, manner or system of governing in which the boundary between organizations and public and private sectors has become permeable... The essence of governance is the interactive relationship between and within government and non-government forces.*' (Stoker, 1998, p38)

It is, therefore, a much broader concept than government, which Stoker defines as 'the formal institutional structure and location of authoritative decision-making in the modern state' (ibid, p34). The standard view until relatively recently was that governments had both the authority and the capacity to govern effectively and to implement their policies and plans. The increased use of the term governance is a recognition that this view of government is no longer valid, if it ever was, and that outcomes depend on the interaction between many actors. Power is fragmented, and not a state monopoly, so that plans and policies can only be achieved through a degree of consensus and partnership. According to UN-Habitat,

> '*Today's governance takes place in a more polycentric system of actors in which the state is less dominant than before. The multiplicity of actors complicates policy-making since no single actor is legitimate enough to direct societal change. Consensus is no longer given by virtue of legitimacy granted to the state's actions but must be socially constructed. This requires alliances, coalitions and compromises.*' (UN-Habitat, 2001b, pp61–62)

Hyden (1992, p12) identifies four essential properties of governance:

- trust (between the various groups in society about the nature and purposes of political action, including the ability to cooperate across basic divisions in society);
- reciprocity (the quality of social interaction among members of a political community, including the formation and operation of associations);
- accountability (the effectiveness of the processes by which the governed can hold the governors accountable, without which trust and reciprocity cannot be sustained);

- authority (effective political leadership which resolves citizens' problems and sustains legitimacy in the public realm).

Hyden's framework has, however, been criticized by Swilling as being too state-centric, under-representing the impact of non-state modes of governance over the distribution of urban resources (Swilling, 1997, p6).

Our analysis of urban governance includes a whole range of actors and institutions, and it is the relationships and interactions between them that determine what happens within the city. The actors and institutions involved include: private sector businesses, both corporate and informal; civil society, including community-based organizations, NGOs, political parties, religious groups, trade unions and trade associations; and the whole range of governmental agencies of national, regional and local government, including traditional authorities where they exist. These are illustrated in Figure 2.1. Urban governance also, crucially, involves individual citizens and households, of all income groups, inasmuch as they have any influence over what happens.[3] Within this, city (or municipal) government is but one element, albeit often the largest and most obvious.

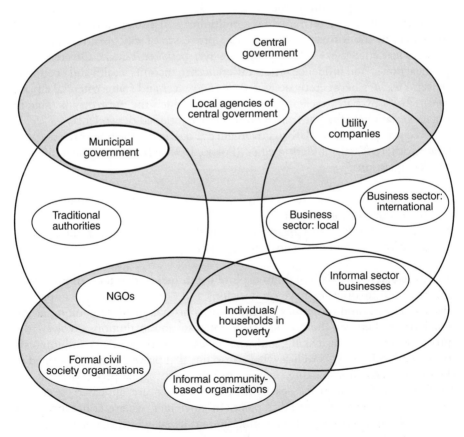

Figure 2.1 *Actors and institutions of urban governance*

If government (including the local agencies of national/state government as well as city government itself) constitutes one large piece of the picture, civil society constitutes another. The term civil society has also been widely adopted in the discourse of international development, but with varying meanings (Mitlin, 2001b; Robinson and White, 1998; Friedmann, 1998). Here we take it to mean associations for common purposes or action, outside the direct control of the state. It includes not just formal organizations, such as NGOs, political parties and trade unions, but a whole range of more informal networks and groups, including community-based organizations, whether formally constituted or not. Civil society is often seen as a counterweight to the state, and an active civil society as essential to the achievement of both good governance and pro-poor policies. However, civil society encompasses a great variety of groups with widely differing objectives, many of which may have no concern with equity or the poor. Indeed, many may have explicitly anti-poor objectives of protecting privilege and vested interests. Nor are civil society organizations necessarily democratically accountable or characterized by the principles of 'good governance' identified above. These issues are discussed further in Chapter 7.

Within this conceptualization of urban governance, informal relationships are at least as important as the formal. Indeed, it is clear that what actually happens in cities is determined by a multiplicity of informal decisions much more than by the formal decision-making processes of city government. But it is also clear that these relationships are not between equals: differences in political power and influence reflect differences in income, wealth and economic power. Dealings between those with differing power and status often take place on the basis of patron–client relationships, in which the poor may be able to obtain certain benefits but from a position of continued dependence.

According to Porrio, 'Urban governance ... deals with the power relationship among different stakeholders in cities' (Porrio, 1997, p2). She goes on to identify two key questions:

- What is the nature of the relationship among stakeholders at certain political and economic conjunctures?
- What are the forms of negotiation that strengthen or weaken the position of stakeholders in urban governance?' (ibid, p2).

In this research we have sought to explore the influence that the various actors, interests and institutions have on decisions and outcomes, and the impact of these decisions and outcomes on the poor. This has involved looking at the relationships between the various actors, interests and institutions involved, the processes of decision-making, and what gives the various actors and interests power and legitimacy, as well as what constrains that power. This is illustrated in Figure 2.2. Decision-making involves not just the formal processes, but the myriad of informal processes by which resources are allocated, access is achieved and development takes place. In particular, we are concerned with processes and mechanisms, both formal and informal, which enable the poor to have influence over, and thereby to benefit from, the decisions and actions of the various institutions of city governance.

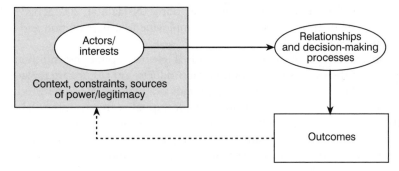

Figure 2.2 *Actors, relationships and outcomes*

Global shifts: globalization, decentralization, democratization

The governance of cities has been profoundly affected by three separate but related shifts in the international scene: globalization, decentralization and democratization. The nature of the impact of these on cities, and particularly on the urban poor, is widely debated. In this section, we briefly review the impact of these processes on urban governance and poverty. In subsequent chapters, we will consider the implications for our case study cities.

Globalization

Globalization is hardly a new phenomenon, but recent developments in technology and communications have brought about far-reaching changes in the patterns of global production and trade, and in the networks between (and within) states. Global competition, and the ease with which capital can flow around the world, have created both opportunities for, and pressures on, cities. Cities no longer relate solely or mainly to their national context but also to international markets and institutions (OECD, 2001).[4] They have been obliged to become more flexible and entrepreneurial, in order to attract inward investment, as well as sustaining local businesses. Bangalore has sold itself as the 'high-tech capital of India', while Cebu promoted itself as 'The Philippines' Best Seller', and the 'economic phenomenon of the South'.

Successful responses by cities to globalization have brought benefits to many. The citizens of Cebu prospered considerably during the 'boom years', and economic growth in Santiago has had a major impact on poverty in the city. But globalization also brings vulnerability, as the inflow of capital which creates employment can just as quickly flow out again.[5] Nor are the benefits equally spread. Just as economic growth benefits some more than others, globalization tends to reinforce existing inequalities. In order to make cities attractive to private capital, resources are invested in facilities that benefit those who make investment decisions. Urban space becomes increasingly segregated, often in the name of security, with privately managed shopping malls and gated housing developments for the rich that exclude the poor (UN-Habitat, 2001a, pp32–38). While some of the poor benefit through employment, others do not, and social exclusion increases.

Globalization strengthens the power of global capital and multinational companies at the expense of labour. Local products and culture are replaced by standardized offerings of the multinationals – a process often referred to as '*McDonaldization*'. Under globalization, while capital is free to move, labour is constrained by border restrictions. The main option for labour seeking to improve its economic opportunities is to migrate to the cities. As cities succeed in responding to the global economic opportunities and experience economic growth, more people – and particularly poor people – move to the city. While this process may help to reduce poverty nationally, it means cities face a never-ending task of meeting the needs of the poor. And while individual countries and cities may have achieved benefits from globalization, the overall trend worldwide has been to greater polarization. In 1996, UNDP reported that the share of global income received by the world's poorest 20 per cent had declined from 2.3 per cent to 1.4 per cent over the previous 30 years, while the share consumed by the richest 20 per cent had increased from 70 per cent to 85 per cent (UNDP, 1996, p2).

One further feature of globalization is that it can undermine city governance as cities compete to offer better facilities, lower taxes and easier regulatory regimes, in what has sometimes been described as a 'race to the bottom'. This process erodes local accountability, as decision-makers become more concerned with the interests of investors than the needs of their citizens. The city case studies identify a number of examples where projects designed to attract international capital have had a deleterious effect on the poor.

Decentralization

Decentralization has been a major feature of the development landscape since the mid-1980s. The World Bank observes that 95 per cent of democracies now have elected sub-national governments, and that governments everywhere are devolving powers to sub-national tiers (World Bank, 2000, p107). But decentralization is not new: many colonial regimes created or strengthened sub-national units as a means of extending control, often using 'indirect rule' through local traditional rulers (Mawhood, 1993; Mamdani, 1996, Kasfir, 1993). During the post-independence period, many countries reversed such arrangements, which they regarded as colonial impositions, centralizing government responsibilities in order to consolidate power and build their nations. This centralization of government was underpinned by economic models of state regulation and central economic planning.

The recent wave of decentralization has been driven by a number of factors. First, the failure in so many countries of the central state and central economic planning to deliver the desired results and to be responsive, particularly to those at the periphery. Second, the political demand from below for greater local autonomy in decision-making. This was particularly strong in Latin America with the re-emergence of democratic governance in the mid-1980s, and in central and eastern Europe, with the political liberalization that followed the fall of the Berlin Wall in 1989. Third, in a number of countries, such as the Philippines, Ghana, South Africa and Uganda, decentralized governance was seen (from the centre) as essential to unifying the state following the transition from autocratic rule or civil strife. There have been other reasons, too. In China, economic decentralization was seen as a means of promoting economic growth, although political control still remains highly centralized.[6] In Indonesia, the threat of secession by resource-rich or ethnically distinct regions precipitated a radical if belated programme of decentralization. Threats of secession were also a stimulus for decentralization in Russia and Ethiopia. In a number of places, particularly in Africa, the decentralization agenda has been driven by international donors, as a means of trying to improve service delivery at the local level.

The arguments for decentralization revolve around three main issues. First, administrative or practical considerations: that it is simply not possible for governments to make decisions at the centre about the detailed management of services and development at the local level. While this issue could be addressed through a deconcentrated administration (ie local offices of the central government), there would immediately arise questions about the accountability of decisions of state officials at the local level, bringing demands for political decentralization.[7] Second, economic considerations: that if decisions about local services and development are made locally, reflecting local needs and preferences, this should result in a better allocation of resources and hence greater economic efficiency. Matching decision-making jurisdictions to the optimum areas for service delivery (within which costs are internalized) is the core of the 'fiscal federalism' case for decentralization (Oates, 1972). Third, political considerations: that, in a democratic state, local people demand the right to make decisions about those things that affect their locality.

There are counter arguments. First, decentralization could result in the fragmentation of the nation state – a particular issue for new and fragile states. Second, local decision-making could undermine the achievement of broader, national goals and common objectives. Third, it could result in economic inefficiency, through the loss of economies of scale (a particular issue with many, very small municipalities created in some central and eastern European countries) and inter-jurisdictional rivalries (an issue with the protectionist development strategies pursued by some provinces in China). Fourth, decentralization could result in increasing inequalities, as rich regions are free to prosper while those in poor regions remain disadvantaged. Fifth, excessive fiscal decentralization (that is, the transfer to sub-national governments of resources and decision-making over taxes and borrowing) could undermine the fiscal position of the central state. There is some evidence of this in both Latin America (Prud'homme, 1995; Tanzi, 1995) and China (World Bank, 2000, p113). Sixth, decentralization may not deliver the intended benefits because of limited technical and managerial capacity at the local level, inadequate systems of local accountability and the increased scope for corruption.

There are, of course, ways of mitigating these negative effects through properly constructed systems of inter-governmental relations, including appropriate assignment of responsibilities, regulations regarding local decision-making and carefully designed fiscal transfer regimes. Many of the weaknesses of recent decentralization programmes arise because of deficiencies in the system of inter-governmental relations. Evidence about the overall impact of decentralization is difficult to establish, because of problems of measurement, comparability and the direction of causality. On the whole, though, it seems that decentralization has neither delivered the significant economic gains some claimed it would, nor has it created the economic and political problems feared by others.[8]

For better or worse, decentralization has focused attention on city governance. Specific issues for this study are whether decentralization has increased the resources available for poverty reduction, and whether it has enlarged the political space for the urban poor to make their voice heard and to improve their position. In relation to the first issue, decentralization certainly has increased resources for some cities, notably Recife, Cebu and Kumasi. Whether or not these have been effectively directed to addressing poverty is another matter. We will return to this point in Chapter 6.

It would be naïve to assume that decentralization automatically ensures that local decision-making reflects local needs and priorities, particularly of the poor. Certainly there is greater knowledge at the local level about local conditions. But elections at any level are a crude mechanism for ascertaining priorities, so that bringing decision-making closer to citizens does not guarantee more responsive and accountable decision-making. Meanwhile, more specific mechanisms of citizen participation are often extremely weak and fail to include the poor (Devas and Grant, 2003). But this is not to say that the poor cannot make use of the enlarged political space at the local level despite the limitations of the mechanisms available.

'Elite capture' is a term widely used (eg World Bank, 2000, p109; Manor, 1999) to suggest that decentralization can adversely affect the poor by surrendering decision-making to a local élite. Manor (1999, p91) has argued that local élites are most unlikely to be more benevolent than those at higher levels. However, there has been little in the way of research on decision-making at the local level or on the behaviour of local élites. Schneider (2002) argues that political decentralization decreases representation of the interests of the poor by reducing the scope for influence at the national level and obliging them to spread their limited organization resources across jurisdictions. By contrast, the rich are able to apply political leverage at the local level without having to organize. From cross-national data, he concludes that there is some evidence that, while administrative decentralization is associated with pro-poor policy (defined as a high proportion of social expenditure in total public expenditure), political decentralization has a negative impact on pro-poor policy. However, von Braun and Grote's (2000) comparison of human development indicators with the extent of political decentralization concludes that decentralization can be beneficial to the poor under the right circumstances, and that it is political rather than administrative decentralization that makes the greatest difference. This is because of the greater scope for the poor both to hold elected officials accountable and to influence public spending decisions when the poor are concentrated in certain jurisdictions. In the end, however, everything depends on detailed arrangements for decentralized governance, democratic control and accountability, as well as the form of resource transfers.

Craig and Porter (quoting Rodrik, 2000) note that 'crossnational statistical studies suggest that decentralized participatory democracies provide for better economic growth, greater predictability and stability ..., and deliver superior distributional outcomes' (Craig and Porter, 2003, p66). However, Crook and Manor's (1998) study of four states in south Asia and west Africa found that, while decentralization had increased participation in all cases, and had increased the performance of government services in some cases, it had no discernable impact on the responsiveness to poor and vulnerable groups. Blair's study of the impact of decentralization in six countries concludes that 'DLG [democratic local governance] initiatives have encouraged participation, and have increased representation, but they have provided little in the way of empowerment, and even less in making the distribution of benefits more equitable or reducing poverty' (Blair, 2000, p25).

The present research does not claim that decentralization per se has an impact on urban poverty, one way or another, but instead looks at how city governance – now accorded a more prominent position as a result of decentralization – affects urban poverty. Nevertheless, we see evidence in a number of the city studies that bringing decision-making closer to citizens opens up greater opportunities for the poor to have an influence and to make at least incremental gains. However, the impact of claims made at the local level may be only localized and piecemeal, often reinforcing clientelistic relationships, rather than being systemic and sustained.

Among our case countries, decentralization has probably had greatest impact in Brazil and the Philippines. In Brazil, the transfer of responsibilities and financial resources has enabled municipal government in Recife and elsewhere to develop a range of social programmes and to introduce participatory budgeting. Decentralization in the Philippines in the late 1980s devolved a range of functions and resources to municipal governments, increasing the scope for cities like Cebu to intervene on behalf of the poor. By contrast, in Ghana, decentralization has remained incomplete: although some responsibilities and resources have been transferred, others remain under the control of the centre, with the appointment of the key officials still resting with central government. In South Africa, there has been a radical restructuring of sub-national government, rather than decentralization in a strict sense, since the former 'white' local authorities have long enjoyed a high degree of local autonomy and substantial resources. By contrast, for those living in the former 'black' local authorities (an imposed and contested form of local government), the reforms of the 1990s have opened up political representation and access to resources.

In our other case countries, decentralization, in as far as it has happened at all, has had much less impact. There has been a long-term erosion of local government responsibilities and resources in Kenya, although recent reforms have begun to address that. Cities in India have not experienced significant changes as a result of decentralization, despite some protection of their political status under the 74th Constitutional Amendment. Indeed, in some cases, there appears to have been an erosion of the role and functions of the municipal government in favour of state agencies and semi-autonomous boards.

Democratization

Probably the most significant change to affect city governance has been the emergence or restoration in many countries of democracy at the national and local level. In some cases, this has been the result of protracted political struggles, helping to place a greater value on the democratic institutions created. This is not to suggest, as some have done (Chalker, 1991; World Bank, 1992), that liberal democracy is a precondition for either development or poverty reduction. But democracy does open up the political space in which the poor have the opportunity to make their voice heard.

In the first post-apartheid elections in South Africa in 1994, the majority of citizens – including most of the poor – had, for the first time, a say in the choice of who would make decisions about the things that affected them. The response of the electorate was overwhelming. But things did not change overnight, and many have been disappointed with the slow pace of change. Those with the economic power still hold that power. Government resources are limited, and changing expenditure patterns in favour of the poor has proved very difficult. Meanwhile, some of those elected to represent the poor quickly lost sight of the interests of their constituents. Nevertheless, the political landscape has changed and the poor have a greater chance of being heard than ever they did under the old regime.

Democracy has swept through large parts of the world since the mid-1980s: Latin America, central and eastern Europe, many countries in Africa and Asia, including the Philippines, South Korea and more recently Indonesia. Even in India, with its long established democratic tradition, élite control through the dominant party has weakened, and constitutional protection has been introduced for democracy at the local level. What is understood by the term democracy does, however, vary considerably, and there is much debate about what elements are essential. The former communist governments of eastern Europe described themselves as democratic and held regular elections, but few would now accept that these states met the conditions for democracy, including a choice of candidates and freedom of information and the press. However, the western model of liberal democracy presupposes certain values that are contested, such as the value placed on individual rights rather than social hierarchies and kinship relationships which are important in other cultures, and the emphasis on winning and 'majority rule' rather than on consensus and inclusion.

Understandings of democracy may clash over issues such as competition between political parties. Political parties provide the opportunity for voter aggregation around common sets of policies, rather than focusing elections on charismatic individuals. But all too often parties fail to develop clear electoral platforms, instead adopting populist rhetoric and reinforcing ethnic or religious divisions (as in Kenya and Zimbabwe, and increasingly in India and Indonesia). They exclude some interests and polarize debate on complex issues in ways that are often unhelpful. The role of traditional authorities (such as chiefs) and traditional decision-making arrangements is another contentious issue. These often command wide respect from local people, despite not being 'democratic'. They may also, in many cases, allow for different voices to be heard, even within a hierarchical framework.

It is clear that democratization does not have any automatic effect on poverty reduction or social inclusion. Despite nearly 20 years of democracy in most of Latin America, incomes and wealth remain far more unequally distributed, and social exclusion remains far deeper, than in countries not noted for democracy, such as China and Indonesia. The emergence or return of multi-party democracy has been blamed in some countries for increased conflict, corruption and declining economic performance. Polidano and Hulme suggest that, while the new populist politics in India has resulted in increased popular participation and improved provision of services in rural areas, it has been accompanied by 'a marked decline in the quality of governance exemplified by intensified communal politics, corruption, the criminalization of politics and the politicization of the bureaucracy' (Polidano and Hulme, 1997, p.6).

Even in the so-called developed democracies of the west, it is apparent that the outcome of the democratic process is more often than not determined by the amount of money that candidates or parties can muster, or by the vagaries of the electoral rules. There is a never-ending debate regarding the relative merits of the majoritarian (or first-past-the-post) system and proportional representation, particularly over how far either system represents the interests of disadvantaged groups. Some countries (for example, India, Sri Lanka, the Philippines) seek to address this by guaranteeing representation of women and ethnic minorities through reserved seats. However, there are questions about how far those who occupy such seats succeed in advancing the interests of those they are supposed to represent (Blair, 2000).

Elections often fall far short of the requirements for proper democracy, with limited understanding among voters about their rights and their choices; the absence of clear manifestos from candidates and information about the issues involved; and electoral malpractices, such as registration fraud, vote-buying, vote rigging and even intimidation. Once elected, representatives may quickly lose interest in those they were elected to serve, concentrating instead on ways, corrupt or otherwise, of recouping the costs of their campaign. Powerful individuals often dominate local politics, maintaining their position through clientelistic control over political agents and local electors. Disillusionment with the performance of those they have elected creates voter apathy and low turnouts at local elections.

Nor is it just the shortcomings of the electoral system. The outcomes of the democratic process for the poor also depend on how far those they elect are able to influence the decisions made, and how far those decisions determine what actually happens. All too often, so-called democratic decision-making structures are subject to excessive pressure from powerful interest groups, marginalizing the voices of those who represent the poor. There are important questions about the accountability of the executive to the elected representatives, about the checks and balances between elected (or appointed) executives and the local legislature, and about the internal organization, functioning and accountability of the paid administration. A particular focus of concern is the budgetary process and the way that this does or does not convert the aspirations of elected representatives (and their constituents) into actual expenditure outcomes. These all emerge as important issues in the case study cities and will be discussed further in Chapters 5 and 6.

Whatever the shortcomings of representative democracy, it does potentially allow the poor to have a voice, not least because they represent the majority in any city in the South. In Indian cities, it is notable that electoral turnout is generally much higher in poor wards than in higher-income wards. Whether for good reasons (perceptions of influence and vote-bargaining with candidates) or bad (naïvety, vote-buying or intimidation) the poor perceive voting as important. Of course, as we have already noted, the poor are not an undifferentiated mass. Divisions by race or ethnicity, gender, income (for example, the poor versus the very poor), economic activity, interest, location and so on, make it difficult for the poor to take advantage of their numbers in the democratic process. Much depends on their ability to organize and lobby. In this, the organizations of civil society – NGOs, community-based organizations (CBOs), trade unions, religious groups and political parties – can play a significant role.

However, civil society is much stronger in some countries than in others. The stronger civil societies have often emerged from periods of political struggle. In the Philippines, NGOs enjoy a privileged position at both national and local government levels. This is also true, to a lesser extent, in South Africa. Of course, not all civil society groups represent the interests of the poor – indeed, the most powerful ones often oppose the interests of the poor, and the institutions of civil society tend to reflect and reinforce existing unequal power relationships. There are also, in many countries of the South, numerous so-called NGOs which are little more than 'briefcase operators' that exploit the poor for their own interests.

Even where the role of civil society has been crucial to the political struggle, once gains have been made there is a tendency for reduced activism and for NGOs to become incorporated by the state as deliverers of services. This tendency has been particularly marked in Chile, where greater prosperity and the achievement of political rights have been accompanied by a retreat from public socio-political space into private space (Rodríguez and Winchester, 1999, p2).[9] There has been a similar, if less marked, tendency in South Africa as many of the civil society activists from the era of struggle have made the transition into government. We will return to the role of civil society in Chapter 7.

Conclusion

The lack of accurate, disaggregated data on the level and trends in poverty at city level is a serious impediment to effective approaches to urban poverty reduction. So too is the lack of understanding by city officials about the differentiated nature of poverty and of the livelihood systems of the poor. These issues will be explored further in the next chapter.

A broadened understanding of urban governance enables us to begin to trace the roles of the private sector, civil society and the various institutions of government at city level – and of the interactions between these actors – in determining what happens at city level. Globalization, decentralization and democratization have all had significant impacts on city governance, although much also remains unchanged. Social exclusion, the vulnerability of the poor and their lack of voice remain, and in some cases have become more severe. But the situation is not hopeless, and there are examples of where the poor have made gains, albeit often only incremental and still fragile. The remaining chapters of this book will explore these issues further, drawing on the city case studies, to enable us to understand better the relationships between urban governance and poverty.

Notes

1   Satterthwaite (1997, p1) points out that the World Bank's 1988 estimate of 300 million 'poor' people living in urban areas implies that less than a quarter of the developing world's urban population at that date were poor, a figure far lower than that suggested by various studies of cities in Africa, Asia and Latin America. One reason for this underestimate is that poverty lines are generally based on minimum food requirements, whereas urban living requires considerable non-food expenditure.

2   Based on an urban population of the developing world of 1.94 billion (UN-Habitat, 2001a, Table A2).

3   It could be argued that individuals and households have no power on their own and therefore cannot be considered as part of urban governance. Yet it is clear that individual and household decisions about where to locate, where to trade and how to move about has a profound impact on the way cities develop and function. At the very least, their resistance to complying with the official regulations limits the ability of city government to govern effectively.

4   Sassen (1994) has argued that globalization has reinforced the dominant position of certain 'global cities', concentrating the power of global capital and effectively controlling the new international division of labour. The implication is that there is little that local actors can do about that situation. Whilst clearly some cities do possess much greater natural and historical advantages than others, there is much that is debatable about what constitutes a 'global city', about the exclusiveness of the concept, and about the room for manoeuvre which city-level actors have (Vidler, 1999).

5   The process can also occur within cities: for example, the shift of business activity from Johannesburg's central business district (CBD) to the suburban centre of Sandton, which was perceived as being 'safer', is now being superseded by relocation even further out to Midrand.

6   Sub-national governments in China actually have a considerable degree of autonomy, in practice if not in principle, especially those with strong local economies (Shirk, 1993).

7   It is common to distinguish between administrative decentralization or deconcentration, which transfers tasks to field offices of central government without local autonomy, and political decentralization or devolution of powers and resources to elected local governments with a degree of local autonomy. A third

aspect, fiscal decentralization, which is about the transfer of resources, and of decision-making over resources, is really a dimension of the other two.

8   Tendler, in her classic study of service delivery in one state in Brazil, concluded that the positive results had much more to do with leadership and the motivation of public servants, and with the particular ways in which central government, local government and civic organizations interact, than with any simplistic notion that decentralization automatically produces better results by bringing decisions closer to citizens (Tendler, 1997).

9   Other writers on Chile (eg Barrera, 1999) note how many of the popular associational movements which flourished during the authoritarian regime have since disappeared. Nickson (1995, p90) observes that mobilization in Latin America tends to be built around specific demands and once these have been accomplished, participation tends to diminish.

Chapter 3

Economic Growth, Urban Poverty and City Governance

Ursula Grant[1]

Introduction

Do the poor benefit from urban economic growth and if so, how? Conventional wisdom suggests that everyone – or almost everyone – should gain from economic growth, including the poor, if only through a process of 'trickle down'. Yet we know that this is often not the case, and that there is no simple relationship between growth and poverty reduction. Nor have all cities been experiencing sustained economic growth: in many cities, the context is one of structural change or even economic decline rather than economic growth. What are the implications for the livelihoods of the urban poor in these circumstances?

As Chapter 2 has indicated, the experience of urban poverty is highly differentiated: some of those living in poverty may gain from economic growth;

others may be disadvantaged, particularly through increasing inequality and exclusion. What happens to particular poor individuals or households depends on a whole variety of circumstances, many – but not all – of which are outside their control. This chapter is concerned with the process of urban economic growth (or more broadly, economic change, since not all cities are growing), and the extent to which the poor benefit from, or are disadvantaged by, that process. It is also concerned with what city governments can do about both the economic condition of their city, and about the impact of economic change on the poor.

In the next section of this chapter we consider whether economic growth (or change) has benefited the poor in the case study cities. In order to do this, we examine the economic structures and trajectories of the cities, what may account for economic change in each case, and what impact this has had on the poor. This is followed by a more detailed analysis of two important aspects of the relationship between economic growth and poverty. The first is the operations of the labour market, including the ways in which the informal sector and the 'local economy' provide economic opportunities. The second is the ability of the poor, through their livelihood and coping strategies, to take advantage of the economic opportunities available.[2] The last two sections of the chapter review how the institutions of city governance in our case study cities have used the room for manoeuvre which they have to address these issues: first to promote economic growth and second to enable the poor to benefit from that economic growth (or to protect them from the negative impact of economic change or decline).

Do the poor benefit from city economic growth?

Analyses of the relationship between poverty trends and economic growth typically focus on national level and proxy statistics. Aggregate data, such as gross domestic product (GDP) per capita, the proportion of the population below the poverty line, and infant mortality have been used, for example by the World Bank (1990), to suggest that the key to poverty reduction lies in the combination of labour-intensive growth, investment in human capital (primary education and primary healthcare) and safety nets for the poor. Growth with equity is the key policy message, implying, first, that the way economic growth is achieved is important and, second, that social policies are needed to enable poor people to take advantage of economic opportunities and to protect them against the adverse effects of economic change.

Economic growth provides opportunities for reducing poverty levels, not least because of the additional resources that can be used for social investment. But whether or not these opportunities are seized depends upon political choices, and in turn on public pressure for these policy priorities (Dreze and Sen, 1989, p181). What matters at a national level is not just the rate of growth but the quality of that growth, and how that growth is distributed. In east Asia, Watkins (1998, p24) asserts: 'the poor ... have benefited from growth not because the gains have 'trickled down' to them, but because the development of their productive potential has been central to the growth process'. The common denominator of successful growth policies in the countries of east Asia has been that they enhanced the productivity of the poor, rather than relying on welfare transfers to raise incomes (ibid, p45).

This chapter attempts to localize and 'urbanize' the debate about economic growth and poverty reduction. In the literature, there are few examples of successful urban growth strategies that have resulted in subsequent poverty reduction. This is partly a reflection of the inadequacy of data at the urban level. This chapter begins to fill that gap while at the same time acknowledging the limitations of the available data.

We adopt a multi-dimensional approach to poverty, drawing largely on Moser's assets/vulnerability framework (Moser, 1998). This framework recognizes that, for poor people, labour represents their most important asset. It is through increasing work opportunities and returns to labour that poor households benefit most directly from economic growth. According to the World Bank, 'the rate of poverty reduction is, on average, proportional to the distribution-corrected growth of private consumption' (World Bank, 2000, p274).

The evidence to support this assumption from the ten cities examined in this book is mixed. A number of cities (Ahmedabad, Bangalore, Cebu, Santiago) clearly show some reduction in poverty with economic growth. This tends to be connected to the performance of the national economies within which they are situated. The economies of Chile, the Philippines and Sri Lanka have all been growing quite strongly during the 1990s, but Santiago, Cebu and Colombo have all outperformed their national economies. Johannesburg seems to have been stagnating in line with the South African economy. The Indian cities included in this study are all located in 'growth states' and tend to perform above the national average. Ahmedabad, Bangalore and Visakhapatnam all provide modest support to the idea that economic growth increases income levels for the poorest.

The other two African case cities, however, are located in countries characterized by long-term economic difficulties. Mombasa shows little evidence of either growth or poverty reduction, and in Kumasi only slight improvements are evident. This partly reflects the limited local management capacity to create an environment for economic growth, but also the dearth of inward investment in sub-Saharan Africa. Mombasa seems to be declining along with the Kenyan economy as a whole, due to a number of factors discussed in Box 3.1. Processing and textile industries have been damaged by economic liberalization, while tourism has been hit by political unrest and insecurity. In Ghana, the disastrous economic policies of the 1970s and 1980s hit the urban poor particularly hard, but by the late 1990s, Kumasi seemed to be experiencing a modest recovery in tandem with the Ghanaian economy. It is not entirely clear what impact this growth has had on the poor, but it seems that at least some of the urban poor in Kumasi have benefited from the overall 'stabilization' of the economy as a result of structural adjustment.

Although measurement and data problems pose difficulties in assessing the relationship between urban economic growth and poverty, it is clear that this

BOX 3.1 MOMBASA: UNFULFILLED ECONOMIC POTENTIAL

Located on the Indian Ocean coast of Kenya, Mombasa has great economic potential. With a deepwater port, it is the centre of well-established coastal tourism and has a multi-country hinterland containing over 50 million people. Yet Mombasa's economy in the late 1990s was stagnant, its infrastructure in disrepair and poverty entrenched.

Poor urban management was an immediate explanation for the lack of support for economic development and the failure to meet basic needs, but the underlying explanations for the present situation must be sought in the wider political economy of the nation.

The primary institution of city governance is the Mombasa Municipal Council (MMC), but many of the important functions are the responsibility of the district offices of central government and the various parastatals. Until recently, local authorities in Kenya received no share of central government revenue, so MMC had to depend mainly on property taxes, market fees, house rents and business licences. The lack of central government support, combined with poor financial management, meant that by the late 1990s MMC was significantly worse off in real terms than it was 30 years previously. Indeed, it had become effectively insolvent, unable to provide adequate services, maintain its housing stock, service its debts, and even at times pay staff wages. Wages absorbed the lion's share of revenue, leaving little for other tasks. Yet the work force – overstaffed at lower levels but lacking professionally qualified senior staff at the top – was unproductive. Outdated organizational structures and lack of planning and management capacity further hindered efficiency. Overlapping responsibilities, rivalry with the district (the boundaries of which are coterminous with the municipality) and poor coordination with the district offices of central government and parastatals exacerbated these management shortcomings.

Underlying this poor performance, however, are adverse economic and political conditions. Trade has been damaged by regional and intra-regional instability and conflict, external shocks and poor management of the national economy. Port operations continue to be significant but are hindered by poor road and rail transport links, congestion, mismanagement and corruption. Tourism declined in the 1990s because of deteriorating infrastructure, competition, attrition of the country's image as a travel destination due to high crime levels and violence associated with the 1992 and 1997 elections, and more recently by terrorist threats. Although some industrial investment has occurred, further investment has been deterred by declining tourism and infrastructure deficiencies. The Moi regime's fear of political challenge and dependence on patronage prevented effective decentralization, fuelled political violence and perpetuated corruption and inefficiency.

Despite this, there have been a number of attempts to address the city's problems by involving the business sector (during the mayorship of Najib Bolala) and community organizations. One project based in the MMC and funded by the Department for International Development (DFID) has sought to develop a participatory approach to poverty reduction through community organizations of the poor. However, all too often in Mombasa, local initiatives and progressive forces have been undermined by those whose interests are threatened, thereby reinforcing and perpetuating the vicious circle of incapacity, illegitimacy and under-performance.

Source: Gatabaki-Kamau et al, 1999

BOX 3.2 SANTIAGO: CAN CITY ECONOMIC GROWTH SOLVE POVERTY?

Over the last 15 years, economic growth in Chile has correlated with a fall in both poverty and indigence. This has provided support for the view that economic growth offers the basis for eliminating poverty, particularly through the generation of employment. Santiago is a relatively prosperous city in a middle-income country where, it is perceived, urban poverty is being successfully eliminated. This perception is well founded, in that poor urban households in Chile have managed to increase their incomes significantly during the 1990s. Nevertheless, the research in Santiago demonstrates three key factors that necessitate qualification of this view. First, there are vicious circles of chronic poverty that are associated with extreme vulnerability and are difficult to overcome solely through economic growth. Second, economic growth and poverty reduction have been accompanied by growing inequalities in income distribution. Third, even where poverty is declining, the coexistence of growth and inequality is associated with social exclusion.

The characteristics of chronic poverty in Santiago are high levels of marginality, a tendency towards inter-generational poverty, low educational levels, little training and few social networks. A more recent phenomenon is that of people remaining outside the labour market for long periods of time, due to economic restructuring or technological innovation. In both cases, those people unable to overcome poverty are most likely to be unskilled workers in the formal economy, particularly women or unemployed young people from the poor *comunas*. Social exclusion in Santiago is related to particular economic sectors, such as elements of the informal economy, and particular social groups, for example the young. Being young and poor is a synonym for social exclusion.

Both poverty and social exclusion also have spatial dimensions. Despite policies of urban improvement and increased employment, the old zones of poverty, usually located in peripheral areas, have remained poor. While the numbers living in 'precarious settlements' have been dramatically reduced, many of these have been relocated to peripheral areas, especially in the south of the city. Forced removals led to spatial concentrations of poverty and generated ruptures in communities, which eroded their social networks and informal social safety nets. Stigmatized and excluded areas are noted not just for their poverty but also for their perceived social pathologies, such as dirt or crime. The policy implications of these findings for local government are two-fold. First, even under conditions of economic growth, the issues of redistribution and persistent poverty still need to be addressed. Second, area-based strategies towards urban poverty reduction and inclusion should be located within broader strategic approaches. Given the division of Santiago's metropolitan area into *comunas* with widely differing income and resource levels, it is debatable whether it is local government or higher levels that are best placed to address the problems of chronic poverty.

---

relationship is complex. The distribution of benefits from economic growth is mediated by social and political as well as economic factors. While the general increase in incomes may result in a reduced incidence of absolute poverty, inequality limits the extent to which this benefits all poor people. In Santiago, for example, although economic growth has been accompanied by impressive reductions in poverty, it has also resulted in increases in inequality, spatial segregation and stigmatization, as outlined in Box 3.2.

Other cities also suggest mixed outcomes. In Colombo, relatively high rates of economic growth during the early and mid-1990s were accompanied by reductions in unemployment, but little in the way of a reduction in poverty – indeed, some of the poverty indicators suggest an increase in the depth and severity of poverty (Fernando et al, 1999, p18). In Johannesburg, the very modest rate of economic growth during the 1990s was accompanied by indications of increasing poverty, particular as a result of unemployment. The performance of the South African economy has been relatively poor over the last 20 years, with per capita incomes rising by an average of only 1.6 per cent per year between 1980 and 1995 (Standing et al, 1996). This is despite a shift from the import substitution policy of the 1960s and 1970s to a more export oriented policy in the 1990s. In Johannesburg, slow employment growth and changes in employment away from primary sectors towards services have been accompanied by rapid urban population growth in the post-apartheid era. The legacies of apartheid include widespread poverty and high levels of inequality. These have been reinforced in recent years by a process of 'white' capital fleeing to suburban areas. Changes in employment patterns include a move away from primary sectors, notably mining, to services. Although manufacturing remains important, manufacturing employment has declined. The fall in demand for labour has resulted in lower wages for unskilled workers and an unemployment rate reaching 20 per cent (or as high as 33 per cent, depending on definitions) by the mid-1990s (Crankshaw, 1997). New entrants to the labour market, predominantly the young and African workers, have suffered particularly.

It is now widely acknowledged that the impact of economic growth on poverty has much to do with the level of inequality within a nation. The same is likely to be true at the city level. According to the World Bank:

> *'Improvements in private consumption per capita are generally associated with a reduction in poverty, but where the distribution is unequal, the poor may not share in the improvement.'* (World Bank, 2000, p234)

Addressing inequality is much more difficult than promoting economic growth. It is not simply a matter of transfers, even if there were the resources available for these, it is also about increasing the participation of the poor. Policy and investment choices are important, particularly investment in human capital. However, a nuanced approach is necessary to ensure that it is the productive assets of the poor that are developed and utilized, and that inequality in access to, and quality of, service provision is addressed. These are issues to which we will return below.

Thus, urban economic growth appears to be a necessary but not sufficient condition for urban poverty reduction. With the general trend to decentralization and local democracy, the room for manoeuvre at the local level has increased, at least in some respects. But the ability of city governments to respond to economic opportunities and to encourage pro-poor growth depends upon the wider context of globalization and structural adjustment on the one hand, and non-economic factors, such as the city's social structure, cultural and religious traditions, and the political order, on the other. The attractiveness of urban areas to investors, and the ability of the urban population to take advantage of the economic opportunities are, in turn, related to the 'soft infrastructure' – healthcare, education, and so on (Harris and Fabricius, 1996, p91). Both local politics and the specificity of urban areas are important in all of this and are further explored in later sections of this chapter.

City economic growth and poverty reduction: Labour markets and economic opportunities[3]

What are the mechanisms through which the benefits of urban economic growth are transmitted to the poor, and how do poor individuals and households respond to the opportunities that emerge from economic growth? The most powerful mechanisms through which economic growth influences poverty are the labour market and employment growth, both formal and informal. If economic growth is to improve the living conditions of the poor it must be inclusive, providing a broad range of remunerative employment. Successful formal sector growth, notably in the manufacturing sector, is often regarded as a prerequisite for poverty reduction (World Bank, 1990; Watkins, 1998). It is the changing patterns of manufacturing and service employment, away from the high wage, unionized and male-dominated industries and business sectors and towards low wage, predominantly female light industries and support services that Sassen (1994) claims can account for the dramatic increases in inequality seen in the cities of the north. As already noted, most of the cities examined in this book have experienced some decline in their manufacturing sectors, while at the same time the service sector has expanded. The impact of this on urban poverty is seen in the changing nature and conditions of the labour market that benefit some and not others.

In Santiago, this pattern largely reflects major transformations occurring in the Chilean economy, with the city becoming one of the main financial centres of Latin America. Johannesburg has experienced a similar trend but generally in a condition of economic stagnation. Between 1970 and 1991, manufacturing in Johannesburg declined from 24 per cent to 16 per cent of total employment, while mining declined from 5 to 2 per cent. During the same period, employment in services increased from 29 per cent to 33 per cent, with financial services increasing from 8 to 13 per cent (Beall et al, 2000, p108). The explanation is partly due to the exhaustion of the gold mines in the area, but also to a more general process of urban de-industrialization. In Cebu, despite its success in encouraging inward investment and export-led industrialization, employment in the manufacturing industry increased only slightly in absolute terms, and declined as a percentage of total employment from 24.4 per cent in 1988 to 20.4 per cent in 1998.[4] Nearly three-quarters of the city's employment is accounted for by the service sector (Etemadi, 1999, Table A2.0).[5]

Macro-economic policy has an impact on the returns to labour, through its support for either capital or labour intensive investment patterns. It is generally believed that labour intensive growth is critical for poverty reduction as it provides more opportunities for the poor to make use of their primary asset, labour. Yet few, if any, of the cities studied appeared to be following labour intensive growth strategies as such. Colombo is perhaps the only one that shows some clear design in promoting labour intensive growth through export production. The Sri Lankan government and the Greater Colombo Economic Commission have actively sought to encourage this sector. Nationally, employment in both manufacturing and services increased between 1980 and 1996.

One approach is through the direct creation of employment in the form of labour intensive public works programmes. Such an approach has long been used in rural areas of the developing world both to create employment and to provide infrastructure (notably roads). More recently, the approach has been used quite widely in urban areas of francophone Africa (Farvacque-Vitkovič and Godin, 1998). Box 3.3 provides an example of one such programme, in Benin. This programme has been used to create employment, to build capacity within local construction firms and to provide much needed urban infrastructure. However, there are also weaknesses, notably the fact that the approach is top-down and engineering-driven, implemented by a special purpose agency with little connection to the city government.

An alternative strategy, through the encouragement of high-tech industries, raises questions about the impact on employment. This is exemplified by Bangalore, where a US$200 million high-tech park was established on the edge of the city, modelled on the American industrial estate and highly subsidized to new business through generous tax concessions and guaranteed power connections. Yet, after several years, many of the units remain vacant and few employment opportunities have been created for the poor. Meanwhile, the effect on land values has been to force out small enterprises and poorer groups in favour of large real estate developers. This failure can be attributed to a lack of understanding by those involved of the way in which much of Bangalore's software industry operates – that is, through complex networks of micro-enterprises working in the front rooms of homes in the middle-income districts of the city. Benjamin (2000) asserts that it is these 'local economies' that form the employment base of urban areas in India. Despite the importance and visibility of the high-tech sector it remains relatively insignificant in terms of total employment in the city – indeed, the silk and garment industries are more significant. Furthermore, it is in the ancillary industries that the greatest employment growth has been generated in both these sectors.

The strength of the labour market as a mechanism to absorb and influence the productivity of the poor has been particularly strong in south and southeast Asia. In the fast growing cities of that region, significant employment increases are evident. In Visakhapatnam, for example, growth has been associated with its large and successful port. The increase in the registered industrial workforce has been combined with a significant improvement in the casual daily wage rate, which doubled between 1993 and 1998. In most Indian cities there are large casual labour markets where individuals turn up seeking work and where contractors go to employ labour. The daily rate for casual labour therefore underpins an entire local labour market, reflecting local economic conditions,

BOX 3.3 EMPLOYMENT CREATION PROGRAMMES: THE CASE OF AGETUR IN BENIN[6]

In 1990, Benin moved from one-party politics to a pluralist democracy and adopted a development strategy based on the market economy. Previously, private initiative had been limited by a state controlled system based on large public sector enterprises and cooperative farming. Private sector employment was restricted and the public sector excessively large, with weak administrative capacity. Since 1991, Benin has received substantial external assistance for economic and institutional reforms and extensive restructuring. These resulted in the loss of over 4000 salaried public sector posts and the closure of a number of public enterprises, contributing to high levels of urban unemployment. Prior to 1989, the economy was in decline, but since then there has been a recovery, with economic growth averaging 5 per cent per year between 1991 and 1999 (World Bank, 2000).

The Agence d'Exécution des Travaux Urbains (AGETUR) was created in October 1990 to provide employment for the many people negatively affected by structural adjustment. This was to be done using labour intensive methods to rehabilitate and construct good quality infrastructure and facilities such as roads, gutters, markets, schools and health centres. Work is carried out through local small- and medium-scale enterprises that are invited to tender for individual contracts. These enterprises recruit both skilled and unskilled labour and are selected for contracts partly on the basis of the number of people they employ.

The AGETUR initiative was specifically aimed at ameliorating the deteriorating conditions for retrenched workers and unemployed graduates. It has been successful in keeping this target group above the poverty line, with supervisory and research roles created in design and consultancy offices, as well as specialist employment with sub-contractors. The employment created varies from professional and managerial jobs such as site managers and technicians, skilled jobs such as bricklayers, welders and carpenters, to temporary labourer jobs for those with no qualifications. In addition, jobs were freed up for others at the ports as port workers moved out to take up skilled and semi-skilled positions within the burgeoning enterprise sector.

One criticism of AGETUR is that employment is available only to a healthy male work force. Moreover, the work available for the least skilled labourers is often piecemeal, temporary and low paid. Thus, rather than addressing chronic poverty, this model has focused on preventing increased poverty among those groups clustered around the poverty line, notably unemployed graduates and retrenched formal sector workers.

That said, the multiplier effect on employment has given a major boost to the local economy, and the infrastructure created has had important community level impacts. The use of locally produced materials has had significant benefits for the wider economy. People are able to trade alongside the newly developed roads and service the workers with food and drink during the contract periods. Much needed infrastructure has been provided, the city's drainage has been improved, and latrines have been installed in public gardens, rest areas, bars and so on. Reduced levels of crime have also been attributed to the increased availability of work.

AGETUR functions as an effective and efficient delegated management agency and has successfully stimulated the growth of an urban SME (small and medium enterprise) sector. However, the arrangement has left the municipal governments frustrated at having lost control over infrastructure projects to a World Bank supported agency. Municipal governments are left with responsibility for maintenance of infrastructure over which they have had no say in construction. This has adversely affected staff motivation and the ability of municipal governments to manage the strategic development of infrastructure. However, because the performance of municipal governments in such works has often been so poor, AGETUR has taken on more and more work, including that directly commissioned by donor agencies. Although this ensures that work is completed efficiently, it may not be the best approach for long-term sustainability or enhancing local governance capacity.

Source: Fanou and Grant, 2001

and is a key mechanism through which the benefits of growth may or may not be passing to poor workers.

We are concerned not only with how economic growth impacts on the incomes of the poor but also with the ways in which poor people are able to access and utilize the opportunities created by economic growth. Assets such as human and social capital are key to these processes. Ill health, for example, plays a major role in reducing the productivity levels of poor people. The Visakhapatnam study shows how ill health and the associated lack of strength reduce the capacity of workers to take on available work. Rather than being lazy, as is often assumed, these workers simply need to take breaks to recuperate between jobs. Those in poverty usually lack the education and skills to access employment opportunities in the formal sector. Accordingly, human capital deficiencies undermine the ability of workers to overcome poverty as well as hindering broader economic growth.

Human capital is an important contributor to welfare changes over time (Grootaert et al, 1995). The longer people are held in poverty, the harder it is to access opportunities. The positive effects of human capital investments at the household or individual level are only felt over the medium- to long-term. Hence, the poor may make choices in favour of immediate needs which contribute negatively to the perpetuation of their low levels of human capital. For instance, rather than attending school, street children in Colombo and elsewhere are engaged in begging and other work. Similarly, the poor in Kumasi reported difficulties in financing their children's education and withdraw them from school during times of hardship. Even when children do attend school they often arrive late due to morning queues for taps and latrines. The effects of inadequate service delivery can similarly impact directly on the productivity of informal economic activities. For example, women and girls in Kumasi spend a large proportion of their time collecting and storing water for food preparation. They use private taps at high cost or sources such as polluted local streams, risking associated health problems. Similar patterns can be found in many cities around the world.

Inadequate service provision directly constrains the capacity of poor people to overcome vulnerability. In poorly serviced areas people use more time and other resources in seeking alternative service provision, often of poorer quality and higher cost. These higher costs often lead to increased indebtedness. Inadequate service provision also reduces their ability to prioritize longer-term asset accumulation, for example through education and health care, which in turn constrains their prospects of rising out of poverty. These are issues to which we will return in Chapter 9.

The importance of local economic activity and the informal sector

Writing about Bangalore, Benjamin and Bhuvaneswari (2001) distinguish between the 'local economy' and the 'corporate economy'.[7] In their view, it is the local economy that provides the main livelihood opportunities to the majority of the urban population, including virtually all the poorest groups. In that city, the bulk of employment generation is constituted by small and tiny enterprises, which cluster to share functional links. For example, in Mysore Road in west Bangalore, an intensive mix of industrial, fabricating and service activities are centred around a host of small enterprises. It is argued that close proximity and high densities allow economic and other linkages to develop between various local groups, thus forming a large and dynamic sector. The diverse and complex ways in which the local economy develops contrast with the corporate sector, located within the 'master planned' areas of rigid land-use controls from which small-scale enterprises (SSEs) and the poor are generally excluded.

Bangalore has become known as the 'silicon valley' of India, with the development of software and high-tech industries, but it is the growth of the small businesses that have developed alongside the formal high-tech sector that has provided the majority of the city's employment growth (Benjamin, 2000). In the case of Cebu, while the national economy of the Philippines was experiencing negative growth during the late 1980s, Cebu City experienced strong economic growth, accounting for 10 per cent of the nation's exports in 1994. However the Cebu boom benefited only certain sectors and it was, as it still is, the informal sector that absorbed large sections of the urban poor work force (Etemadi, 2000).

It is the informal sector that offers the main income opportunities for poor households since barriers to entry are lower. Increased employment of household members within the informal sector is often required during times of hardship, perhaps as a result of a shock such as the illness or death of a family member. Coping strategies include the entry of previously non-earning household members into the informal sector, and wage earners taking up supplementary activities. In Mombasa, women are disproportionately represented in the informal sector, mainly selling foodstuffs, brewing and so on. Children also play an important role in contributing to the informal strategies of households. However, those engaged in informal sector activities face many obstacles: inadequate access to credit and appropriate sites or premises; bureaucratic licensing requirements and regulatory restrictions; and demands by the police for bribes to operate without licences or in non-permitted locations (Rakodi et al, 2000). Similar patterns are found in each of the ten cities.

The local or informal economy often involves the use by individuals or households of their homes or land as productive assets, for example by the conversion or addition of rooms to provide space for economic activities. Letting out rooms previously occupied by the owners' family is one coping strategy during times of hardship. Relaxation of the enforcement of the planning laws in South Africa has resulted in the construction of backyard shacks in the townships and in the use of housing as productive capital. As a result, the townships are less homogeneous and the use of public and private space has changed. Prohibition of trading in townships has been ended and hawkers, retail outlets, taxis and so on are now an important part of local life. In Bangalore, small-scale weavers such as those belonging to the traditional weaving caste (*Devangas*) mostly operate from their homes, with minimal cost and easy access to markets for both inputs and finished products.

Successful small business development in Bangalore, both informal and formal, can in part be attributed to a land tenure system that is flexible, diverse, and allows for mixed uses. By operating outside of the formal planning process, with access to relatively cheap land with loose land-use regulations, small local enterprises can start up and develop in 'messy' but effective ways. These locations provide proximity to markets and suppliers, allowing for financial and subcontracting linkages to develop easily. In turn, productive forms of social capital can form and significant employment can be generated.

Controls over land and planning are, therefore, important tools that municipal governments can use to promote local economic activity. Conventional 'master planning' can disrupt the productive activities of the poor, whereas linkages between formal and informal businesses can be enhanced through incremental development, mixed land use and diverse tenure. Similarly, planning regulations can affect how households are able to use housing as a productive asset. Indeed, as Moser (1998, p11) has suggested, the removal of tenure insecurity and other obstacles that constrain households from using their homes as productive assets may be the single most important poverty reduction intervention that urban governments could adopt. These issues will be discussed further in Chapter 8.

City governance and economic growth: What room for manoeuvre?

A city's economic growth prospects are framed both by its national context and by global pressures. All nations and cities ultimately face common pressures to integrate globally in order to attract investment and grow economically (Vidler, 1999, p4). However, governments, both national and local, respond differently to these pressures, and, through the policy choices they make, can have a significant influence over local economic growth patterns.

There is a growing realization that cities need to respond flexibly to a changing global market-place and to 'market' themselves in order to encourage inward investment. Striking differences emerge between cities with respect to how they have marketed themselves to the international economy, and how successful they have been in attracting inward investments. Cities like Johannesburg, Santiago, Cebu and Bangalore have developed strategies to market themselves. Johannesburg has sought to position itself as a high-tech centre under Gauteng province's slogan of 'Smart Gauteng'. Bangalore has marketed itself as India's 'silicon valley' in order to claim for itself a dominant position in India's high-tech industry, in competition with Hyderabad. However, as already noted, this high profile sector has contributed only modestly to employment in the city, particularly for the poor. Kumasi and Mombasa, by contrast, seem to have been unable to establish a coherent strategy to promote economic development and employment.

Sassen (1994, p120) draws a clear distinction between 'winners' and 'losers' amongst cities, in reference to their ability to respond to global opportunities. Ruble et al (1996, pp5–15) similarly distinguishes between the 'new age boomtowns', namely those cities which have seized upon post-industrial technologies to emerge as financial service centres, 'partially marketized cities' and the 'marginalized' city. The last refers to those that have failed to integrate in the global economy and are concentrated particularly in Africa. The African city is characterized by an absence of export-led industrialization, weak infrastructure and state apparatus, and a low skilled labour force, failing to engage effectively in global competition and becoming 'relatively poorer and more peripheral' (Simon, 1992, pp48–50).

Vidler (1999) examines the agency of the local within the context of this 'global game'. She asserts that a city's relative economic success is shaped in part by its specific starting point and by the resources potentially available to the city government. These starting points include a city's economic position in the national and international economy, its historical legacy, its political and institutional frameworks, and its local culture and social structure. Different levels and combinations of resources are available in each city, some of which are beyond the city government's control while others are potentially subject to their influence, such as infrastructure provision or the development of a skilled labour force. As Vidler argues, a city's starting point does not mean that its growth (or decline) is predetermined. Indeed, 'one of the keys to city economic growth is an appreciation – on the part of city governments – of the resources they have at their disposal, coupled with an understanding of how these might be productively exploited or developed' (Vidler, 1999, p13). Cities face different challenges, opportunities and local circumstances, and therefore different levels of manoeuvrability or relative autonomy.

Attracting corporate investment is often seen as crucial to urban economic growth. For this, city marketing efforts, sometimes in partnership with the private sector, seek to present positive images and gain international exposure. However, such an approach seems questionable where resources are lacking to provide even the most basic infrastructure. Indeed, there are risks that such promotion results in the destruction of livelihood opportunities for the poor, through repression of the informal sector for the sake of the city's image (as in Mombasa and Kumasi), or through pre-emption of well-located land for prestige developments (as in Bangalore).

The challenge facing city governments is both to attract inward investment and to develop a skilled labour force while simultaneously protecting the productive activities of the poorest. One approach is to develop partnerships or alliances with other institutions such as private enterprises and community organizations for the purpose of developing and implementing growth strategies. Such 'growth coalitions' or productive alliances can harness opportunities in ways that might not be possible for city governments on their own. The requirements for successful partnership include a reasonably buoyant and influential private sector, active community organizations and a suitably capable and authoritative local government, together with some common economic interest motivating them to join forces. Box 3.4 reviews the case of Ahmedabad, where a fairly progressive local administration has been able to negotiate innovative partnerships with business and community organizations for urban development. Cebu also provides examples of such alliances. Mombasa,

BOX 3.4 CITY GOVERNMENT – BUSINESS – CIVIL SOCIETY PARTNERSHIPS IN AHMEDABAD

Ahmedabad, the state capital of Gujarat, is historically a textile city with a resilient economy and a substantial industrial and commercial base. Over the last 20 years, the textile industry has been subject to major decline and restructuring, witnessing a loss of about 60,000 jobs. However, the city benefited from India's economic liberalization policy in the 1990s. Indeed, recent growth trends in income and employment have strengthened the city's economy. The city has a proactive local administration, a dynamic corporate sector with a long tradition of participation in civic affairs, and a large array of NGOs and CBOs. The improved fiscal position of Ahmedabad Municipal Corporation (AMC) has enabled it to work in partnership with these other agents. Keen to promote this partnership to generate economic opportunity, AMC plans to set up an international exhibition centre in the city to promote local industry and trade.

Relations between the business community and the municipality reflect changing economic circumstances and opportunities. Arvind Mills, one of Ahmedabad's largest textile companies, for example, claims 'enlightened self-interest' as a compelling reason for its engagement with AMC and city NGOs in stimulating the local economy, improving the city slums and raising city living standards, in order to attract management personnel from all over the world. One proposal mooted by this company was to set up a modern garment park in the centre of the city, utilizing land and labour left unemployed after mill closures.

One partnership project that has been implemented focused on increasing the economic potential of a prime business and commercial artery of the city – the CG road. Here, Arvind Mills met the capital costs of redevelopment and will recover its contribution from advertising and parking revenues. The project involved other business partners in planning, construction and management work. The road was widened and footpaths constructed to become a major shopping street. The project has successfully met many of its objectives but there has been concern that, despite the employment created, the project has displaced smaller businesses and hawkers. In other initiatives, AMC has involved private companies in upgrading and maintaining parks, gardens, vacant land and roadsides in return for advertising rights. These initiatives have increased the city's green areas, provided employment opportunities and generated new forms of investment partnership.

Perhaps the most significant example of partnership is the Slum Networking Project (SNP) established in 1995 as a partnership between the city government, the private sector, NGOs and the slum communities themselves. Arvind Mills set up a trust (SHARDA) in order to execute this project. The AMC facilitated the project, and SAATH, an NGO, took responsibility for community mobilization and development. Overall, the project has outperformed earlier piecemeal efforts at slum improvement. Box 9.4 provides further details.

Despite the clear achievements of these partnerships, problems have been experienced. There has been little long-term thinking or strategy to link this approach with the wider issues of city economic growth, so that in most cases these initiatives work in isolation from wider social and economic dynamics, with implications for their sustainability. Perhaps unsurprisingly, there have been serious difficulties in maintaining partnership relationships, as a result of differences in work culture and decision-making structures between the private sector businesses, NGOs and the municipal authority. Arvind Mills actually pulled out of the Slum Networking Programme after the pilot programme. Nevertheless, they are still involved in other projects and there is still clear commitment to working together to realize the city's economic potential.

Source: Dutta with Batley, 1999

however, demonstrates how ethnic and political tensions can frustrate attempts to build alliances by undermining trust between local government and entrepreneurs, and between enterprises of different scales and types.

City governance and poverty reduction: What are the possibilities?

There is clearly a significant relationship between local economic change and the lives of the urban poor. However, there is no automatic correlation between economic growth and poverty trends, either positively or negatively. Evidence from the cities is mixed. The relationship is affected by inequality, by the limited availability of infrastructure and services, and by government activity. While there is scope for city governments to influence the performance of the local economy, that scope is highly constrained by national and global economic factors. Furthermore, city governments often do not have – formally, at least – any role in promoting local economic development.[8] City government may have rather more room for manoeuvre in enabling the poor of the city to benefit from any economic growth, or in protecting them from the adverse effects of economic changes.

The productivity of the urban economy can be much influenced by the actions of city government. Ensuring that basic infrastructure and services are provided and are accessible to all can have a profound effect on businesses, enabling them to function without resorting to costly alternatives. This is especially important for the informal and local economic sectors that are so often inadequately served. Ensuring access to land and secure tenure for embryonic enterprises, on terms that are appropriate to the ways in which they operate, is also a strategically important role for municipal governments. These aspects will be discussed further in Chapter 9. City governments also have a role, whether directly or indirectly, in ensuring access to primary healthcare and primary education, through which the poor build up their human capital and so are enabled to benefit from new economic opportunities. Few of our case cities performed noticeably well on these aspects, and many performed badly, for reasons that will be discussed in subsequent chapters.

All too often, the role of city government has been destructive towards the income opportunities of the poor. Demolitions, re-settlement in remote locations, repressive regulation of informal sector trading, and poor quality of services all increase the vulnerability of the poor and undermine their capacity to take hold of local livelihood opportunities. Formal systems of 'master planning', as in Bangalore, designed to serve the interests of formal sector businesses, make it difficult for the poor and the informal sector to establish their claims. Over zealous enforcement of inappropriate regulations, along with 'mega projects' which pre-empt well located land and displace the poor, diminish economic opportunities.

Failure to provide adequate security leads to fear and unease, particularly about the use of public space. This in turn inhibits the development of networks and social capital on which the economic activities of the poor depend. There are examples of where city governments have sought to address these issues, such as the provision in Johannesburg of street lighting to lengthen the day for trading and to facilitate socializing without fear. Upgrading of slum areas in Visakhapatnam has had a profound effect on local level economic activity by poor groups. But the case studies show that it is far easier for municipal governments to destroy jobs, livelihoods and social capital by ill thought-through policies and actions, than it is to create or rebuild them. A first step, therefore, is to prevent such 'bad governance' – a point to which we will return in Chapter 8.

Notes

1   This chapter draws on an earlier working paper written with Philip Amis (Amis and Grant, 2000).
2   A fuller analysis of the livelihood strategies of the poor will be provided in Chapter 4.
3   It should be noted that the city studies did not focus on labour markets and employment as such, so the comments in this section are based on general observations from the city studies and elsewhere rather than on detailed analysis of what is occurring in labour markets in the cities concerned.
4   Since 1998 was the time of the east Asian financial crisis, employment in manufacturing is likely to have been lower in that year than it would otherwise have been.
5   However, it is important to note that statistics on employment may vary in terms of how they treat informal sector workers. This can affect the service sector in particular, since this is where the bulk of urban employment is located. Also, the service sector is sometimes used as a residual category. This might help to explain the very high proportion of workers counted in this category in Colombo, Cebu and elsewhere.
6   A short, supplementary case study was undertaken in Benin, examining the role of employment creation programmes in the city of Cotonou. This work was carried out by Blandine Fanou and Ursula Grant in 2000.
7   Benjamin's concept of the 'local economy' overlaps with the more widely used concept of the 'informal economy', but is rather broader, including much of the small-scale industrial sector, and without the pejorative connotations of illegality often associated with the latter concept. By contrast, the 'corporate economy' covers the formally constituted, mostly large and medium sized enterprises.
8   However, in India, the 74th Constitutional Amendment assigned to municipal corporations responsibilities for economic development and poverty reduction.

Chapter 4

Surviving in the City: Livelihoods and Linkages of the Urban Poor

Jo Beall

Introduction

Chapter 2 provided a discussion of how urban poverty has been defined and measured and how issues of definition and measurement can affect policies targeting the urban poor. It was pointed out that urban poverty is multi-dimensional and more dynamic than implied by poverty datum lines and static policy analyses. Indeed, poverty can be characterized by cumulative deprivations, and one dimension of poverty is often the cause of or contributor to another dimension (World Bank, 2000). The dynamic responses to poverty on the part of the urban poor themselves, combined with the complexity of urban institutional life, leads us to suggest that urban social disadvantage needs to be understood relationally, in terms of analytical constructs that explain processes of social exclusion and marginalization, as well as the relative powerlessness and absence of voice among the urban poor in respect of governance.

In this chapter we explore the livelihoods of the urban poor, understood not simply in terms of the strategies by which they survive and make a living in the present, but how they seek to secure their long-term future. In particular we look at their connectedness and the linkages they make towards these ends. The networks of the urban poor include those of mutual support among close family and wider kin as well as neighbourhood and community-level groups. They also include more extensive associations that assist in the access of information and resources, or that link them into the decision-making arenas of urban governance. The question is asked whether the social resources of the urban poor constitute a form of social capital that extends beyond mutuality and enhances urban governance.

Framing urban livelihoods

For most poor people in cities, when asked what they need most, they say jobs or money. Indeed, jobs and income earning opportunities were found by our study to be the most fundamental preoccupations of the urban poor. This is hardly surprising given the almost total dependence on money for survival in city economies. However, pursuing secure livelihoods is not only about activities directly associated with income earning but includes a much wider range of endeavours. A single household might see different members employing livelihood strategies as diverse as competing in formal labour markets, undertaking seasonal and casual work, earning incomes in the informal economy and obtaining credit. Moreover, it is difficult to divorce a focus on urban livelihoods from concerns over basic needs. Both day-to-day and in terms of longer-term security, commercial relations are often the key to accessing health, education, housing, services and decent living environments. It is important, therefore, to explore the pursuit of urban livelihoods not only in terms of productive economic activities but also in terms of the arena of reproduction, understood both at the household level and in terms of the provision and consumption of services in the city.

The productive life of the working poor in cities requires above all a healthy body, in turn dependent on access to basic services and a decent living environment. Access to basic services such as a safe and reliable water supply and sanitation were major preoccupations of the urban poor in the cities studied, while extending services at the same time as maintaining existing supply constituted a critical challenge to local authorities. In Mombasa, for example, the majority of households are officially said to have access to piped water but, in reality, very few parts of the city received a continuous supply, forcing residents to buy water from vendors or to rely on water boreholes managed by women's groups or mosque committees. Such providers are often more reliable and accessible than providers of formal services. However, they may also be more costly. In the case of inadequate sanitation, the poorest are often resistant to deploying limited income to this end, resorting instead to performing ablutions in streams and drains, or using plastic bags for defecation, with serious health implications for themselves and the whole community. In Kumasi, for example, the inadequacy of public toilets and having to 'go to the bush' was an issue that loomed large for people.

Access to land and housing is a critical element in combating urban poverty and achieving livelihood security and is an area that is mediated most particularly by commercial transactions. As a productive asset, housing is a vehicle by which home-based work can be generated. It can be used as collateral for accessing credit and can generate a rental income, which may be important as the only or as a supplementary income for poor urban households (Beall, 2000b). As important, if not more so, is the need for housing as shelter and as a social asset without which it is difficult to fully participate in society. In Cebu, for example, the poor were identified as squatters or renters living in makeshift shanty houses. In both social and economic terms, security of tenure was perceived to be important for livelihood strategies in the present and for greater livelihood security in the longer run.

In the urban context, locality and place are important dimensions of the way in which poverty is experienced. Distance from work opportunities or proximity to environmental hazards can play their part in urban social disadvantage and this was found to be the case in a number of our city studies. For example, in Bangalore, location was shown to critically influence the ability of poor people to secure livelihoods. In Johannesburg, the spatial legacy of apartheid saw the poorest citizens forced to reside in the most far-flung residential areas of the metropole. Santiago is also a very segregated city in socio-economic terms (as illustrated in Box 3.2), and although conditions for the poor have improved markedly since 1990, the spatial distribution of poverty has changed very little, while those areas where poverty persists are socially stigmatized.

Like health and housing, education holds benefits in terms of short-term coping strategies as well as a household's ability to recover and move permanently from vulnerability to self-sufficiency (de la Rocha and Grinspun, 2001). Seen across the generations, securing education for younger family members is an important livelihood strategy, but one found to be evidently under stress among the urban poor. In Cebu this involved failure to access secondary and higher education. In Mombasa, low and declining school attendance was reported, attributed both to inadequate household resources and rising education costs, making it increasingly difficult for children from poor families to attend even primary school. Similarly, in Kumasi, a major issue for people was not being able to afford school fees. Even in higher income cities such as Santiago, issues of inequality were evident, where the level of service provided by the under-resourced municipal schools fell well below subsidized and private schools.

Perceptions of poverty were not only associated with material lack but also with issues of respect and dignity. We found people were deeply fearful of social stigma and exclusion. Social exclusion can derive in part from lack of access to labour markets and economic processes, and in part from exclusion from political and decision-making processes. Both forms of exclusion can impact negatively on the livelihoods and linkages of the urban poor. In Kumasi, for example, low-income people were sensitive to being excluded by those in authority and identified the poorest amongst them as being those who were not respected in society, who had little access to basic needs and who lived in relative isolation. In Mombasa too, among their many problems poor families emphasized feeling powerless to improve their situation.

Perceptions of insecurity were found to accompany the experience of social exclusion and these in turn affected the ways in which poor urban dwellers engaged in social and public life. Trends detected in Johannesburg, Santiago and Indian cities such as Bangalore included a decrease in social contact and use of public space, exacerbated by declining levels of public safety. This in turn tended to lead to self-confinement and disengagement with the urban environment and urban processes, with negative consequences for state–society relations and urban governance. In Kumasi the poor felt themselves unfairly labelled as thieves. While gated communities are most often associated with high-income urban residents protecting themselves from crime and violence, barricading themselves behind high walls and gates, research in Johannesburg found gated communities among the urban poor as well. Here migrant hostel dwellers were just as likely to shut themselves off in bounded compounds, both to protect themselves from violent crime and hostility in the broader environment as well as to pursue illicit livelihood activities in the face of exclusion from job markets and other forms of income generation (Beall et al, 2002).

There is no doubt that the urban poor are energetic and resilient in the face of both adversity and opportunity. Individuals, households and communities use their existing endowments and capabilities to survive, to secure livelihood stability, and to increase their security. They secure themselves against shocks and stresses by working, saving and investing, including in social networks and relationships. It is the poorest who are most susceptible to shocks because it is they who have the least by way of endowments. Understanding vulnerability, therefore, requires building a picture of the resource endowments of poor households as well as the income earning activities in which they engage (de la Rocha and Grinspun, 2001). Moser (1998) has pointed out that the 'resilience' necessary to exploit opportunities and to resist and recover from adversity is closely linked to the assets held by the urban poor.

For Moser, it is people's ability to effectively transform these assets into income, food or other basic necessities that can enhance productivity and constitute a 'resilience' strategy. Such transformation can occur either by intensification of existing livelihood strategies or through developing new or diversified strategies (Moser, 1996, p2). Chambers and Conway (1992) conceptualize livelihood strategies as activities that are improvised and sustained by household members through utilization of tangible assets such as stores and resources, and intangible assets such as claims and access. Efforts might include gaining and retaining access to information, resources and opportunities, dealing with risk, negotiating social relationships and managing social networks within families, communities and the city itself. Every household's combination of strategies will be different, depending on their tangible and intangible asset base. In what follows, we explore intensification and diversification of urban livelihood strategies at the household level, before going on to examine the importance of linkages beyond the household towards enhancing livelihood security.

Household livelihood strategies

Household relations have been considered a livelihood asset and are often crucial to the survival of one urban household relative to another in a similar external environment (Moser, 1996, 1998). The composition and structure of urban households as well as their stage in the domestic cycle, along with other factors such as headship and internal/external relationships, all provide or limit a household's ability to mobilize additional labour, to diversify livelihood strategies and to consolidate life-chances in the city (Beall, 2002a). The importance of household consolidation and family ties for escaping poverty was underscored in our research, as was the position of individual household members. Relationships across generations often operate alongside gender relations to inform the ways in which livelihood strategies are consolidated and diversified, with both children and older people playing an important role in contributing to overall household income, withdrawing from household consumption and expenditure and engaging in domestic work and childcare (Beall, 2002b).

Working for a wage and generating incomes

As pointed out above, urban livelihoods are crucially linked to employment or income earning opportunities. Access to formal sector employment is everywhere quite limited and in all the cities studied, recourse was taken to casual labour or informal income generating opportunities. Even for those in permanent and salaried employment, sustainable livelihoods often demand engaging in additional work in the informal economy. This was certainly the case in the African cities studied. In Visakhapatnam, it was not simply whether one was in employment or not that was a marker of poverty, but the position held within the labour market. Indeed there was a definable hierarchy established in people's minds between regular, contract and casual work.

While the paid work of the urban poor is invariably badly remunerated and executed under difficult if not dangerous conditions, some groups are particularly vulnerable. For example, in all the cities studied it was found that large numbers of children engaged in livelihood activities on their own account or more often on behalf of their households. They inevitably did this at the expense of their education and future potential. In Johannesburg, for example, where post-apartheid government policy is firmly focused on getting the children of historically disadvantaged populations into schooling, it was found that excluded populations escape the net. In particular, children of street traders, many of whom are foreign African migrants, are not easily being recruited into South African schools. In Bangalore, it was the case that the number of children living and working on the streets runs into the tens of thousands. Even when education or vocational training opportunities are on offer, these are often eschewed due to the lack, or perceived lack, of employment opportunities following on from them (Beall, 1997).

Women are also recognized as being disadvantaged in urban labour markets, having weaker access both to formal jobs, except in the most exploitative of

BOX 4.1 KUMASI: WOMEN TRADERS FORGE LINKS IN SUPPORT OF URBAN LIVELIHOODS

Market trading forms the main occupation for over 70 per cent of urban women in Ghana, and the Kumasi Central Market (KCM) is the largest in the country. The majority of women traders are not among the city's poorest but it is precisely the income from market trade that is instrumental in keeping them and their households out of poverty. Moreover, it is difficult to calculate those who indirectly benefit from their trading activities, whether as dependents or as paid workers. Market income also plays a central role in underpinning the financial autonomy of trading women – important in a context where non-pooling of household resources and gender-specific budgeting responsibilities are customary.

   Social networks are critical to market trading and, in the absence of any official information sources, for example on prices or the source and availability of commodities, women traders rely on their social networks to direct and sustain market business. These social networks are also important in the longer-term social and economic security of trading households, and have been sustained longer than more formally organized market associations. Formal market associations in the KCM have tended to collapse due to the inability of commodity leaders to resolve problems among their large and heterogeneous membership. Moreover, busy women traders have scant time to engage in formal collective action. A lack of accountability and communication on the part of the Kumasi Metropolitan Assembly (KMA) has also undermined formal associations.

   Although the role of women traders as family breadwinners is vitally important, as is their contribution to tackling poverty at the local level, they are rendered invisible by policy and planning. Despite the KCM playing a major developmental role in the city, accommodating trade, creating employment and providing the main source of revenue for the KMA, the market sees little government support. Market trade is treated residually by both national and local policy makers. For things to be different, a change in attitude towards women's economic and social contribution is required, and a breaking of the political hegemony that fails to support the social and economic contribution of market trade. In the meantime, the trading women of Kumasi are fighting poverty for themselves.

sectors, and to certain assets, notably capital and land. Women are found to be over-represented in the non-conventional or informal economy and to pursue such livelihoods largely as workers rather than as entrepreneurs (Beall, 2002a). Again our city studies proved to be in line with these findings. In Mombasa, for example, it was found that women were not only disproportionately represented in the informal economy but were engaged mainly in selling foodstuffs, brewing and selling illicit liquors, while men were dominant in more lucrative activities, such as the hawking of curios, manufacturing, renting out rooms and water vending. Even in Kumasi, where women had more opportunities as traders than in most other places, opportunities for the poor were constrained by acute competition. This applied both to informal livelihood options such as petty trading as well as to urban agriculture where there were competing demands for land by other uses, notably construction. Moreover, women's central role in the economy of that city is largely ignored by the municipal government, as indicated in Box 4.1.

In Kumasi, marginalized trader groups were found to experience severe problems with land availability and were allotted no permanent working place. For instance, retailers were constantly being threatened with relocation, being driven away from pavement stalls and having their stalls demolished by the city authorities. In Cebu too, working conditions associated with the poor included not having permanent stalls or vending spaces, having only limited capital or none at all and thus being unable to redeem confiscated goods or to repair vending units when threatened or harassed by the authorities. In Johannesburg, the well-meaning Metropolitan Local Council cleared the streets of vendors, offering them a covered market in Yeoville instead, but depriving the street traders of prime positions and opportunities in terms of passing trade.

Casual labour, characterized by very low and irregular wages, constitutes a critical source of income for poor urban households. This was found to be the case in the local economic clusters in Bangalore described in Chapter 8, and casual work was a prominent feature of livelihood strategies in other cities too. Even in Santiago, a city in the study with one of the most developed economies and where economic growth had impacted to a degree on urban poverty, the poor were found to earn very low wages as casual workers in the formal sector. However, in Ahmedabad, by contrast, there was evidence of an upturn in activity in both the formal and informal economies and a corresponding decrease in casual work.

Not only was the type of work conducted important but also the location of the income-earning activities undertaken. Home-based work had implications for the living environment, while factory-based work often took its toll in terms of travel expenses. In the African cities in particular, linkages between urban and rural populations were found to be strong and to play a crucial role in family survival, as households diversified their livelihood activities across the rural–urban divide. For example, many men in Mombasa were temporary migrants who might return home either to invest in a business or when work was not available in town. The same applied to the migrant hostel residents of Johannesburg for whom some livelihood activities, such as the sale of crafts and of marijuana, were dependent on supplies from rural areas. Hence, agricultural seasons could affect the availability of produce and labour in urban centres as well as patterns of migration. Intra-family resource flows included not only urban–rural remittances but other forms of reciprocity that indicate important interdependencies between rural and urban environments. Indeed, such flows were found to be particularly important to survival in times of economic hardship among the poor in the African cities studied. These linkages, along with the broader dilemmas of employment creation, have important policy implications, suggesting that urban planners and managers cannot be expected to address the problems of urban poverty outside of the wider policy picture and interventions at higher levels.

Cutting down on consumption and the care economy

It goes without saying that strong and well-supported livelihood strategies lead to more secure urban households. However, livelihood income and outcomes often do not meet even the most basic of household needs, increasing the vulnerability of those already marginalized from the social and economic life of the city. Important among the strategies of the urban poor were found to be modulating patterns of consumption in order to adapt to shifts in household income or shocks to the household resource base, such as price rises, loss of subsidies or periods of illhealth on the part of breadwinners. Our studies confirmed that women generally spent a greater proportion of their income on household needs than did men. As such, in family efforts to cope with urban poverty, they were the household members most likely to engage in belt tightening exercises. Even among better-off households, the study of Kumasi Central Market showed that when both spouses were traders and earning similar amounts, women nonetheless allocated over half their income to household expenditure while men allocated far less.

In Kumasi, poor people talked of cutting meals from three to just one a day and buying smaller (and less cost effective) bags of rice. In Mombasa it was found that the poor engaged in expenditure saving by walking to work, eating only once a day, gathering fallen items from the ground to sell or to eat, withdrawing children from school, postponing medical treatment and using self-medication. Consistent with much of the literature on urban poverty (Bradley et al, 1991; Harpham and Tanner, 1995) illhealth emerged as a critical issue in precipitating poverty and one that was strongly linked to problems of indebtedness. In Visakhapatnam linkages were drawn between the impact of household debt and breakdown in family relations, leading to alcoholism and, in extreme cases, suicide among people living in the slum areas. Going into debt was itself seen as part of everyday household financial management in Visakhapatnam.

In many cities credit taken from friends and family with no or low interest was regarded as the simplest way to manage household budgets in times of hardship. In the absence of this option and in times of serious financial crisis, moneylenders were favoured. In Kumasi, the use of petty credit from storekeepers was also cited as a mechanism regularly used for buying necessities such as food, while larger forms of borrowing and savings associations were invoked if collateral were needed for less regular expenditure. Asking for assistance from relatives in times of hardship was cited as a key coping strategy for the poor in Mombasa. It was asserted that seeking material and financial assistance from relatives is not regarded as begging – although begging at religious buildings for food and money was also regarded as a crucial strategy for many without family support. Supporting family members is clearly reciprocal, implying that everyone is at one time or another indebted to someone in the family.

Other important adaptive institutions for the poor can include mechanisms for pooling income and other resources within households and communities (Moser, 1996). Although our city studies did not identify anything as formalized as the community kitchens found in many Latin American cities, there was ample evidence of arrangements for sharing consumption. For example, in Kumasi, the extended family system played a significant role and, among the Asante people in particular, served to soften the impact of unequal social disadvantage across different members of an extended kin group, through the practice of sharing homes by family members of different class backgrounds. However, while extended families can provide networks of mutuality and support, this is often an unequal process more burdensome on some members than others. For example, a poor person can expect business support from a rich relative or to have utility bills paid. Rich relatives may take on the responsibility of paying school fees for the children of a poor brother, sister, cousin or a distant relative. However, the obligations to provide for and support the poorest members of a family or community can constitute a drain on the resources of the almost poor, significantly increasing their vulnerability.

Reciprocal obligations or social indebtedness can be a particular problem for migrant groups, who are prevailed upon by rural relatives and urban counterparts, and at a time when their own position within the city may be fragile and contingent. Under such circumstances some family members are more vulnerable to refusal than others. In Kumasi, while old age is traditionally associated with respect and wisdom, it was reported as often being experienced as loneliness and neglect as household members struggled to balance multiple social obligations against limited livelihood opportunities. The position of older people was reported to have worsened also due to a weakening of traditions and the scattering of family members in and from urban areas. As care of the elderly is dependent on informal family support systems, increasingly older people in Kumasi are left without social protection or are sent back to their villages to escape urban hardships.

The vulnerability of older people in cities was not matched by the contribution they made to livelihood strategies within family and household structures. Importantly, they were found to provide care and to adopt 'parenting' roles when younger adult members were engaged in paid work. In South Africa it was found that for many older people, especially women, their reality was one of responsibility for rearing first their own children and then their grandchildren. In the context of HIV/AIDS, greater numbers of older people are finding themselves heads of households comprising many young children and few contributing members. In these and other household structures, in the context of high levels of poverty and unemployment, whole families are dependent on the pensions of older household members.

Wider social networks of the urban poor

Beyond families and households, we found evidence across the African and Asian cities especially, of resource pooling within communities and more commonly, through associations such as savings and self-help groups. Such activities, and the social relations associated with them, can provide an essential buffer for the poor against deepening vulnerabilities and shocks. There is a tendency to assume that community networks of support and reciprocity are stronger in rural than in urban areas. However, city studies revealed that there is ample evidence of community networks and other civil society groups being vital support mechanisms for the urban poor, although there is also evidence of commercialization of reciprocal relations, for example in relation to gifts and rituals associated with weddings and funerals. Nevertheless, informal institutions and organizations remain important and act as rule-enforcing mechanisms for reinforcing customs, norms, values, religious beliefs and social and solidarity networks in urban communities. These in turn can mediate access to employment, commodity markets, land and housing, services, personal security in the home as well as sources of wider social support.

Social networks are important, therefore, as an asset that poor people in cities can exploit to advance themselves or, in times of adversity, use to help dampen the effects of poverty. Ethnic or hometown associations are important in urban areas of Africa, for example. They were identified in Kumasi, Mombasa and Johannesburg as being active and beneficial among migrants, who rely on ethnic affiliation to counter feelings of insecurity and isolation in these cities. Generally, such ethnic networks tend to operate at community level and are not citywide. In Johannesburg, for example, they were found to operate often within or between migrant hostel complexes, with residents of a particular hostel building all originating from one rural area or town and socializing with people in other hostels from the same rural area. These networks constitute a social function but also act as welfare associations, providing financial support to members in need, such as for funerals.

Basic needs or insecurities often compel the urban poor to form new, urban-based informal support networks. In some low-income neighbourhoods of Kumasi, for example, a communal lifestyle enabled pseudo-kinship relationships to emerge within these urban communities, resulting in family-like reciprocal behaviour. For example, a mother needing to go to the market would leave her children in the care of another household. In return, she would feel obliged to undertake the shopping for them or even feed their children when she minded them in return. In Ghana, communal labour has always been an asset the poor have exploited to meet some of their basic needs, and poor communities in Kumasi were found occasionally to mobilize and use communal labour to provide community facilities such as schools, clinics, drains and bridges, public latrines, and to clean their living environments. Among groups of working people, this system was also used. The mechanics at Suame, the traders of the Kumasi Central Market and the carpenters at Anloga, along with several other poor groups in the city, were noted to have specific days on which they cleaned their surroundings before starting work.

Such activities are dependent on a degree of mutual interest existing within a community or group and it was asserted that levels of solidarity were less strong in Kumasi than those that might be found in Ghana's rural areas, where stronger communal traditions still prevail. Moreover, mutuality was not a feature of communities across all our city studies. In Santiago, for example, it was found that, unlike during the dictatorship years when they shared disadvantage and a common struggle, people, including poorer citizens, had retreated into family groups with the arrival of peace and relative prosperity. They were both apathetic and suspicious of efforts at social mobilization beyond the household. The experience of Santiago notwithstanding, evidence from Cebu demonstrated that local level social networks are an important way for people to glean information about employment opportunities as well as access to government resources and services.

Pooling resources as a livelihood strategy was also found to extend beyond household sharing to community level systems for savings and for credit. In Bangalore, for example, it was found that customary rotating savings mechanisms, known locally as chit funds, constituted a critical resource for the urban poor and fed into complex informal markets of one kind or another. In Colombo, traditional funeral societies (*Maranadara Samiti*) and savings groups (*sittu*) were found to exist alongside sports clubs, trade unions and community development organizations. The same patterns were observable in Johannesburg, with *stokvels* or informal savings clubs, bulk buying schemes, communal eating arrangements and burial associations existing side-by-side with church-based and religious organizations in a city which historically has boasted an active civil society. Even for Santiago, evidence was provided of broader social networks in operation, such as the *allegados* committees. This is a Chilean practice and term applied to extended family or friends living in households where they do not pay rent but contribute in non-monetary ways. As shown by the cases of the *allegados* committees for Latin America and the hometown associations in Africa, informal social networks often become semi-formalized and in turn, come to constitute a more complex web of associational life.

Informal support networks and associational forms can lead to more sustained and organized forms of collective action, not least when livelihoods are threatened. In Cebu, for example, trading groups had organized themselves to fight against stall demolitions. Trade-based associations were among the most active community organizations in Kumasi. Membership groups, by definition, seek to promote the interests of their members. As such they do not always assist in addressing community level or citywide concerns and can work to exclude the most destitute or vulnerable in a society. Among the latter, loose organization can sometimes be found, for instance among the street children of Bangalore. However, these fluid associations are often exploitative. They are rarely sustainable and cannot easily be scaled up into more formalized groupings capable of effective collective action (Beall, 1997).

Our findings also point to the need not to romanticize social networks and relations of reciprocity. Moser (1998) has argued that under stresses and shocks, social capital can be eroded and de la Rocha and Grinspun (2001) also suggest that social resources seem to diminish under the pressures of poverty itself. Our research confirmed that the poorest people were those in isolated households unable to rely on supportive social networks and that low-income areas were those most likely to be situated in stigmatized localities, with crime, violence and fear becoming self-fulfilling prophesies. As our study of Johannesburg showed and as illustrated in Box 4.2, social networks can be characterized as much by exploitative relationships and antisocial behaviour as by reciprocity, support and cooperation.

Box 4.2 Johannesburg: Antisocial networks hurt urban livelihoods and public safety

Social networks are important in advancing the livelihood opportunities of the urban poor. However, such networks are not always benign. They can be characterized as much by exploitative relationships as by reciprocity. Sometimes the livelihood strategies of one group are advanced at the expense of another, severely compromising public safety. In Johannesburg criminal gangs, shacklords, drug lords, pimps and rival taxi operators have intimidated streets, neighbourhoods and whole areas. These areas in turn have become characterized by high levels of crime and interpersonal violence.

Globally, most urban crime is property-based and Johannesburg is no exception to this. In a survey conducted in the late 1990s, two-thirds of its residents reported being victims of crime, most commonly burglary. Johannesburg also experiences high levels of violent crime and has the second highest murder rate in the country. Although the fears of the affluent white population of the city are widely publicized, in fact the black population is just as likely to fall victim to violent crime. For example, a recent survey in Johannesburg found that over 70 per cent of victims of violent car theft and armed hijacking in the city were black. Since 70 per cent of the population of the city is black, this suggests that the issue is not one of race.

Interpersonal violence is also a growing problem in the city and a significantly large proportion of victims are women. Despite the fact that domestic violence and rape are known to be notoriously under-reported, nevertheless official figures for Johannesburg point to an average of 2.27 rapes per 1000 population. Police reports suggest that the highest incidence of reported rapes were in the high density, low-income areas of Soweto, Alexandra, Hillbrow and the inner city. Most crimes involving interpersonal violence are likely to take place at home or in a tavern or bar, with heavy involvement of guns and alcohol.

Causes of high levels of violent crime in Johannesburg are difficult to determine and a number of interpretations have been offered. They include the impact of the legacy of institutional violence under apartheid and the political violence that accompanied its demise. Socio-economic explanations have been offered, related to rapid urbanization, a sluggish economy and high expectations on the part of historically disadvantaged people, especially the young. Contingent explanations relate to the prevalence of gun ownership and an environment of poverty. What is clear is that the actual experience of crime and fear of crime has led to social retreat. The dominance over certain areas by criminal gangs has threatened and eroded prior neighbourhood level social networks, founded on social homogeneity and cohesion. The disappearance or mistrust of social organization serves to reduce the linkages of the urban poor and their connectedness into their communities and the city.

Urban governance and the social assets of the poor

A question critical to our concern with urban governance is whether the social assets of the poor, and more particularly their reciprocal networks and local level associations, can have multiplier effects, sometimes understood as 'bridging social capital' (Foley and Edwards, 1999). In other words, as Putnam (1993) would have us believe, does a rich associational life lead to concerted civic action and the engagement of a responsive local government? Our evidence suggests that no such automatic relationship exists. We found that community level associations and membership organizations reinforce social assets amongst the urban poor but that these are often predicated upon what has been dubbed 'bonding social capital' (Foley and Edwards, 1999) among exclusive groups whose activities benefit the group itself but do not have a wider impact on urban poverty reduction. Kinship networks and very localized forms of association constitute and give rise to important community level assets but ones that rarely go beyond the group.

For example, it was found in the case of one informal settlement in Johannesburg that the group which had arrived and established themselves there earlier excluded new migrants from access to land, housing and services (see Box 7.2). We found across our city studies that endowments of such forms of bonding social capital constitute important, if fragile, resources for the urban poor. They can provide safety-nets when social deprivation is exacerbated by shocks, stress and other sources of vulnerability. The question as to whether bonding social capital benefits urban development is more vexed. To the extent that it does, it is when poor urban communities engage in self-help initiatives to provide urban goods and services in the absence of adequate provision by the relevant authorities. In other words, activities such as cleaning market places, maintaining public toilets or looking after neighbourhood infrastructure have a substitution effect, allowing local authorities to abdicate responsibility for providing these services for low-income areas or groups. However, the fact that they are invariably performed in the interests of an exclusive group means that the benefit to the city concerned is fairly limited.

The question remains, therefore, under what circumstances if any, are localized and in-group activities scaled up for more generalized goals and ends? The ten city case studies provide some evidence of organizations scaling up and scaling out, a process described in some detail in Chapter 7. However, the move from bonding to bridging social capital, for example through the formation of federations of smaller organizations and their engagement with local government, is neither automatic nor easy to forge. Nevertheless, the city reviews did yield evidence of local organizations of the poor forming themselves into loose but wide federations that afforded them greater voice. The best example was the formation of the Cebu City United Vendors Association, described in Box 7.3. Other examples included informal networks of *sangas* (revolving credit groups) in Bangalore, 'caste-based organizations' in Visakhapatnam, traders' associations in Kumasi and committees for local improvement and development in Santiago. The more formally constituted federations of community-based organizations (CBOs) were found to emerge most particularly in response to government provided services, such as the Home Owners' and Water Users' Associations in Cebu City. Another example was the rents and rates boycotts in the 1980s and early 1990s in Johannesburg, where township residents, on an organized basis, refused to pay what they saw as illegitimate apartheid local authorities for sub-standard services.

When neighbourhood or community-based organizations are scaled up to city level, various forms of capture can come into play. Examples of this were provided by the studies of Visakhapatnam, Bangalore and Johannesburg. In these cities it was found that, in their individual capacities, community level organizations were often concerned with meeting immediate felt needs rather than taking on wider concerns. Even when their ambitions were greater, such organizations generally have no social, legal or political status, can often claim no right of access to decision-making forums, or find that the representatives of informal local structures are relatively powerless in the more formal political arena. Another problem is that organizations active at the local or even city level can become subverted to national-level agendas and ambitions. For example, in Johannesburg the civic organizations affiliated to the South African National Civics Organization (SANCO) became preoccupied with that organization's oppositional agenda in respect of the national government, rather than with local issues of urban development and governance.

A number of the city case studies provided examples of community-based organizations being created by the state or other developmental institutions for project-based and sometimes political purposes. For example, in Santiago, large numbers of organizations were formed to support community projects related to state programmes for poor areas. In Bangalore and Colombo, the Urban Basic Services Programme (UBSP) established Neighbourhood Committees and Community Development Councils (CDCs) respectively, in order to ensure consultation and participation in service delivery. Once objectives were achieved, many such organizations became moribund and ceased to function. In Johannesburg user involvement in local decision-making is not only encouraged but is constitutionally required. Here it was found that organizational pluralism was prevented due to one dominant group or community organization emerging and usurping the consultative process. These city-level experiences also demonstrated that the artificial imposition of community-level structures sometimes served to undermine existing organizations and erode spontaneous social participation. This suggests that government cannot easily construct or forge bridging social capital for its own purposes of urban development.

To the extent that partnership relationships that build bridging social capital can be fostered and nurtured between organizations of the working poor and local government, this was found to depend on the intervention of representatives of the former. The obvious example to emerge from the city studies was that of the Self-Employed Women's Association (SEWA) in Ahmedabad, which has successfully engaged local authorities and the business community on behalf of its constituency of women pursuing home-based livelihood strategies or earning a living in the informal economy. SEWA was created in 1972, initially as a response to loss of jobs in the city's textile industry. Today it runs credit, healthcare and social insurance programmes as well as engaging in policy advocacy and political lobbying. In the absence of organizations such as SEWA, the resources of the poor are often destined to remain operative at the micro-level alone, poorly harnessed towards advancing livelihood opportunities through organized linkages.

Conclusion

What is clear across all the cities studied is that social networks and the many different forms of associational life described above are crucially important in maintaining and developing urban livelihoods. However, while clearly being a resource to the urban poor, they are very fragile and take their toll on people, some more than others. People do support each other and communities cooperate. Under certain circumstances they organize themselves more widely. However, under conditions of poverty and stress, without some sort of security in place, it is difficult for poor urban households to engage in reciprocal gestures and for low-income communities to sustain self-help initiatives. Even more difficult to sustain is organized and scaled-up public engagement, except under conditions of extreme provocation, such as during the twilight years of apartheid in South Africa or under the Chilean dictatorship, or when sympathetic representatives and interlocutors work with and on behalf of the urban poor. Under these circumstances, it is very easy for city governments to destroy or damage survival and livelihood strategies by their actions, even when well intentioned. Hence, it is vital that urban policy-makers and planners understand the livelihood strategies, networks and other social assets of the poor, in order to anticipate and respond to the possible impact of interventions. This is illustrated most clearly in relation to policies towards the informal sector, as recounted in Chapter 8.

When intentions are less noble, it is also easy for city governments to abdicate responsibility for the urban poor altogether, allowing them to substitute their scarce resources and their limited time and energy for the public provision or coordination of service delivery. What does this mean for urban governance? Clearly as much as they benefit poor households and communities themselves, the social assets and social networks of the poor also constitute a resource for city governments. Moreover, when the urban poor do engage in scaled-up public action around community-based or work related issues, they can and do rock the boat. This confirms that there is no substitute for extending the linkages of the urban poor in pursuit of sustainable livelihoods, not simply in self-help networks of mutuality and support but towards engagement in local governance.

Chapter 5

Urban Politics: Exclusion or Empowerment?

Carole Rakodi[1]

Introduction

Urban governance refers to the interactive relationships between and within government and civil society actors in cities. It includes the overlapping domains of political and administrative processes of decision-making and is also about how government organizations react to the needs and demands of urban actors, both organized and unorganized. Chapter 6 concentrates on the organizational and administrative arrangements and practices of city governments. This chapter explores political systems and processes at the urban level, including the creation and operation of political institutions, government capacity to make and implement decisions, and the extent to which those decisions recognize and respond to the interests of the poor. Its aim is to analyse and explain how urban political systems and processes operate and the extent to which they give the poor political voice and influence.

For what purpose and in whose interests government actions are taken depends on three main factors:

- The political context, which has both local and supra-local dimensions. The former refers to the socio-political public space available to urban actors, including the poor, and their ability to take advantage of that space. The outcome depends on the character of that local political space, the capacity of citizens to engage in politics, the distribution of power between them and how they exercise that power. The supra-local dimensions of the political context include the institutions and rules that govern political behaviour, the political culture and the nature of the national political regime.
- The way that political intermediation mechanisms (the formal structures and procedures of the urban political system) are designed and how they work in practice.
- The political actors involved – their goals and demands, the resources they bring to the political system, the power relationships between them, and the strategies and tactics they adopt, that is their political practices.

The interrelationships between political structures, actors and practices in particular contexts have varied characteristics and differing outcomes with respect to effective and pro-poor governance. As explained in Chapter 1, this research stops short of a rigorous analysis of outcomes, although it has identified illustrative examples of pro-poor results. Instead, it concentrates on how and in what circumstances poor people are able to gain access to decision-making processes and influence political agendas, with the result that public agencies (especially local government) address poverty through their practices and resource allocation decisions.

The discussion will first explore dimensions of the political context of the cities under study, to identify what local and supra-local contextual characteristics are most likely to produce urban political space in which avenues of influence are open to poor citizens. Second, it will analyse the structures and procedures of alternative urban political systems, including forms of democracy and representation, arrangements for executive control and, briefly, mechanisms for accountability. Third, it will analyse the articulation between political structures and a variety of urban interests, identifying key actors, explaining how they behave, and revealing relationships between them through an analysis of political practices. Particular attention will be given to the concerns of poor people, their capacity to press their demands and the responses of political decision-makers to such demands.

Democratization, decentralization, rights and regime change: The political context

Political contexts, in which authoritarian centralized rule advances the interests of the ruler, who exercises coercive, economic and bureaucratic hegemony, were common in many of the countries in which the case study cities are located in the 1970s and 1980s. These gave way in the 1990s to more democratic regimes in which it was intended that citizenship rights would be exercised through the electoral system and that the voting power of poor people would ensure that their concerns were addressed. In addition, decentralization would improve efficiency and local responsiveness. Even in the well-established democratic system of India, there was recognition that democratic practices were being undermined at the local level by the periodic suspension of many elected local governments and the failure to decentralize effectively. This led to attempts to strengthen local democracy by constitutional change at the beginning of the 1990s.

Political arrangements are embedded in a wider set of rules and practices. These are based in part on the constitution and associated law, which specifies political and civil rights and ensures that these rights can be protected. Such 'rules' or norms of political behaviour also arise from socially constructed identities, meanings, informal rules and institutions, and political practices. The latter, in turn, influence the framing of constitutional and legal frameworks. All are shaped by history, previous experiences of democratic arrangements and the nature of the (re-)democratization process. Together, they constitute the political culture and incorporate a conceptualization of citizenship as active or passive.

Liberal democratic theory (like liberal economic theory) gives primacy to the individual. It assumes that politics aggregates the prior desires or preferences of individuals into collective interests through the mechanisms of elected government, guided by what have come to be a commonly accepted cluster of rules and institutions. These include universal adult suffrage, regular elections, political competition, associational autonomy and the separation of executive, legislative and judicial powers (Held, 1993; Parekh, 1993). According to this theory, government is constituted and leaders selected by individuals exercising their right to choose. Once voted into office, the elected representative is trusted to act as promised, although it is also recognized that he or she has considerable leeway to make detailed decisions, and that additional political practices such as lobbying can supplement periodic elections.

All the city governments studied operate within the context of a formal liberal democratic regime at the national level. However, the political culture, the nature of the previous regime and the characteristics of the processes of regime change vary, helping to explain the nature of the post-transition constitutional settlements and the embeddedness of democratic practices. In some of the countries, earlier authoritarian regimes were cloaked in formal democracy, providing some political space for the organization of opposition. For example, in Brazil between 1964 and the end of the 1980s, the military enlisted the aid of the traditional political élite and the executive branch of government to distribute state resources in order to manufacture consent, and to demonstrate this consent through façade democracy. The regime's need to use the traditional political élite in this way enabled the latter to protect its position, jump onto the democratization bandwagon when pressure for regime change grew too strong to resist and protect its own interests after democratization (Hagiopan, 1994). Countering élite dominance, however, labour unions have remained a potent political force, despite the attempts of the military to reduce their influence. Allied to broader social movements, they were able to exploit the widening of national and local political space to strengthen their political organization (through the Workers Party), influence the new constitution (and thus the form of new political structures) and develop new political practices. Because, in Brazil's federal system, *local* political arenas provided a modicum of political space, local opposition politics and social activism made a significant contribution to the process of regime change, which was rewarded by a commitment to decentralization in the post-transition settlement.

Similarly, in the Philippines, democratic formalism allowed political competition within an élite oligarchical regime. Such competition pitted factions of the élite against each other, resulting in political instability, and excluding many groups from political participation (Rüland, 1992). Regime change occurred both because of competition between the ruling families and as a result of wider social struggles to end authoritarian rule. As in Brazil, the Catholic Church played an important role in supporting community-based organization (CBO) and building grassroots awareness. Again, as in Brazil, sections of the old oligarchy continue to play significant roles in democratic government at both the national and local levels. However, organized civil society played a key role in the process of bringing about democracy, increasing general levels of political awareness and winning for it formal recognition in representative political structures.

In South Africa, because opposition political parties, especially the African National Congress (ANC), were proscribed, the long and often violent struggle against the apartheid regime depended on other forms of social organization, especially trade unions and civics,[2] as well as on widespread mobilization and resistance amongst the population at large. The length, intensity and form of the struggle has resulted in a constitution crafted to ensure political representation of the previously excluded majority and an unambiguous political commitment to redressing apartheid's legacy of extreme inequality and widespread poverty. However, fiscal constraints have made it difficult to consolidate the new democratic institutions, achieve the necessary administrative reforms and reduce poverty. Moreover, many of the organizations, including the civics and many non-governmental organizations (NGOs), which were critical to the struggle against the previous regime have had difficulty adapting to the new political and financial situation.

In Brazil, the Philippines and South Africa, therefore, the struggle to end authoritarian rule depended on organized civil society as well as wider societal opposition. Despite their difficulties, they have a combination of strong democratic constitutions, political commitment to decentralization and provision for civil society inclusion in representative political institutions. As a result, these countries probably have the best prospects for achieving consolidated and stable democracy at both national and local levels.

Chile, India and Sri Lanka provide contrasts. In Chile, although an active civil society played a key role in ousting the Pinochet regime, its role under democracy has not been sustained. Economic growth, following neoliberal economic reforms in the 1990s, and targeted welfare policies have reduced the incidence of poverty. However, the individualist ethos of Chile's model of democracy, its liberalized economy and the focus of its poverty policies on the most vulnerable has led to social fragmentation and the weakening of collective organization. Social exclusion and spatial segregation have undermined the ability of the poor to make effective claims on the political system. In India the prospects for a more effective and responsive democratic local government system to develop were improved by the 74th constitutional amendment. However, the broad-based Congress Party has lost ground to parties with narrower regional, caste or religious bases, reducing the legitimacy of national democratic processes and hindering progress with decentralization. Local politics remains essentially clientelist, despite the presence of fairly well developed civil society organizations (CSOs) and a relatively independent judiciary. In Sri Lanka, national electoral competition has resulted in peaceful transfers of power (except in the north of the country, where a long-standing civil conflict had at the time of the study superseded democratic politics). However, for Colombo, political and bureaucratic rivalry between local, provincial and national levels of government reduce the city government's room to manoeuvre. In addition, political competition at the city and neighbourhood levels manifests itself in electoral politics, which, as in India, are an uneasy mixture of representative democracy and clientelism.

The fragility of democracy, limited political space and undeveloped civil society, especially organizations of the poor, are most marked in the countries where, until recently, one-party rule was accompanied by a refusal to tolerate independent organization outside government and the ruling party. Many such countries also suffer from recurrent crises and their governments lack any real commitment to decentralization. These conditions apply especially to Ghana and Kenya. In Ghana, a legacy of authoritarian politics and state-led approaches to development seems to have resulted in a limited appreciation of the need to secure public support. In addition, the traditional authority structures of the Asante kingdom, which is centred on Kumasi, and which are characterized by hierarchy, deference and unquestioning loyalty to established authority, have an important continuing influence on political culture and behaviour. For example, in Ghana the President nominates (subject to approval by the metropolitan assembly) the metropolitan chief executive (MCE). From 1995 to 2001, the MCE who governed Kumasi in an autocratic, idiosyncratic and ineffective manner was a wealthy member of the Asante royal family, as well as a supporter and financier of the ruling party and personal friend of the President. Presidential support, control over resources and the deference due to a member of the traditional élite enabled the MCE to command majority support in the elected Assembly or sideline it when necessary, despite widespread criticism of his management and allegations of corruption. In Kenya, multi-party elections were restored in 1992 in response to domestic and external pressure, but for a decade there were abuses of the electoral rules. Opposition parties were sometimes refused permits to operate and were denied access to the media; and there was violence, harassment and gerrymandering. Moreover, parties continue to have an ethnic base, the democratic process is seen as an opportunity to capture personal power and President Moi was able to manipulate state resources to stay in power until the December 2002 elections (Wanyande, 2000).

Of all the case study countries, Chile's approach to democratization most closely resembles that recommended by liberal democratic theory. It illustrates many of the shortcomings of that model of representative democracy, especially the passive concept of citizenship that entrusts decisions to elected representatives who may in practice pursue their own interests, and the marginalization of minorities that occurs in majoritarian systems (Held, 1996). Where history and culture have fostered conceptions of active citizenship and organizations of poor people, in contrast, the latter show greater capacity to exercise their political rights. In addition, in such an environment, the legislative base for the democratic system is more likely to incorporate ways of ensuring that the interests of disadvantaged groups are recognized and to provide for forms of direct, deliberative or participatory democracy (Miller, 1993; Held, 1996).

A further criticism of liberal models of democracy is that they fail to recognize values, bases for identity and behavioural rules that value consensus and impose obligations on kin and ethnic group members to support each other. While this moral public sphere is deeply rooted in countries such as Ghana and Kenya, the new democratic institutions still lack roots and legitimacy. As a result, voting follows old allegiances, fragmenting those (especially the poor) who share common economic interests, exacerbating conflict and rivalry between ethnic groups and undermining controls on rent seeking and corruption (Dia, 1996; Enemuo, 2000). The implications of these differences in political culture and history for local politics in the case study cities will be explored further below.

Forms of democracy: Urban political structures and arrangements in theory and practice

The scope for local decision-making depends on the extent to which powers and responsibilities are decentralized to local government, both in theory and in practice. Earlier research has demonstrated that, to respond to local needs, operate effectively and develop legitimacy, local government needs a sound legislative framework, a range of significant responsibilities, an adequate resource base, and political and administrative capacity (Davey, 1996; Crook and Manor, 1998; Blair, 2000). Without these, it is likely to be locked into a vicious circle in which it has little legitimacy in the eyes of urban residents and businesses but lacks the political and financial resources to improve its performance. As a result, citizens and potential candidates for electoral office are not encouraged to take the political process seriously. These earlier findings are borne out by the experiences of the case study cities.

In Ahmedabad, for instance, despite an almost uninterrupted tradition of elected local government since 1950, the general malaise of democratic institutions in India, together with local communal violence arising from caste and religious divisions, had eroded the Ahmedabad Municipal Corporation's (AMC's) legitimacy. The appointment of an effective Municipal Commissioner in the mid-1990s, however, enabled the AMC to realize a financial surplus for the first time. This enabled it to leverage additional capital funds, initiate innovative partnerships and improve service delivery. As a result, confidence in its capacity to deliver increased and its legitimacy in the eyes of citizens improved.

In this section, the legislative basis for decentralization will be discussed first. This will seek to demonstrate how different political interests in central and local government interact with the distribution of responsibilities between central and local agencies to influence responsiveness to the poor as well as effectiveness of service delivery. Second, arrangements for electoral participation at the city level, including the location of legislative and executive control, will be analysed. Finally, the potential contribution of other forms of democratic practice will be reviewed.

Responsibilities and resources: Democratic decentralization or token local government?

In theory, all the national governments in this study are committed to democratic decentralization. In practice, however, their willingness to devolve significant responsibilities, revenue generating powers and autonomy in decision-making varies, depending on several factors. These include central government's own hold on power; concern about the development of autonomous power bases, potentially under opposition control; a (sometimes legitimate) concern that central policy aims would be undermined by local decisions; and the disdain of central bureaucrats for local administrative capacity. Two contrasting cities, Cebu and Bangalore, are analysed in Boxes 5.1 and 5.2.

The Philippines constitution guarantees both significant functions and assured resources for local government, creating a meaningful political arena at the local level. In Cebu City, the electoral arrangements have encouraged the emergence of effective leadership and active engagement by civil society, resulting in a considerable degree of both responsiveness and accountability. In Bangalore, in contrast, many of the most significant service provision and urban development responsibilities remain the responsibility of the Karnataka State government, reducing the scope and effectiveness of local government, which is left with limited powers and resources to deliver local services. Powerful political interests at the state level are not concerned with poverty reduction, although some national programmes attempt to address the needs of poor urban people (see Box 5.2).

The wide remit and substantial resources available to local governments in South Africa and Brazil are similar to the Philippines. However, in Johannesburg the long process of reorganizing local government, together with the Metro council's recent fiscal crisis and the retention of some significant responsibilities (eg housing and education) at national or provincial levels, has constrained the city's ability to tackle widespread poverty despite its relative wealth. In Brazil, following democratization, a decade of left wing municipal government and a history of community-based organization, the allocation of increased powers and resources to local government provided scope for more pro-poor municipal politics. These were implemented in part through a process of participatory

BOX 5.1 CEBU: TOWARDS DEMOCRATIC DECENTRALIZATION AND PRO-POOR LOCAL GOVERNMENT

In Cebu City, the restoration of democracy in 1986 brought with it a political commitment to decentralization and democratic local government enshrined in the Local Government Code 1991. According to this legislation, municipal government has responsibility for a range of services and can also play an agency role in delivering certain national programmes, such as the Community Mortgage Program (CMP), which provides loans to enable residents of informal settlements to purchase land and install infrastructure. In line with the constitution, local governments receive a substantial share of central government revenue and also have a range of local revenue raising powers (see Chapter 6). Cebu itself benefited from rapid economic growth in the 1980s and early 1990s. With substantial local taxes and significant revenue sharing from central government, Cebu City is reasonably well resourced.

In the first mayoral elections of the current era, first Osmeña and then his deputy, Garcia, were brought to power, each for two successive terms, on the basis of a high voter turnout and with clear majorities. Half the councillors elected in 1988 and all of those elected in 1995 and 1998 were affiliated to their party. The mayors had a vision of Cebu's economic future as a port, industrial and service city potentially attractive to Asian foreign direct investment, and a clear local identity and commitment.

In accordance with the Local Government Code, along with a directly elected mayor and members of the legislative assembly, local bodies with wider representation have been established. Most power rests in the hands of the executive mayor. However, the local bodies provide for mandatory representation of NGOs and 'people's organizations' (registered community-based organizations, or CBOs). They have functions related to development and poverty reduction, housing and upgrading, schools, street children, street vendors etc. In addition, a sub-city level of government increases responsiveness to neighbourhood concerns (see Box 6.4). Policy consultations are common, for example during the preparation of city development plans. Municipal governments in the Philippines are obliged to allocate 20 per cent of their total financial resources to implement their development plans, together with an additional 5 per cent earmarked for a gender component.

Since 1986, municipal decision-making in Cebu has contained significant pro-poor elements. In part this can be explained by the city's relative prosperity: according to government figures (although these are challenged by local civil society), the economic boom years reduced poverty. This also enabled the city government to generate resources for large-scale infrastructure investment as well as basic services, despite a downturn associated with the Asian financial crisis of the late 1990s. In addition, organizations and advocates of the poor formed coalitions to lobby for pro-poor policies. They were able, in successive elections, to lobby and secure the commitment of the successful mayoral candidate to a pro-poor political agenda in return for delivering political support. They were also able, to some extent, to hold the Mayor to account following each election. The strength of civil society can largely be attributed to the number of NGOs, some of which cut their teeth on the politics of confrontation during the struggle to end authoritarian rule. Some NGOs provide continuing support for community organization and some participate in local government through the political structures which provide for representation of NGOs and organizations of the poor.

The pro-poor orientation of local policy can also be attributed to national policy commitments which themselves result from strong civil society organization and influence. In particular, a Presidential Commission of the Urban Poor was mirrored in the Cebu City Commission of the Urban Poor (subsequently the Division for the Welfare of the Urban Poor). The DWUP coordinates the implementation of national and local poverty reduction policies with a focus on social housing, services and the upgrading or relocation of informal settlements. Despite the limitations of these programmes, they contribute to a mosaic of pro-poor expenditure and actions.

Cebu City, therefore, has a relatively stable and consolidated democratic political system, which has given voice and influence to the poor. However, local politics still has strong oligarchical and clientelist features. Successive mayors have come from the two most important local families. While their actions have provided some benefits to poor groups, their responses to competing interests have often not favoured the poor. Significant resources have been allocated to prestige projects. The concentration of power and resources in the hands of the mayor and the inability of assembly members to exercise effective scrutiny have reinforced a tendency to allocate resources to meeting the needs of the poor on appeal and by favour rather than by right – a tendency exacerbated by the non-ward based system of political representation. People's organizations (POs) and NGOs can and do successfully articulate the interests of the poor through a variety of formal and informal mechanisms at both neighbourhood and city levels. However, representation in formal decision-making mechanisms is not always meaningful and often the only effective strategy is a direct appeal to the mayor. Thus, although poor residents have obtained improved access to the resources distributed by the political system, their relationships with the mayor are characterized by an uneasy balance between an electoral contract, indirect access mediated by NGOs, and dependent clientelism.

budgeting (PB). Recife, the case study city, followed in the footsteps of Porto Alegre and Belo Horizonte in instituting such a system (see Box 6.3).

The remaining cities bear a closer resemblance to Bangalore than Cebu. In Kumasi, central ministries have been reluctant to cede their functions, as intended under the decentralization programme, to municipal government, which lacks financial and administrative capacity. In Colombo, opposition control of the Colombo Municipal Council (CMC) led central government to retain control over key functions, including urban development planning, housing, water supply and staff recruitment. In Kenya, the retention of key services such as water under the control of national agencies and, until recently, the absence of any central–local financial transfers, rendered Mombasa Municipal Council (MMC) unable to deliver services effectively. Finally, in Chile, central government keeps firm control over all the most significant services and programmes (including those intended for the poor) and ensures that Santiago does not become an independent source of political power by dividing it into 34 municipios.

Structures and processes: the arrangements for urban electoral politics

Especially where local governments have wide responsibilities and significant resources, but even where their roles and capacity are limited, the formal arrangements for electoral politics and the characteristics of day-to-day political practices both matter. Particular formal electoral arrangements are not inherently more effective, responsive to the poor and accountable than others.

BOX 5.2 WEAK LOCAL GOVERNMENT AND INFORMAL POLITICS IN BANGALORE

The metropolitan area of Bangalore is administered by the Bangalore City Corporation (BCC), together with eight County and Town Municipal Councils. However, major infrastructure installation, water and sewerage, curative health, strategic planning and land administration are responsibilities of Karnataka State rather than the city government. Although there is provision for the BCC to be represented on the boards of some state agencies, the state government appoints most of the members on political or business criteria. The wide range of state developmental powers and resources attracts representatives of business keen to promote the economic development of Bangalore as a leader in high-tech industries into standing for political office at the state level. Their priorities are to improve infrastructure, make land available for commercial and industrial activities together with high and middle income housing, and enhance the city's ability to compete for international and domestic investment. On the heels of large-scale investment in infrastructure projects come construction industry interests, which are also influential at state level. The corporate sector (business and finance) therefore works with an 'upper circuit' of state agencies responsible for formal planning, land allocation and comprehensive infrastructure development (as illustrated in the diagram in Box 5.3). Large NGOs funded by external development assistance are also part of this circuit.

The BCC is left with what Benjamin and Bhuvaneswari (2001) call the 'soft' aspects of urban management – trying to influence implementation and service distribution. It is also involved in implementing a number of Union Government poverty alleviation schemes but has little scope for policy-making, except in certain aspects of primary healthcare, education and community development. In the local political system, councillors are elected on a ward basis, and sit on executive standing committees, with the dominant party exercising executive leadership. However, state appointment of the Municipal Commissioner reduces the power of councillors to direct and control administrative officers. In addition, the control of national and state governments over policy and programme design decisions reduces the potential role of councillors. For example, the earlier Urban Basic Services Programme (UBSP) allocated resources for infrastructure improvement at the ward level, allowing councillors to play a role in directing investment to under-serviced settlements. However, under the current Swarna Jayanti Rozgar Yojana programme, state and national level elected representatives are supposed to play a role in identifying individual beneficiaries, thereby sidelining local councillors.

In this context, rather than trying – with little chance of success – to influence policy through the formal processes, residents concentrate on developing the necessary political and bureaucratic relationships to advance their struggles over land tenure and service provision. In accessing land (through squatting or informal subdivision), prospective settlers and subdividers make political contacts. Once occupying the land, CBOs (called *sangas*) are formed to start the long processes of tenure regularization, or at least protection from eviction, and securing basic infrastructure. Residents try to develop a variety of political relationships, especially with the local councillor, but also, where possible, with the MLA (Member of the State Legislative Assembly). The scope for developing such relationships is influenced by ethnicity, party political affiliation and stability of residence (owners are generally more influential than tenants). Moreover, candidates for municipal or state office often stand precisely *because* they have interests in land or construction. Settlers can often, through local leaders or party workers, bargain for secure tenure, the relaxation of formal regulations, or the next stage of infrastructure installation. Although residents do vote in state elections, those elected represent large and mixed constituencies, are too remote for much personal lobbying and rarely have a pro-poor political platform. Municipal politics, in contrast, is more accessible and councillors are likely to be more responsive. The outcomes of local elections depend largely on the perceived capacity of candidates to obtain resources. Whereas high-income residents and larger enterprises can pay individually (for private services or bribes), low-income and (many middle-income) residents can only obtain secure tenure and services with the support of an elected representative. This can only be obtained if electoral support is given – thus voter turnout (at around 80 per cent) is much higher in low- rather than high-income areas. Local leaders, in turn, owe their position to their ability to maintain appropriate political contacts on the one hand and to deliver votes for relevant candidates on the other. All those involved gain in some way from this hierarchy of patron–client relationships.

However, political links are not always necessary and are rarely sufficient – councillors, community leaders, entrepreneurs and residents also cultivate contacts in the middle and lower levels of the municipal and state bureaucracies (see Box 5.3). Social and ethnic connections or petty bribery enable many to get permissions, exemptions or services they cannot otherwise access. Often, in residential areas, 'connection men' (the locally resident employees of service providing departments) will enable service connections to be made in return for a 'fee'.

Thus small enterprises and low-/middle-income residents depend on the politicians and bureaucrats of municipal government and the lower level bureaucrats of the State government. This lower level circuit is a sphere of clientelist inter-dependence, characterized by informal connections – referred to by Benjamin and Bhuvaneswari (2001) as 'politics by stealth'. It is far from the ideal of consolidated democratic decentralization, in which elected representatives balance the interests of their constituents with the need for strategic investment and redistribution, and all citizens gain access to land and basic services as of right. Nevertheless, Benjamin and Bhuvaneswari argue that the informal municipal politics and 'porous bureaucracy' of Bangalore serve low- and middle-income residents much better than State level politics, large-scale decision-making and formal planning. Allocation of responsibility for most policy and investment decisions to the state government, which is more remote and unaccountable than the city government, disadvantages the poor.

In practice, their operation is influenced by the political context and culture, the extent of local autonomy and resources, the configuration of political interests at the city level and the strategies and tactics adopted by different urban actors. However, certain formal political arrangements do seem to provide more opportunities for the poor and marginalized to influence decision-making than others. The most relevant features of those political arrangements include the basis for electoral representation, the location of executive authority, the rules about terms for holding office and provisions for wider societal representation in governance.

The basis for electoral representation

The evidence from the city case studies and other research (eg Crook and Manor, 1998) is that a ward-based system of representation tends to encourage local representation and accountability. Especially where poor (and lower middle-income) citizens are geographically concentrated in certain residential

BOX 5.3 BANGALORE: COMPETING GOVERNANCE CIRCUITS

Bangalore: Competing Governance Circuits

CORPORATE INTERESTS
(Mostly richer groups)
- Industrial/bureaucratic/ IT sector élite/media
- Ex-senior government employees

Contact Points
- Staying in the same neighbourhoods
- Professional associations/clubs/ resorts
- Relatives
- Children to similar schools
- Consultants

Who are the 'contacts' or 'connections'?
(into the system)
- Senior bureaucrats
- Senior professional government staff
- Higher level political heads
- Corporate media

Political circuits:
State level political interests and to an extent national political interests via the party system

INSTITUTIONS
Parastatals/state level bureaucracy
- Infrastructure development agencies
- Financial agencies
- Development authorities
- Metropolitan planning agencies
- Dedicated service providers

INSTITUTIONAL OUTPUTS
- Dedicated infrastructure/ civic amenities
- Central locations
- Larger parcels of land
- Fiscal benefits

INTERVENTION PROCESSES
- Dedicated mega-projects
- Master planning: policing

COMPETING CLAIMS IN PUBLIC POLICY SHAPING PUBLIC INVESTMENTS AND REGULATIONS

INSTITUTIONAL OUTPUTS
- Upgrading infrastructure
- Secure land tenure while maintaining a diverse tenure regime
- Basic civic amenities

INTERVENTION PROCESSES
- Regularization
- Upgrading

INSTITUTIONS
Mostly local government (some lower level bureaucracy of parastatal agencies)
- Standing committees (especially Works and Finance)
- Mayors/Deputy Mayors
- Councillors
- Senior technical staff
- Middle and junior bureaucracy

LOCAL ECONOMY COALITIONS
(A spectrum of richer, middle and mostly poor groups: depending on the particular local economy)
- Local landed élite; larger entrepreneurs; commercial traders; local politicians, lower and middle level bureaucracy, real estate agents
- Subcontractors; renters, sales agents, fabricators, political workers, lowest level government workers
- Workers, hawkers

Contact Points
- Staying in the same neighbourhoods
- Professional associations/ clubs/resorts
- Relatives
- Children to similar schools
- Liaison agents

Who are the 'contacts' or 'connections'?
(into the system)
- Middle and junior bureaucrats
- Middle and junior professional government staff
- Lower, middle political agents, and some senior political heads

Source: Solomon Benjamin, Environment and Urbanization Vol 12, No 1, April 2000, p55

neighbourhoods, candidates depend on their votes and in turn need to respond to their constituents' concerns. Such an outcome depends, however, on a number of other factors. First, it depends on councillors having influence on executive decisions. Second, it relies on voters having a conceptualization of 'representation' that leads them to expect political promises to be kept and tangible benefits to be forthcoming, rather than political office being regarded primarily as a means of conferring status on the elected representative. It also depends on ward boundaries being appropriately defined. In urban areas which are rapidly growing or where densification is occurring, tardy redefinition of ward boundaries can result in a democratic deficit, in which the population size of wards (or constituencies) is very large, particularly in those wards where the poor reside. For example, in Mombasa, each councillor represents an average of nearly 30,000 residents, compared to about 15,000 in Johannesburg, Colombo and Kumasi. Indeed, national governments may deliberately adopt such a strategy (together with gerrymandering or reserving seats for its own appointees) where opposition parties tend to win urban parliamentary seats and control over powerful local authorities. In Mombasa for example, the provision for seven nominated councillors in addition to 24 elected councillors enabled the national government to secure a clear majority on the Council.

In addition, the positive benefits of a ward-based system may not be realized if votes are mobilized on other bases (eg ethnicity or caste), the Council does not have jurisdiction over relevant activities or lacks resources (as in Bangalore), or councillors are prohibited from standing in successive elections (see below). In Kumasi, for example, the domination of a nominated Mayor, together with the Metropolitan Assembly's limited resources and capacity, gives Assembly Members little scope for positive action. In contrast, in some local authorities (eg Ahmedabad) councillors may be given a development budget to spend at ward level. This enables them to increase their responsiveness to the needs of residents (as well as increasing their chances of re-election). Particularly where boundaries for national constituencies and local administrative jurisdictions coincide, rivalry between the candidates may lead to attempts to capture public programmes in order to command the resources needed to reward constituents and supporters. These are contests which mayors or councillors may lose. This occurs, for example, in Santiago, where the boundaries of national constituencies coincide with those of lower level local government.

Although ward-based elections may give more political voice to the poor, other things being equal, they also share the main disadvantages of majoritarian democracy, which limits the influence of minorities and potentially exacerbates rivalry between groups. It is to overcome this weakness that systems of proportional representation (PR) have been adopted in many places. However the closed party list system, which is the usual basis for PR, puts power into the hands of the political parties and reduces the responsiveness and accountability of those elected to their constituents. In Johannesburg, in the 1996 elections, 162 of the 270 councillors were directly elected on a ward basis and 108 under a PR system, to try and get the best of both worlds.[3] However, designing an appropriate system of PR is by no means straightforward, as illustrated by Colombo's experience: the closed party list system introduced in 1979 was amended in 1987 and 1991 and proposals to abandon it in favour of a ward-based system were under consideration by the time of the 1997 elections.

Other reforms that may increase the representativeness of electoral systems include:

- Mandatory voting (as in Santiago), which may be one of the few ways of counteracting the worldwide pattern of low (sometimes very low) turnout in local government elections, at least in the short term. However, disillusion with Chilean politics in general and the incumbent government's policies in particular have still led to declining turnout (especially in high-income areas) and increasing numbers of spoilt papers (a means of protest adopted by more vulnerable groups including the young and poor people).
- The reservation of seats for under-represented groups. The 74th Constitutional Amendment in India, for example, provides for a third of the seats on local councils to be reserved for marginalized social groups (women and scheduled castes and tribes (SC/ST)) and for the largely symbolic office of mayor to be rotated between a scheduled caste, female and general candidate each year. However, those elected to reserved seats are not necessarily accountable to their constituents, as class or other interests may take precedence over the interests of the marginalized group concerned.

The responsiveness of a political system to poor citizens depends only partly on the design of formal arrangements for the election of representatives. A further dimension that affects the relative power of councillors is the location of executive power and whether the chief executive is directly or indirectly elected. In addition, the outcomes of electoral politics reflect the tactics adopted by elected representatives. These depend not just on their reliance on the votes of particular groups, but also on their judgement as to whether formal decision-making or informal clientelist strategies will produce better results. Both these aspects are discussed further below.

The location of executive authority

In theory, political systems in which the mayor is directly elected and performs the role of chief executive generate strong leadership and a clear line for accountability. Accountability may be increased further if the mayor shares decision-making power with an executive committee or the full council, which typically approves the budget. However, direct election of a chief executive is also a high-risk system, since an overwhelming share of power is vested in a single individual, who may turn out to be a bad leader. The risks may be reduced and power more widely distributed if the chief executive is indirectly elected and thus shares power more equally with councillors, although the outcome of such systems is sometimes said to be indecisiveness and unclear accountability. For example in Ahmedabad, most power at the municipal corporation level rests with the Standing Committee of the AMC (12 elected from 129 councillors, by convention reflecting party representation on the Municipal Corporation General Board as a whole). However, the existence of other Standing (and ad hoc) Committees with executive powers diffuses executive responsibility and clouds lines of accountability.

Whether an elected chief executive holds effective power also depends on whether s/he, the council or an external body is responsible for appointing senior paid officials. The Latin American tradition, in which a directly elected mayor makes his or her own appointments to senior posts (confidence posts), has both advantages and disadvantages. The advantages are control and strong direction of policy by a like-minded team if the mayor provides good leadership. The disadvantages include discontinuity between administrations, poor promotion prospects for career officials and weak or partisan leadership if the mayor is ineffectual or biased (Nickson, 1995). If the mayor or council as a whole is responsible for such appointments, their ability to direct policy and implementation is increased but so is the scope for using local authority jobs as patronage resources (for example in Mombasa). However, if central government makes senior appointments, including the chief executive, local responsiveness and accountability are reduced. Although a characteristic of authoritarian regimes, this also occurs in supposedly democratic political systems. The most glaring example in the case study cities is Kumasi.[4] However, in Indian cities also, the local authority's agenda can be largely set by state-appointed senior executive officers (commissioners). For example, in Ahmedabad, good leadership was for a time provided by an able, far-sighted and energetic Municipal Commissioner. However, the government practice of transferring commissioners frequently reduces their ability to achieve much.

Terms of political office

The rules governing terms of political office also make a difference to the efficacy and accountability of local political systems. If successful candidates are limited to a single term, their political tactics may well focus on maximizing their personal returns, especially if the costs of fighting an election are high. Unless their ambitions include a higher-level political career, responsiveness and accountability are likely to be limited. Where successive terms are permitted, candidates have more of an incentive to be responsive and to demonstrate their probity, although the latter may be threatened by obligations to reward their campaign financiers and supporters. A second term may enable representatives to tackle longer-term and more difficult issues, since the priority during a first term, especially if it is short, must be to deliver visible results. An example was the 100 Day Programme of Colombo's new Mayor, elected in 1997, which included improvements to solid waste management, and securing NGO and private sector inputs to renovate out-patient dispensaries, roundabouts, traffic lights, roads and public toilets. Mombasa's new mayor, elected at the beginning of 1998, adopted a similar strategy of prioritizing immediate visible improvements. However, if cross-party support is not secured for longer-term initiatives, these are vulnerable to electoral reversals. For example, the development of participatory budgeting in Recife was temporarily threatened between 1997 and 2000 when a right-wing mayor held power. In Colombo, the Colombo Municipal Council (CMC)/central government collaboration to implement the national Million Houses Programme (especially its settlement upgrading component) was seriously undermined by electoral reversals at national and local levels in the mid-1990s (see Box 5.4).

On the contrary, the absence of restrictions on the number of successive elections for the same office that may be contested by a candidate may provide opportunities for the abuse of patronage resources, lessen accountability and fail to provide sanctions for poor performance. The same applies to appointments – without mandatory restrictions on the duration of an appointment, it may be hard to displace unsatisfactory incumbents. Citizens and many Assembly Members in Kumasi breathed a collective sigh of relief when the expiry of the term of office of the city's Chief Executive enabled his removal and replacement.

Responsiveness, accountability and sustainability at the local level may, therefore, be undermined by a poorly designed electoral system, inadequate arrangements for the exercise of executive authority and dysfunctional rules on terms of office. Local electoral arrangements are important in securing effective and legitimate local politics. However, additional provisions for securing wider societal participation in local decision-making can supplement them. Some alternative arrangements are explored below.

Provisions for wider societal representation in local electoral politics

Some of the ways in which representation that reflects society at large can be secured have been mentioned above – partial proportional representation and reserved seats. Further ways of obtaining wider societal inputs in municipal decision-making include the establishment of advisory mechanisms, increasing transparency by making information and decision-making bodies publicly accessible, and increasing accountability by the establishment of external scrutiny bodies.

Legislative provision for the mandatory establishment of consultative/ advisory bodies is more common in Latin America than Africa or Asia (except for the Philippines). Thus the Consejo Económico y Social Communal in Santiago is comprised of representatives of organized civil society (40 per cent representatives of Neighbourhood Boards, the official CBOs, 30 per cent of other CBOs, 30 per cent of business and commercial entities). The forums that play a role in PB in some Brazilian cities and the consultative Municipal Councils in Filipino cities have similar compositions. Non-governmental urban actors may also be included in non-mandatory standing or ad hoc policy-making, administrative or coordinating arrangements. In Cebu, NGOs are included as members of commissions for the welfare of children and women and family affairs; people's organizations (POs) are members of committees for the registration of POs and committees with functions related to informal settlement upgrading or relocation; and the members of a committee on street vendors include an NGO and vendors' association. In Colombo, the Housing and Community Development Committee, the members of which included the Mayor, CMC officers, NGO representatives and six district leaders, was, between the mid-1980s and the mid-1990s, a regular forum for coordinating the implementation of the Million Houses Programme in the city. Such arrangements do give greater representation to various societal interests. However, their standing in relation to elected bodies or to each other is not always clear, and the lack of a mandatory basis may weaken their influence.

Extending local democracy and participation

Formal electoral and executive arrangements at the city level provide a basis for representative city government. However, they are insufficient to ensure pro-poor decision-making and accountability to citizens without ways of reducing the remoteness of citywide government, increasing its responsiveness and ensuring transparency. In many cities, there is recognition of the need for a local or neighbourhood level of local government to increase responsiveness and improve service delivery. However, as with city government, the representativeness and effectiveness of lower levels of government depend on their legislative basis, the powers and resources available to them, the arrangements for representation, the nature of their leadership and the relations between them and higher levels of city government. Democratic representation at this level may be based on elections but it is also at this level that opportunities occur for other democratic practices, involving direct, deliberative or participatory democracy. In the cities studied, sub-city or neighbourhood levels of representation have been established as part of the hierarchy of local government administration (eg in Cebu City) or specifically to create avenues for more direct democratic involvement of residents (eg in Recife and Colombo).

Administrative decentralization of service delivery and regulatory processes can improve service provision by providing a local interface between the responsible agencies and residents. However, it does not necessarily give citizens a say in decision-making. Local levels of deliberation and representation can play an important role not only in making the bureaucracy more effective and accessible to residents, but also in providing channels for consultation, participation and accountability, as in the *barangays* of Cebu City (see Box 6.4). However to be effective, they depend on political commitment at the municipal level and can founder if they are seen as rivals by the mayor or councillors elected to represent citizens at the municipal or city level. They can also be easily sidelined if they do not have a sound legislative basis (as in Colombo – see Box 5.4) or are not allocated resources as of right (as in both Colombo and Kumasi). Further, their effectiveness and representativeness may be reduced if, in establishing them, city government sidelines existing leaders or recognizes representatives who reflect the views of only sections of a local community.

The foregoing discussion suggests that any arrangements for institutionalized community representation or participatory democracy are likely to have mixed outcomes. The best established of such arrangements in the cities studied is the system of participatory budgeting in Brazil, as described for Recife in Box 6.3. Although the system is far from perfect, Melo et al (2001) conclude that:

BOX 5.4 THE RISE AND FALL OF PARTICIPATORY DECISION-MAKING IN COLOMBO

In the early 1980s, the National Housing Authority and the Colombo Municipal Council Health Department established Community Development Councils (CDCs) in most low-income areas in Colombo in order to implement a UNICEF-funded Urban Basic Services Programme. Their roles included consultation and resource mobilization. In 1985 they were adopted as the main vehicle for implementing the Million Houses Programme and were used to prioritize needs, develop solutions and smooth local implementation of informal settlement upgrading. Between 1979 and 1998, 623 CDCs were registered, although the number of new registrations fell off after the mid-1990s. Each adult from participating families voted annually for the CDC committee, and Health Instructors hired and trained by the CMC's Health Department provided support. Unresolved problems were referred to monthly meetings at either district level, which residents were free to attend, or to a city level committee. In the second half of the 1980s and the early 1990s therefore, community level organization played an important role in the detailed local design and implementation of a large-scale programme of regularization, infrastructure installation and house improvements.

However, since 1994/5 over 600 of the CDCs have collapsed or become dormant. The explanations are largely political. First, the CDCs were established by government and used more for cost recovery than consultation. Their legitimacy therefore depended on improvements and services being delivered. Thus when resource flows linked to the national programme declined without any substitute means of generating local funds for continued improvements, their legitimacy was reduced. Second, the programme was associated with the United National Party government of 1977–1994; where CDC leaders and selected beneficiaries were also predominantly supporters of the ruling party, CDCs were discredited not only in the eyes of opposition politicians but also in the eyes of many residents. Third, elected councillors were ambivalent towards the CDCs – they resented them as political rivals, but also used them to deliver local benefits. When a councillor failed to channel resources to his ward or favoured some residents over others he might also blame the CDC. Finally, relationships between CDCs and NGOs were similarly ambivalent. Some NGOs provided support but others were mistrusted by residents, were non-participatory in their approach, took the credit for CDC initiatives, and tempted able CDC leaders into their employ, with adverse impacts on the already limited capacity of many CDCs.

International support was made available for building the capacity of CDCs and relevant government agencies. However, the support was sometimes channelled ineffectively through NGOs to CDCs, and often did not last long enough for CDCs to develop sustainable capacity, especially as their leaders often lacked experience, status and knowledge of English. As a result, when faced with declining resident support, an unresponsive bureaucracy or political opposition or indifference, the CDCs lacked the resilience and capacity to take their own initiatives. The limited attitudinal change achieved in public sector agencies and the limited resource generating capacity of the local authority also hindered the viability and sustainability of the approach.

Many of these flaws could have been tackled with continued political and organizational support. Ultimately, it was the withdrawal of political support for a programme associated with the previous government and the lack of a legislative basis for CDCs that led to the decline of both the programme and a promising form of community organization. This is not the end of the story, although the future is uncertain. The Million Houses Programme benefited large numbers of poor people using participatory approaches and realistic components, and the years of CDC organization will have left a legacy of social capital. Perhaps, in the future, demand for further improvements in the living conditions of the poor and the need for an organizational vehicle through which they can express their demands will prove that, far from collapsed, CDCs are merely dormant. Perhaps, given appropriate political space, they will revive, albeit in modified form and with fresh leadership, as mechanisms for organization, participation, implementation and monitoring.

Source: Russell and Vidler, 2000.

'PB does increase the capacity of excluded social groups to influence the decision making process regarding the allocation of public resources. In addition, it increases the access of the poor to basic urban services and contributes to making local expenditure reflect the priorities of the poor. While the accountability mechanisms in the process are fragile, it allows for consultation and deliberation on the use of public resources. Although resources allocated through Participatory Budgeting are small, the evidence is that in an extremely unequal society like Brazil, these programmes are one of the few ways to transform public investments from favours into rights.' (Melo et al, 2001, p170).

The *barangay* level of local government in Cebu also appears to benefit poor residents. Elsewhere, such arrangements are less well established and their weaknesses tend to outweigh their strengths. Nevertheless, they have potential for increasing the responsiveness and accountability of government to local communities and poor citizens. For example, the Integrated Development Planning (IDP) process in South African cities is still in its infancy. However, with political commitment at metropolitan and sub-metropolitan levels, there is still scope to support disempowered groups to develop the skills to enable them to play a full role and ensure its representativeness.

A prerequisite for exercising voice, increasing responsiveness and securing accountability at both city and local levels is transparency. This depends on the political culture and legislative provision, such as Right to Information legislation or provisions in the local government or planning legislation. It also relies on media coverage of local government issues and openness to resident views. Although there is, in theory, a free press in all the case study cities, in practice it varies in importance, coverage of local government issues and freedom. The local press actively covered a range of city government issues in Ahmedabad and Visakhapatnam and, more unexpectedly, in Mombasa. Elsewhere, its role was more limited, generally concentrating on service delivery problems (eg in Colombo), especially where it practised self-censorship or was vulnerable to legal action or other sanctions (eg in Kumasi). In the latter, local radio had started to adopt a more active role, although the previous Municipal Chief Executive limited media coverage by selecting those journalists permitted to attend the (irregular) Assembly meetings. In Johannesburg community radio plays a significant role, although in some areas, such as Soweto and Alexandra, it had started to come under the control of the local élite.

The evidence from the case study cities shows that, for sub-city levels of government and other mechanisms for participation to be effective, representative, accountable to citizens and capable of holding higher levels of local government to account, they need:

• a supportive political context in which higher levels are committed as a matter of principle to neighbourhood representation and participation, or see effective lower levels as being in their own political interests;
• a strong civil society, to play an advocacy role on behalf of the poor, act as a watchdog to ensure accountability and organize citizens to claim their rights to land, services and a say in decisions;

- considerable ongoing support from NGOs and other organizations, to inform and empower citizens, elected representatives and local leaders to fulfil their roles and responsibilities;
- transparency, based on legislative safeguards and a free and active local media.

Actors, power relationships and political practices

In the introduction to this chapter it was noted that the characteristics and outcomes of local political activity are shaped by the actors involved in urban politics. These actors have varying goals, demands and resources. In addition, the strategies and tactics they adopt differ. The influence that poor people have on political decision-making depends, therefore, not just on their capacity for organization and the tactics they adopt, but also on how they relate to other political interests. These other political interests include high-income groups, formal businesses, trade unions and NGOs. Formal systems of representative democracy are necessary. Middle- and upper-income residents and formal businesses can afford to pay for services and to invest in compensatory measures such as water storage tanks if services are deficient. They are, therefore, often uninterested in municipal politics and reluctant to get involved. Poor people can influence the political agenda where they have democratic rights and are not precluded from exercising them by their place of residence or regulations governing electoral registration. However, the research shows that formal democratic politics alone is insufficient to provide poor residents with influence over decision-making, access to services as of right and fair treatment with respect to regulatory procedures. They depend, therefore, not just on periodic elections but also on other forms of political activity and a variety of allies. The allies that potentially have the greatest sympathy for the concerns of poor citizens, as well as having some capacity for organization and political influence, include political parties, trade unions, NGOs and religious organizations.

Political parties and political agents

Only in a minority of the case study cities are political parties well organized, with a clearly defined policy platform, implying a contractual relationship with voters in which a representative has committed him/herself to specific policies. Where powerful parties, such as the ANC in South Africa or the Workers' Party (PT) in Brazil have a clear commitment to reducing poverty, the nature of politics changes, with considerable benefits for the poor. However, the need of such parties to maintain a support base among wider social groups and to juggle potentially conflicting economic objectives limits the extent to which their political aims are translated into practical outcomes. Elsewhere, political parties are weakly organized and lack the will or capacity to formulate policy platforms. Many appeal to voters on ethnic, caste or religious grounds rather than those of common economic interests. In such circumstances, the relationships between supporters and elected representatives may be deferential – the representative is trusted to make decisions on behalf of the electorate. Alternatively, the representative may be regarded as an agent, elected in the expectation that he or she will deliver particularistic benefits to individuals or communities. This may require that the agent places him or herself in a position in which access to resources can be secured, for example by joining the ruling party.

Poor people *may* identify with a party because of its stated policy commitments, but seem to be more likely to behave instrumentally. They trade votes for specific promises of assistance, or support the candidate they believe is most likely to be both responsive and able to assist with the many problems that characterize informal settlements and the lives of poor households in the city, as illustrated for Cebu and Bangalore in Boxes 5.1 and 5.2. In so-called 'vote bank' politics, the poor are far from passive. Sometimes votes are purchased or candidates appeal to sectarian allegiances. However, vote bank politics can work in the interests of the poor. Local leaders in a competitive political situation such as Bangalore often form alliances with more powerful groups and use their ability to deliver votes to win rewards and concessions for residents. Nevertheless, merely voting for a candidate may not result in the promised assistance, because politicians may be unwilling or unable to fulfil their campaign promises.

The most common political practices by poor residents focus on developing personalized ties with elected representatives, party leaders or street level officials. Such ties may be expressed in vote bargaining and clientelism (as in elections for Cebu's Mayor, or the support base of ward councillors in cities such as Bangalore. They also take the form of petty bribery – as when a minor official is 'tipped' (Kumasi) or given 'tea' (Mombasa) or 'speed money' (Ahmedabad). However, where necessary, residents will approach others who may be perceived as more sympathetic or more likely to secure a positive response. For example, in Kumasi, residents will often approach their MP or the local chief, who can, if they are willing, bypass the Kumasi Metropolitan Assembly (KMA) and contact more senior central government officials or politicians on their behalf. In Bangalore, they will, if they can, contact state level bureaucrats or, less easily, politicians. Because the building of political capital requires long-term relationships with local politicians and bureaucrats, the sheer persistence of the poor is critical to their survival and success.

Political alliances

Poor residents or small-scale enterprises (SSEs) may also form alliances and organize to increase their political influence. But there are obstacles to effective organization. In Bangalore, for example, caste-based and religious rivalries hinder the political alliances of the poor. However, local residential environments and economies bring multiple poor groups into close contact and their mutual interdependence forces informal collaboration across these primary divisions. People are highly conscious of their distinctiveness, but ready to sink their differences in common party allegiances and cross-class activities such as religious festivals in order to maximize their political influence. CBOs in informal settlements generally form around the need to obtain secure tenure and infrastructure. Once these objectives are achieved, they may become dormant, as in Colombo, unless access to decision-making processes or further resources depend on a CBO being present. Indeed CBOs may be initiated by or in response to external bodies, as in the Philippines Community Mortgage Program (CMP) or South Africa's Integrated Development Plan (IDP) process. Their roles are discussed in more detail in Chapter 7.

SSEs are generally organized on an occupational or sectoral basis – for example taxi drivers, auto-repair workers and market traders in Kumasi. Sometimes they are able to successfully protest an undesired policy or regulatory change, or lobby for support from local government. In some political circumstances, a combination of an open and flexible local political culture and well-organized civil society has led to outcomes that are favourable to small and micro-enterprises. For example, in Cebu City, policy towards street vendors has been worked out locally, through threats of demolition, protest, and resistance, leading to concessions and 'unwritten policies' (see Boxes 7.3 and 8.2). Thus the authorities have conceded tolerance in return for compliance with informal rules. The operators in turn have learnt that they have rights and understand the need for engagement with regular processes of policy and rule-making. Individual vendor groups have formed into federations and common interest organizations of informal sector operators have emerged at city level. The result has been that confrontation and favour seeking behind closed doors has gradually been replaced with more open processes of negotiation between informal sector operators and the local authority. More commonly, however, SSEs are weakly organized, especially across sectors. In addition, as explored in more detail in Chapter 8, their gains are limited or temporary, especially if their interests conflict with those of formal business.

High-income residents and formal enterprises have greater organizational capacity and when they organize collectively can exert more influence on decision-making than organizations of more numerous but less economically powerful and socially well-connected poor residents. In 1998 in Johannesburg, for example, the Sandton Residents' Association resisted an increase in property rates by organizing a boycott and a large number of appeals against property revaluation, worsening the city's financial crisis. If enterprises are sufficiently large and important to the local economy, they can lobby individually and informally to protect their own interests. Sometimes, business organizations may be represented on city level advisory or decision-making bodies. However, often the relationships between businesses and the local political system are ambivalent. Moreover, such arrangements may not represent the enterprises on which the poor depend. For example, it is the government, not the traders, which appoints a traders' representative to the KMA.

Trade unions

In cities with large formal sector wage-based economies and a history of trade unionism, trade unions may play an important political role. However, they are also primarily concerned to protect the interests of their own members, who are unlikely to include the poorest. Trade unions concentrate on workplace rather than neighbourhood issues, for example, the dockworkers in Mombasa. Their activities may contribute to a leftward leaning political culture, as in Brazil, but they may also resist pro-poor changes where they perceive these to be against the interests of their own members. For example, in Indian and South African cities, municipal workers have resisted reorganization of service delivery, especially when it involved corporatization and private sector participation, because of fears for their jobs, even when one purpose of the reforms was to raise capital to extend services to low-income areas. Where traditional industries, such as textiles in Ahmedabad, have declined, or where economic liberalization has made waged employees more insecure, as in Visakhapatnam, unions are unlikely to be important political actors.

NGOs

The presence, purposes, resources and capacity of NGOs varies between the case study cities, but their contribution to supporting poor people's organization and political engagement or pressing for pro-poor policies is generally limited and contradictory. The majority of NGOs are concerned with welfare and are engaged with national or local government only insofar as they may deliver a service on its behalf. In this role, they may act as intermediaries between government and poor residents, but their relations with the state are either dependent, or, where the government perceives them as competitors for external resources, competitive. Many such NGOs (especially indigenous ones) are small and poorly resourced. Those NGOs engaged in advocacy on behalf of poor citizens or supporting the organizations of the poor are relatively few in number in most of the case study cities. Moreover, NGOs are often distrusted both by poor residents and by governments, as being self-interested, unrepresentative and unaccountable. If they adopt conflictual tactics, these may be resented by government and, especially if they are used repeatedly, lead to resistance rather than positive change. Where NGOs have played a role in gaining benefits for poor residents, as in Cebu, they have worked alongside local government on particular issues or projects (see also Chapter 7).

Religious organizations

Religious organizations are widespread and numerous in low- and middle-income countries and their number and membership are often growing. Sometimes (as in India) political affiliation is, at least in part, on religious grounds. Sometimes also, the concern of specific religious organizations for social justice has been an important direct or indirect political influence. In the case study cities, for example, branches of the Roman Catholic church in both Brazil and the Philippines were instrumental in conscientizing and organizing the poor, while in Kenya the churches joined other civil society actors in pressing for democratization, constitutional reform and the rule of law at the national level. On the whole, though, in these case study cities, religious organizations are not actors in local politics, concentrating instead on the spiritual and sometimes material welfare of their adherents.

Poor residents are sometimes passive in political terms, because of their lack of knowledge of how government operates, disillusionment with their experience of the political process, preoccupation with day-to-day survival or social sanctions against participation, especially by women, in public life. However, more often they devise active tactics and strategies, many of which diverge considerably from the expectations of traditional liberal democratic theory. Sometimes they are successful in securing political representation, influencing decisions and obtaining redress for grievances. However, even in the minority of countries where there is political commitment to addressing the needs of poor people, conflicting interests and inequalities of knowledge, capacity and resources may result in outcomes falling far short of intentions. Even more commonly, the greater economic, social, organizational and informational power of high- and middle-income residents and formal sector businesses reduces poor residents' access to political influence and decision-making processes and forces them into clientelist strategies. Conflicts of interest among poor residents and between groups of informal sector operators exacerbate the problem.

Conclusion

The characteristics of urban political systems are influenced by the ways in which societal interests interact with formal and informal political structures and processes. The characteristics of the articulation have implications for the nature of government and the way government bureaucracies operate. They also affect the political practices of politicians and citizens, as expressed in the relationships between those with political power and the electorate, as well as in the preoccupations of everyday politics. In addition, they influence the ways in which civil society is organized and engages in political activity. Using ideas about the nature of democratic political systems and the research findings, an attempt is made to develop a typology of urban political systems in Table 5.1. Notionally, this represents a progression, from authoritarian regimes on the left side of the table, to consolidated representative democracy on the right. In practice, of course, not only is such a progression by no means certain, but also most contemporary urban political systems have mixed characteristics. Nevertheless, we can distinguish between them with respect to the basic features of the political system and power structure. Such features tend to be associated with characteristic relationships with the administrative apparatus, citizens and civil society organizations. These in turn have different implications for the ability of poor residents to exercise political voice and the strategies and tactics employed by CSOs, as well as for the responsiveness and accountability of government. The cities studied have, with considerable hesitation, been located in the suggested typology, although this risks being both much too static and also greatly over-simplified.

In both autocratic and oligarchical authoritarian regimes, 'participation' in politics means demonstrating support for leaders, who use their control over resources to respond selectively to citizens' needs and priorities, using

Table 5.1 *Forms of urban political system*

	Articulation of urban government with societal interests						
	Command, under monarch; autocracy	Command, under oligarchy; populism	Formal representative democracy + clientelistic political system			Inclusive representative democracy	Inclusive substantive democracy + strong social contract
			Pro-patron clientelism	Balanced clientelism	Lobbying and pressure		
Power structure	Command, under monarch; autocracy	Command, under oligarchy; populism	Pro-patron clientelism	Balanced clientelism	Lobbying and pressure	Inclusive representative democracy	Inclusive substantive democracy + strong social contract
Bureaucratic mode	Subordinated bureaucracy		Porous bureaucracy			Administration	Administration and management
Basis for inclusion	Personal favours by windfall		Personal favours by exchange	Group favours by exchange	Group favours by lobbying and pressure	Rights	Rights and effective voice
Focus of open politics	Gratitude	Mass acclaim	Implementation, crisis management			Policy and implementation	Policy, implementation and partnership
Relationship with civil society	Welfare CSOs tolerated if they do not challenge the regime and supplement government resources. Advocacy CSOs demanding political reform suppressed.	Welfare and development CSOs tolerated if they do not challenge the regime. Compliant CSOs may be used to deliver services. GONGOs sponsored by the state. Advocacy CSOs demanding political reforms bought off by concessions.	CSOs organize to lobby patrons, press claims and demand reforms to make the democratic system more responsive and accountable. Welfare and development CSOs tolerated. Compliant CSOs may be used to deliver services. Alternative models developed by CSOs may be influential.			Governments selectively respond to CSOs organized to defend rights, increase voice and improve accountability.	Governments respond to CSOs organized to express voice and call government to account. CSOs enter into partnerships with public agencies.
Case study city	Recife to 1980s Mombasa to 1990s Kumasi to 1970s Santiago to 1990s	Cebu to 1980s	Kumasi Mombasa	Bangalore Visakhapatnam	Ahmedabad	Johannesburg Cebu Recife Santiago	

government resources to coerce the population or manufacture consent. In such circumstances, only CSOs that do not challenge the regime are tolerated. Independent or government sponsored NGOs may be used to deliver services on behalf of the state or fill gaps in the services it provides; sometimes in populist regimes with formal democratic systems, development oriented NGOs may be tolerated. However, advocacy organizations demanding political reform are suppressed or co-opted. Nevertheless, welfare NGOs may start to question state service delivery policy and performance, and development NGOs may develop the capacity of citizens to organize and articulate their demands for political and other changes. Many of the cities studied showed these political characteristics in the 1970s or 1980s.

As demands for democratization gather pace, the space for political activity is likely to widen, either gradually (with many setbacks) or suddenly. With the introduction of formal democracy, urban governments have to become more responsive. They continue to use compliant CSOs to deliver services and may respond to criticisms of their performance by expanding such use. They may introduce other reforms such as the use of private sector or community organizations to improve service delivery, sometimes drawing on alternative models developed by NGOs. The increased space for political activity makes it possible for civil society to organize, demand reforms to make the democratic system more accountable and develop the capacity of voters to exercise their political rights. However, the limited capacity and legitimacy of government agencies, especially at the local level, the limited efficacy of mechanisms to ensure good performance and accountability and the immaturity of political institutions result in pervasive clientelist relationships and corrupt practices. These may bring some benefits for citizens, including the poor, but at considerable cost, both in terms of time and money to residents and entrepreneurs, and with respect to the legitimacy of the political-administrative system. Although all the cities studied were located in countries which had re-established or reinforced democratic politics, in all of them systems of formal democracy coexisted with more or less pervasive clientelist politics, providing differing levels of access to the poor.

Given favourable political circumstances and increasing levels of political awareness, democratic consolidation may occur. There is arguably potential for this, at least in Recife and Johannesburg and perhaps in some of the other cities studied. If a virtuous circle of increased responsiveness, leading to increased willingness to pay taxes and user charges, better performance, increased accountability and greater political legitimacy occurs, then access to political influence and basic services may be assured as of right. In turn, the capacity of public sector agencies to deliver is likely to increase and, while CSOs continue to lobby for improved performance and other reforms, they are increasingly likely to be willing to act in partnership with public sector agencies. Gradually, state–society relations come to be based on an (implicit) social contract, and levels of trust, while always provisional, start to increase. Although conflicts of interest persist, and economically powerful actors often win in battles for resources, the deeper embeddedness of democratic values and the more influential political voice of poor citizens increase both the pressure for redistribution and the proportion of resources directed to reducing poverty. That the conflicts and contradictions do not disappear, even in societies with well-established democratic systems, strong welfare states and effective and well-resourced local government, is illustrated by the experience of many developed countries. Ironically, low and declining turnout in countries such as the UK demonstrates that local politics is not always alive and well even in these circumstances.

The road from democratization and decentralization to consolidated local democracy, effective local government, and constructive dialogue between local government and poor citizens is long and rocky. Some of the case study cities have made greater strides than others towards consolidated democratic institutions and mature political processes capable of resolving conflicts of interest and responding to the poor. These differences can be explained by their political history and culture, the characteristics of the struggle for democratization, the nature of the democratic transition, their administrative capacity and the levels of resources available. Even in these systems, many gains made by the poor are achieved by fostering patron–client relationships with elected representatives and officials at all levels of government, rather than as of right. Where patron–client relationships are pervasive, although poor people may be able to gain limited benefits and prevent harm to their livelihoods and living conditions, local politics is essentially extractive and inefficient. It is a politics in which government is seen as a source of goods to be consumed privately by officials and residents alike. However, it has little to offer on how publicly available goods can be expanded so that all citizens can access basic services as of right, or if these are not delivered, how the responsible agencies can be called to account. It is a politics based on favouritism and special pleading – not entirely dysfunctional but ultimately limited in its capacity to reduce poverty and inequality.

Notes

1   Richard Batley also reviewed the findings of the city case studies with respect to political aspects of pro-poor governance. His insights are acknowledged with thanks, especially the typology included in the conclusion of this chapter, which has been developed from an initial draft he prepared. However the views put forward here are those of the author.
2   Civics (civic associations) were community-based organizations that were ostensibly apolitical structures that mobilized around quality of life or development issues in the black townships, represented communities in township-based politics and linked them into the mass democratic movement (Beall et al, 2002).
3   The number of councillors was reduced and the relative proportions of those elected through each channel changed (to 50:50) following the reorganization of Johannesburg's local government.
4   Strictly speaking, district and metropolitan chief executives in Ghana are only nominated by the President, subject to the approval of the district/metropolitan assembly, which can reject the nomination. However, the position of the former MCE of Kumasi was exceptionally strong because of his close family relationship to the First Lady, his financial backing for the governing political party and his link to the Asante royal family.

Chapter 6

Urban Government: Capacity, Resources and Responsiveness

Nick Devas

New opportunities for responsive city government

City government is only one actor within urban governance, but it is the most obvious. Many city governments are locked into a historical model as monopoly suppliers of basic public services, with decision-making concentrated in the hands of a small but often ill-equipped group of officials, and minimal participation by, or accountability to, citizens. However, there is evidence of change in some of the case study cities.

Decentralization has focused attention on city governments, often after years in which their powers have been eroded and their functions transferred to other agencies. The search for increased efficiency and the pressures of global competition drive city governments to seek alternative ways of doing things, including building partnerships with the private sector and non-governmental organizations (NGOs). The heightened international concern with poverty puts pressure on them to consider how to respond to the needs of the poor and excluded. Perhaps most significantly, the process of democratization, accompanied by the increasing strength of civil society, has forced city governments to start becoming more accountable and more responsive to citizen demands. While the performance of city governments in the South generally remains very poor, there are examples in the case study cities of at least the beginnings of more responsive urban government.

What accounts for differences between city governments in terms of performance and responsiveness? And what accounts for whether and how they change? Chapter 5 has examined the issues in terms of the urban political processes, both formal and informal. This chapter focuses on the organizational, financial and administrative aspects of city government. But these aspects are closely inter-related. As indicated in Chapter 5, the ways in which city governments respond to the situations they face depends greatly on the national and local political context, including the legal and institutional framework, and the nature of political processes at national and regional level. This includes the extent of political space available to civil society, and the ability of civil society organizations (CSOs) (particularly those of the poor) to make use of that political space to influence the political and administrative processes. This aspect will be considered further in Chapter 7.

City governments themselves face a number of specific constraints – institutional, organizational and financial – on their ability to respond to the needs of citizens, particularly the poor. How far they are able to overcome these impediments depends in turn on both the national political context and on the qualities and abilities of local leadership. In this chapter, we will examine some of the constraints facing the city governments in the ten case study cites, how these constraints affect their ability to respond to the needs of the poor, and how far they have been able to overcome these constraints. The greatest obstacle in many of the cities is finance. We therefore look in more detail at how city governments generate the resources they need, and how this process of revenue generation impacts on the poor. We also look at how far cities' spending patterns benefit the poor, and the processes of decision-making about the use of available financial resources. In the last section we look at some of the specific ways in which city governments have sought to become more responsive to the poor, and at the crucial role of civic leadership in this.

Constraints on city government

The ability of city governments to respond to the needs of the poor is, in practice, highly constrained – by tight boundaries, limited range of responsibilities, out-dated bylaws, limited management capacity, inadequate financial resources, and so on. In this section we review some of these impediments.

Boundaries

The boundaries of several of the cities in this study have not been extended to take account of the city's growth. Many of the urban poor settle on the periphery, beyond the city government's jurisdiction. This is where population growth is most rapid and where infrastructure and service needs are greatest but resources are most limited. In Ahmedabad, for example, the urban periphery is divided between 163 village, town and municipal councils, together with a number of special purpose agencies. The capacity of the adjoining local governments to address the needs of the poor may be very limited indeed. 'The result is an uncertain patchwork of provision, or no provision at all' (Dutta with Batley, 1999, p72). A similar situation applies in Bangalore.

In Santiago, the city is divided among 34 municipalities, with the poor concentrated in certain municipalities, and a ten-fold difference in municipalities' revenues per capita between the richest and poorest (Dockemdorff et al, 2000, p182). Cebu City covers only the core of the metropolitan region yet contains a substantial proportion of the conurbation's industrial and commercial resources. A similar situation applies in Recife. Under apartheid, the Greater Johannesburg area was divided into 13 racially separate jurisdictions with vast differences in autonomy, political legitimacy, and fiscal and management capacity. The interim post-apartheid arrangement of four local councils under the Greater Johannesburg Metropolitan Council (GJMC) was an attempt to introduce a greater degree of equity between areas of the city. The effect was unsatisfactory, with bizarrely shaped jurisdictions and political resistance to transfers of resources between the local councils (Beall et al, 1999). Consequently, from 2001, the lower level was abolished, leaving a unitary city council for some 4 million people. Whilst this has brought about the objective, long cherished by the African National Congress, of 'one city, one tax base', it has made for a huge institution remote from its electorate.

Responsibilities

Responsibility for many of the services most vital to the poor often does not lie with the city government. In a number of countries (the Philippines and much of Latin America) decentralization has expanded the powers and responsibilities of city governments. However, in several of the case cities, city governments have quite limited responsibilities: waste management, sanitation and local roads, but not primary healthcare, education, electricity, police and security services, and often not even water, land and housing. These services are typically provided by central government, parastatal agencies or even private companies. This severely constrains the ability of city governments to respond to the needs of the urban poor.

In south Asian cities, responsibilities are often divided between a great range of special purpose agencies such as development authorities, slum clearance boards, and public utility companies. These tend to operate in competition with each other and with the municipal government, creating problems for long-term operation and maintenance, and breaking the accountability link with local voters.

For example, out of 23 people on the board of the Bangalore Development Authority (BDA), only two are elected members of the Municipal Corporation (Benjamin and Bhuvaneswari, 1999, p52). Benjamin (2000, p54) observes that, compared to the access which the poor have to the municipal corporation through their elected councillors, state agencies and development authorities are more accessible to middle- and upper-income groups (see Boxes 5.2 and 5.3).

In Kumasi, the decentralization law placed education and health services under the Metropolitan Assembly, but in practice the resources for these, and therefore effective control, remain firmly with the central ministries (King et al, 2001, p65). Similarly, Mombasa Municipal Council (MMC) nominally has responsibility for primary education, but with central government paying the teachers, head teachers being responsible for running the schools, and maintenance of schools being met largely from fees, the municipal council has little more than an advisory and supervisory role (Gatabaki-Kamau et al, 1999, p112).

With decentralization, some municipal governments have been given increased responsibilities for welfare and poverty alleviation, but often without the resources to meet those responsibilities. In Johannesburg, this 'unfunded mandate' has become a major political issue. According to the Ghanaian Local Government Act, Sub-Metro Assemblies are legally responsible for formulating poverty reduction interventions but they have no resources for this. In India, the 74th Constitutional Amendment proposed that local bodies should be responsible for poverty alleviation programmes but this has not been backed up with commensurate financial resources.

Conflicts between levels of government

The limited powers and responsibilities of city government have much to do with the way in which decentralization has been framed and implemented, and with the vested interests at national or regional level. Thus, while in the Philippines and South Africa legislation assigning powers and responsibilities to local government has been implemented fairly completely, in Ghana resistance by central ministries, together with perceived incapacity at the local level, has prevented effective transfer of responsibilities. In Kenya, there has been a steady erosion of local responsibilities during a long period of national economic and political stagnation. In India, there is often a three-way tussle between union, state and local administrations, in which the weakest element – local government – finds its powers eroded in favour of special-purpose agencies of state or national government.

Political conflicts between municipal, state/provincial and central governments can undermine the capacity of municipal governments to respond. In India, where different parties may be in power at each level, state governments may oppose actions by municipal governments simply on political grounds. This has occurred in all three of the Indian case study cities. Because land is a state matter, municipal governments are effectively prevented from regularizing land and thereby increasing their tax base (Benjamin and Bhuvanswari, 1999, p57). Although the 74th Constitutional Amendment was intended to offer protection to municipal governments from arbitrary interference from states, problems continue. In Colombo, the provincial government has on a number of occasions obstructed the municipal government's attempts to invest in poor communities, perceiving this as a political threat. It has also sought to control the flow of central government funds to the municipal corporation, creating delays and preventing services from being improved.

Overlapping responsibilities and rivalry between central and municipal government has also been an issue in Mombasa, where the centre's District Administration has the same boundaries as the Municipal Council. There have been numerous examples of central government interference in the local political scene in Kenya, including the curbing of the powers of mayors in opposition controlled local authorities and the reassignment of senior officials. Bureaucratic controls imposed by the centre often do little to improve local performance, resulting instead in delays, costs and rent seeking opportunities for those charged with enforcement. In Kumasi, the tight control exercised by the government appointed Chief Executive has much to do with the fact that the region is a centre for opposition politics. By contrast, one of the factors in Cebu's success in the late 1980s and early 1990s was the good relationship between city and provincial governments, although that seems to have broken down in recent years.

Legal constraints and outdated bylaws

Outdated legislation inhibits constructive engagement in informal housing areas. A number of countries have regulations prohibiting the expenditure of public resources on 'illegal' or irregular settlements, or areas that are not paying property tax. This was the case in Colombo until the mayor was able to obtain a dispensation. In India, there is an elaborate system for defining categories of 'slums', and the ability of authorities to intervene depends on their classification. Thus, the Slum Clearance Board in Bangalore cannot provide water or remove waste from 'non-notified' slum areas, and the municipal government cannot regularize land tenure without state government sanction. It may suit some municipal governments to hide behind such regulations if they wish to ignore informal housing areas, but in other cases it can be a genuine obstacle.

Inherited planning bylaws and building standards are usually unsuited to the needs of the poor and their ability to pay. In Colombo, 90 per cent of residents in the city's under-serviced settlements occupy plots that are less than a quarter of the minimum plot size specified in the regulations (Fernando et al, 1999, p23). In Mombasa, applicants for official plot allocations have to show their ability to undertake permanent construction within two years, while regulations regarding plot sizes, land use and building materials are unachievable by the poor. Of course, such regulations are rarely enforced, but their existence can provide rent seeking opportunities for the enforcers. Even where municipal governments wish to revise their bylaws, there may be legal obstacles to doing so. For example, Cebu's policy of 'maximum tolerance' of street vending (see Chapter 8) has to remain unofficial since the Supreme Court has ruled that street trading is illegal.

Availability of information

As noted in Chapter 2, the data which city governments possess about urban poverty is woefully inadequate and does little to illuminate the differentiated nature of poverty or the livelihood systems of the poor. City governments also lack essential data about environmental conditions and the impact of these on different groups. In some cases, they lack even basic information about the services for which they are responsible: service levels by area, service reliability, who benefits, who pays and how much, and so on. Citywide statistics sometimes exclude informal or irregular settlements, making nonsense of aggregate figures. Without such information, no meaningful poverty strategy can be developed or implemented.

Capacity and performance of municipal government staff

Services under the control of local government are often significantly worse than those provided by central government or parastatal agencies. This may be partly because of the nature of the service (sanitation may be more difficult to provide and manage than electricity, for example), and partly because of the greater resources available to central government and parastatal agencies. But it is also due to the weak technical and management capacity at the local level.

A key problem is the poor rates of remuneration, so that capable and ambitious staff move elsewhere. At the same time, municipal governments are often seriously over-staffed at the lower end.[1] Because of the weakness of local technical capacity, important services and large projects are often transferred to special purpose agencies, thereby making local governments even less attractive for professionals to work in. Political interference and malpractice compound the situation. In Colombo, recruitment is the responsibility of the Public Service Commission, so the Municipal Corporation has little scope to do anything about its staffing situation. In Kenya and Ghana, key local government staff are posted to local authorities from the centre. While this may enable municipal governments to benefit from qualified staff, it weakens the allegiance of senior officials to the local government and contributes to demoralizing disputes between officials and elected members. But even where, as in Johannesburg, city governments are well staffed with professionals, problems remain, as illustrated in Box 6.1.

Financial resources

Lack of financial resources is perhaps the most significant factor preventing urban governments from addressing the needs of the poor. Most of the case study cities have potentially substantial resource bases but are unable to exploit them effectively. Local tax instruments are often unsatisfactory – low yielding, politically sensitive, difficult to collect, economically damaging and impinging on the poor. Large amounts of tax remain uncollected because of political, administrative or legal obstacles. Mombasa Municipal Council, for example, is effectively insolvent, and is barely able even to pay its staff.

Despite its vast revenue base, Johannesburg was forced into financial crisis because of low collection rates on electricity and water charges as well as

---

BOX 6.1 JOHANNESBURG: TRANSFORMING THE
POST-APARTHEID CITY GOVERNMENT

Apartheid left a damaging legacy in terms of the city's administration. Under apartheid, the city was run by whites for whites, while those areas occupied by blacks were managed by an imposed, segregationist administration. There were marked differences between the two in terms of the skills and capabilities available to them. Attempts to unify the system and redistribute staff resources through a succession of reorganizations during the 1990s led to the demoralization of staff, loss of experienced personnel and skill shortages in critical areas. The system remains quite dualistic, with a clash of governance cultures. In certain parts of the city, strong bureaucratic codes and rules are enforced, so that, for example, planning applications in the wealthy areas follow slow but due procedures. Elsewhere, in the fast growing areas where the poor live, there is a fractured system of informal political control, with increasing scope for patronage and corruption.

The inherited approach of the city government has been one of providing high standards for the few, with an expenditure-led budgeting system in which resources were always assumed to be available. Adapting to the demands of the hitherto under-served majority in a situation of limited resources has required a major shift in administrative culture.

Nevertheless, attitudes of metropolitan and municipal staff have changed. Today it is not unusual to find local officials with an activist or NGO background being supportive of NGOs and community-based organizations (CBOs) with good 'anti-apartheid credentials'. There is widespread recognition of the role that civil society organizations played in the transition to democracy, and can play in the city's reconstruction and development. A number of the major personalities from the oppositional NGO Planact, as well as from civic associations in former townships, now occupy senior positions in the city government. But that too has its problems, as activists have to make the transition from opposition and 'struggle politics' to the grind of institutional change and service management. Meanwhile community groups of the poor find themselves confronting in government those who were formerly their comrades.

Increasingly, the core business of city government is being more rigorously defined in order to make best use of limited fiscal resources. Participation is more generally and formally institutionalized, and the struggle-based personal connections between officials, politicians and communities are fading. While it is difficult to predict the future character of city government in Johannesburg, it is hard to believe that it can ever again be as unfair and inequitable as it used to be under apartheid.

Source: Beall et al, 2001

---

property tax (see Box 6.2). Unwillingness to pay in Johannesburg is a legacy from the days of political struggle but has proved difficult to change. As an example of the tensions surrounding the issue, two councillors were murdered during the government's campaign to improve utility charge collections. Enforcement action against defaulters is undermined by intimidation against utility company staff, and the ease with which illegal (re)-connections can be made. Whilst some of the poor may benefit from non-payment, there are serious problems of inequity between those who pay and those who do not. Later in this chapter we look at the attempts cities have made to address their financial constraints.

Some cities receive significant transfers from the central (or state) government. For example, transfers provide two-thirds of Kumasi's budget, through a combination of salary support and the District Common Fund (a national tax sharing arrangement). In Recife, national tax sharing represents over half of the city's budget, although the proportion is declining. In Cebu, decentralization increased the proportion of transfers in the city's budget from 30 per cent to 40 per cent, although cuts in the national tax-sharing rate in 1999 reduced this again. In both Recife and Cebu, these transfers allow the cities concerned full discretion in the use of the money.

By contrast, in South Africa, redistribution of national resources in favour of poorer local governments has meant that the transfers received by Johannesburg have steadily declined. These now stand at less than 5 per cent of the city's budget, most of which is in the form of grants for specified purposes (mainly health services). In India, state and central transfers represent only 10–20 per cent of the budgets in Ahmedabad, Bangalore and Visakhapatnam, and much of this is in the form of specified grants. Mombasa now receives around 12 per cent of its budget from national tax sharing, but until 1999/2000, there was no system of inter-governmental transfers in Kenya, so Mombasa received nothing at all from the centre.

Failings of city government

While city governments face many obstacles, not everything is beyond their control. Internal organization – all too often centralized, departmentalist, hierarchical and inward-looking – inhibits access by and responsiveness to the poor. In Kumasi, every decision had to be approved by the (then) Metropolitan Chief Executive (MCE), whose behaviour was autocratic and whose response to the poor was generally negative.[2] Conflicts between elected representatives and officials and inter-departmental rivalry can be major impediments to effective delivery of services, even where there is a political commitment to addressing poverty. Professional training and negative attitudes towards the poor may also be obstacles. In Ahmedabad, engineers were reluctant to divert service lines into slum areas for fear of reducing supplies to the regularly serviced areas (Dutta, 1999, p76). In Bangalore, the pursuit of master planning has generally been at the expense of the poor (Benjamin and Bhuvaneswari, 2001, p246). In Johannesburg the culture of high infrastructure and service standards for the few has made it difficult to address the needs of the poor majority within the available resources.

Officials – and elected representatives – are often too concerned with crisis management and with maximizing their own income opportunities to be willing or able to engage with the poor. Corruption has a negative impact on the urban poor in numerous ways: in reducing the resources available to the municipal government, in biasing the allocation of those resources, and in preventing access by the poor to services (UNDP, 1997a; Gupta et al, 1998).[3] At the lowest level, 'connections' are needed in order to get anything done, rather than the system being responsive to legitimate demands in a transparent and routine way. Demands for 'speed money' to process an application or issue a permit are

---

BOX 6.2 JOHANNESBURG: IMPACT OF THE CITY'S
FISCAL CRISIS

Johannesburg is a wealthy city. The city government has substantial revenue sources, as well as technical and managerial skills to manage them. Under apartheid, those resources were heavily skewed to the needs of the well-off. With the political changes of the early 1990s, newly elected councillors saw the opportunity to redirect spending to meet the needs of the historically disadvantaged communities. But this came to an abrupt end in 1997 when the city ran into a fiscal crisis requiring severe cuts in its budget.

There were many reasons for the fiscal crisis. One was the costs and difficulties associated with a series of reorganizations of local government in the city. Another was the difficulty of spreading the resources which had hitherto served a minority to meet the needs of all. A third was the failure to collect all the revenue due. The city government inherited a culture of non-payment of charges and taxes in the former black local authorities – losses that had previously been borne by the national budget. At the same time payment rates in the former white local authorities started to decline – something made much worse by a tax boycott by the wealthy property owners of Sandton.

Nevertheless the fiscal crisis seemed to take the city by surprise. This was partly because the system of accruals accounting in use tended to disguise the problem. Accruals accounting credits revenues when they are due rather than when they are actually paid, with non-payment being recorded as a debtor. As a result, unless the debtor's position is taken into consideration, the revenue accounts can give the impression that more resources are available than is actually the case. The city government (GJMC plus the four Metropolitan Local Councils) continued to spend as if they were collecting 100 per cent of their revenues, when actually they were collecting only 90 per cent. Since a large part of the city's revenue comes from water and electricity charges, out of which it has to pay the utility suppliers, it soon ran into unsustainable cash-flow problems. The position was shored up by expensive, short-term borrowing.

The central government stepped in and imposed a new executive (Committee of Ten, subsequently the Transformation *Lekgotla*), with a brief to develop a radical restructuring plan. Heavy cuts were made in the capital budget and plans were developed to improve revenue collection, restructure certain activities along commercial lines and privatize others. The redirection of resources to the poor was put on hold and, until the elections at the end of 2000, local democratic accountability was effectively suspended.

---

commonplace. In Kumasi, while the official charge at a health clinic is Cedis 500, it is common for people to have to pay ten times that amount if they want to be treated (Devas and Korboe, 2000, p130). In Bangalore, it is routine for the police to require daily payments from street traders for protection. Elected councillors often perceive their position primarily in terms of the rents they can extract, in order to finance their re-election campaigns. In Kenya, land-grabbing by well-connected politicians has been a major issue.[4]

Generating and managing the financial resources

All cities face financial problems, but some manage to do more than others to address them. In this section, we look at the ways in which cities have sought to increase resources, and the impact of this on the poor. We also look at the impact of cities' spending patterns on the poor, and the processes of decision-making about resource use.

Improving local revenues

Table 6.1 provides an indication of the scale and types of local revenue in seven of the case cities for which sufficient data were available. It shows not only that cities in relatively richer countries (South Africa, Brazil) have greater total resources per capita than those in poorer countries (Kenya, Ghana, India), but also that these resources represent a larger proportion of per capita gross national product (GNP) in richer countries than in poorer ones.[5]

Table 6.1 also shows that locally raised revenues provide between one-third of the city's budget (Kumasi) and nearly all of it (Johannesburg). In all cases, the cities have quite a high degree of local discretion about the use of resources as a whole.[6] All the cities levy property tax, and this is the largest single revenue source in four cases. However, revenues from property tax lack buoyancy, and a large proportion of the tax remains uncollected in most cases.

With the exception of Recife and Ahmedabad, per capita revenues have been static or declining in real terms. In Recife, decentralization has been accompanied by substantial increases in both transfers and local tax revenues, the latter as the result of new taxing powers. This increase in resources opened the way for the adoption of 'participatory budgeting' (PB) (see Box 6.3). Ahmedabad Municipal Corporation (AMC) has been highly successful in counteracting the evasion and corrupt practices that undermined collection of *octroi*, thereby dramatically improving yield and helping to turn around the city's fiscal position during the 1990s. Yet at the same time, efforts to improve collection of property tax, including a successful High Court case that cut the number of appeals by taxpayers, seem to have had only limited impact. Although property tax yield went up during the 1990s, the rate of arrears remains one of the highest in the country. One of the reasons was the closure of textile mills, which accounted for a significant proportion of the city's tax base.

Cebu had considerable success in improving the performance of property tax, with a 150 per cent increase in tax yield in real terms between 1988 and 1992 (Etemadi, 1999, p44), but revenue growth in subsequent years has been much smaller. Following its fiscal crisis, Johannesburg embarked on an ambitious plan to improve revenue collection and hive-off non-core businesses. Credit control measures succeeded in raising collection rates from 85 per cent to 92 per cent over three years, although those averages mask big variations across the city. Meanwhile, in Mombasa and Kumasi, tax arrears just keep mounting up. In some cities, the failure of central government and parastatal agencies to pay their dues is a major problem.

Cities with a variety of buoyant revenue sources, particularly those levied on some form of economic activity, are generally in a better position than those that depend mainly on property tax, such as Bangalore and Mombasa. Besides Ahmedabad, with its substantial receipts from *octroi*, Recife, Johannesburg and Cebu all get a significant share of their revenues from business-based taxes. In Kumasi, market revenues are the largest revenue source. In the end, city

Table 6.1 *Analysis of city revenues*

	Cebu 1999	Ahmedabad 1996/7	Bangalore 1998/9	Mombasa 1999/2000	Johannesburg 1999/2000	Kumasi 1998	Recife 1996
Total revenue per capita ($) (excluding borrowing)	$40	$34	$14	$12	$120	$4.50	$160
Total revenue per capita (as % of GNP/capita)	3.9%	9.0%	3.1%	3.2%	3.8%	1.1%	5.3%
Local own revenue (as % of total revenue)	65%	88%	75%	88%	97%	34%	46%
Total revenue growth in real terms	Overall: static (Business tax: good)	Good (4–5% pa) (esp. Octroi)	Static	Static	Modest (c.3%)	Negative	High
Total per capita revenue growth in real terms	Slight decline	Modest increase	Negative	Negative	Static	Negative	Positive
Main local taxes (as % of total revenue)	Property tax 26% Business taxes 20% Amusements 7%	Octroi 58% Property tax 24%	Property tax 30% Stamp duty 5% Betterment 7%	Property tax 34% Bus.licences 17% Market fees 7%	Property tax 65% Bus.turnover 25% Electricity 5%	Market fees 12% Bus.licences 7% Property tax 5%	Services tax 20% Property tax 11%
Property tax collection performance	60–86% (dep.on definitions)	<20%	<60%	79%	90%	67%	N/A
Transfers (as % of total revenue)	IRA tax sharing 35%	Mainly conditional grants for education 12%	Deficit/ conditional grants plus compensation for abolished taxes: 23%	General grant (LATF): 7%; specified grant for roads: 5%	Specified grants 3% (District Common Fund) 45%	Salaries subsidy (20%); tax share	Tax share (mainly FPM) 54%
Degree of local discretion in use of overall resources	High	High	High	High	High	High	High
New borrowing (as % of budget)	45% (mainly for one big project)	N/A (but significant)	20% (mainly for roads and infrastructure)	None	Small (mainly refinancing)	None	N/A

Note: All figures are approximate only.
Source: City case studies

governments can only levy those taxes which are specified in national (or state) legislation, and national regulations often limit the scope for increasing tax rates.

Borrowing is one way that cities have used to augment their resources for capital expenditure. With the development of the municipal bond market in places like India, the opportunities for borrowing have increased. However, loans have to repaid, so unless they are used for projects that generate an adequate return, the burden on city finances increases. In Cebu, borrowing for the South Reclamation Project (a project to reclaim a large area of land close to the central business district) nearly doubled the size of the city's budget in 1999–2000. Although this project was expected to generate substantial returns, the debt burden was considered to be too great, and a large part of the project was transferred to a state agency. Both Ahmedabad and Bangalore have issued bonds for road construction, and for water and sewerage in the case of Ahmedabad, and both have borrowed from HUDCO (the national housing finance institution) for housing and urban infrastructure. While Johannesburg borrowed substantially in the past, recent borrowing has been mainly to re-finance previous loans. The weak financial positions of Mombasa and Kumasi have prevented those cities from borrowing at all in recent years.

Impact on the poor of resource mobilization

To what extent do the revenues collected by municipal governments – and the attempts by municipal governments to mobilize more revenues – impinge on the poor?

Property tax, if properly administered, should have relatively little impact on the poor, especially where low value properties are exempted (as in Cebu and Ahmedabad), or taxed at a lower rate (as in Kumasi and Visakhapatnam).[7] However, where there are high rates of arrears on high value residential or commercial property – the situation in many cities – the burden of the tax falls proportionately more heavily on the less well-off. In such circumstances, increasing tax rates without improving collection performance could be inequitable. In Johannesburg, it has traditionally been the poor who have not paid – a legacy from the anti-apartheid struggle, but increasingly owners of higher value properties are failing to pay; the value of tax arrears on city centre commercial buildings now far exceeds that on all low value residential properties.

Local business taxes tend to be arbitrary and regressive, particularly since accurate assessment of profitability or turnover is difficult. Certainly, flat-rate business licences tend to burden small businesses much more heavily than large ones, although some systems exempt informal sector traders. In Kumasi and Mombasa, the burden of market fees – the largest revenue source in Kumasi – undoubtedly falls mainly on the relatively poor.

Cities have also sought to improve their financial situation by levying, or increasing, charges for services. Charges have an obvious impact on the poor, but city-level information does not always reveal the extent of charging or its impact. It is widely acknowledged that charges for health services represent a burden for the poor and may prevent them from accessing health services (Mills et al, 2001; Sepeheri and Chernomas, 2001). Yet charges for health services rarely come anywhere near covering the costs of the services: typically, they cover about 10–15 per cent of expenditure on health in the case cities. A much greater problem for the poor is the unofficial charge levied by those controlling access to the service, since these are often much higher than the official charges. Charging for sanitation (such as public toilets) also has an impact on the poor, but can be justified as a way of covering maintenance costs, thereby ensuring that the service continues to be usable. However, this has been highly problematic in Kumasi, where contracts were awarded to members of the Metropolitan Assembly who then failed to use the revenues for maintenance, thus imposing significant burdens on low-income households (see Box 9.2).[8]

Charges may be justified where only certain people receive the service. In Kumasi, household waste collection is provided only in the high-income areas, and a charge is levied. However, the charge is not commensurate with the cost of the service, so that high-income residents effectively benefit from a large subsidy. Charging for water can also be justified on the grounds that finance is needed to maintain and expand the system. General under-pricing of water is likely to mean that there are no resources to extend water supply to areas where the poor reside, obliging them to continue using much more expensive vended water or polluted sources. In Bangalore, there is a system of free public standpipes, but resources are lacking for maintenance and extension of the network. In Mombasa, while the piped network nominally serves most of the city, in large areas no water flows because there are no resources to repair the network or increase bulk capacity.

In Johannesburg there is near universal provision at relatively high standards, but the problem is the absence of a system of targeted subsidies to enable the poorest to pay the relatively high bills. Low-income households, for example pensioners, can face utility bills that may exceed their entire income (Beall et al, 2001). Although the city established an 'Indigence Register' to identify those against whom enforcement action would not be taken, this did nothing to enable those on the register to pay their accumulated debts. In addition, the register soon became outdated, and there was scope for abuse such as meter switching.[9] Alone among the case cities, Santiago has a comprehensive system of relating water bills to ability to pay, based on household income data, although how well it works is open to question. A more common approach is to use progressive block tariffs to charge more to large volume consumers, on the assumption that the rich consume more water than the poor. But in Kumasi that system takes no account of how many households use one tap, thereby penalizing those living in communal blocks, whatever their income.

Spending patterns and their impact on the poor

To what extent do municipal expenditures actually benefit the poor? To answer that would require a more detailed benefit–incidence analysis than is possible from the available municipal budget data. Comparisons between cities are also difficult because of the differing ways in which information is compiled. However, Table 6.2 indicates broad areas of expenditure that can be regarded as benefiting the poor.

Table 6.2 *Analysis of city expenditures*

	Cebu 1999	Ahmedabad 1996/7	Bangalore 1998/9	Mombasa 1999/2000	Johannesburg 1999/2000	Kumasi 1998	Recife 1996
Range of expenditure Responsibilities	Wide incl. health, education (shared) (water indirectly)	Wide incl. education, health, water	Moderate incl. public health, water distribution excl. education	Moderate incl. public health, education (shared) excl. water	Quite wide incl. water and electricity, some health excl. education	Limited incl. health (shared), excl. water education	Wide incl. health, education, social welfare
Capital expenditure (% of total expenditure)	45% * 2.5% **	20%	10–20%	2%	16.6% ***	40%	16%
Administrative expenditure (incl. Mayor/Council)	25% *	30%	6.5%	27%	32% ***	c.25%	N/A
Debt-service ratio (approx) (% of revenues net of loans)	2.3%	9%	8.8%	5% (but defaulting on most loans)	15%	0	?3%
Expenditures/subsidies benefiting the poor (% of total expenditures)	Health 9% Div. for Welfare of Urban Poor Purchase of lots/ slum upgrading Grants to barangays	Health 14% Primary educ. 20% Water taps 9% Slum improvement Economic opportunities	Health 14% Water taps 4% Provision for SC/ST 2%	Public health 10% Waste 11%	Health 7% Waste 4% Housing 4%	Nothing significant	Urban infrastucture in poor areas Education Health Social assistance
Sub-city levels of government	80 barangays (receive share of national/city revenues)	Part of budget handled through Zones and Wards	None formally but Wards have some significance	None	GJMC budget incorporates 4 MLCs (now abolished)	4 Sub-metros 20 Town councils 403 Unit committees but none really functioning	None but 6 regions and 15 micro-regions for participatory budgeting

Note: All figures are approximate only. * Including South Reclamation Project. ** Excluding South Reclamation Project. *** Percentage of net budget (including only net revenue from water, electricity)
Source: City case studies; GNP data from World Bank 2001a

The most obvious area of expenditure to benefit the poor is that on health, since the benefits of publicly provided health services are – in principle – available to all, while higher income groups are likely to opt for private services. Expenditure on health typically represents 10–15 per cent of city budgets. Similarly, where the municipality provides primary and nursery education for free, the poor may be expected to benefit, so long as access is not dependent on unofficial charges. In Ahmedabad, 20 per cent of expenditure goes on education. The Indian cities subsidize a network of free public standpipes which are clearly of benefit to low-income groups. In Ahmedabad, water provision accounts for about 10 per cent of the budget, in Bangalore about 4 per cent. But many areas are not served – often the areas where the poorest live, and maintenance problems and lack of capacity in the system mean that many standpipes operate only intermittently or not at all. In Johannesburg, waste collection is provided virtually throughout the city, so that some of the 4 per cent of the budget spent on that could be considered as benefiting the poor.

Some cities spend money on slum upgrading and local level infrastructure and services. This could be expected to benefit the poor directly, although benefits generally accrue more to property owners than to tenants. By contrast, in many systems, subsidies for public housing provide little benefit for the poor, since they rarely occupy such housing. Cebu has a specific department for the Welfare of the Urban Poor, although its budget is minimal. By law, the city is required to set aside 20 per cent of revenues for a Local Development Fund, and some of this is used for projects that benefit the poor, such as artesian wells, fire hydrants, drainage, purchase of plots and so on. But actual expenditures from this fund are much lower than the statutory requirement. In Bangalore, the law requires 18 per cent of the budget to be allocated for Scheduled Castes and Tribes (SC/ST), but in practice actual expenditures are more like 2 per cent (depending on definitions). By contrast, in Ahmedabad, the city is required to assign 10 per cent of revenues to slum areas and in most years this proportion has been exceeded. In Kumasi, 20 per cent of the District Assemblies Common Fund (DACF) is supposed to be allocated to income-generating activities for the poor. But this has not generally been complied with, and what little has been spent in this way has been allocated in a most opaque manner (King et al, 2001, p155). By contrast, participatory budgeting in Recife has resulted in some shift, albeit modest, in the pattern of expenditures towards social expenditure and infrastructure in poor neighbourhoods (Melo et al, 2001, p118).

Other expenditures are less obviously of benefit to the poor. Most cities spend 25–30 per cent on administration, including the mayor and council, and revenue collection, but figures vary depending on what is included. Most cities spend large amounts on public works, much of which is for roads. The benefits to the poor of such expenditure are likely to be marginal at best, through the effects on economic growth, or negative at worst, as the poor are displaced for new road construction or to enable traffic to flow freely. Expenditure on street lighting, drainage and public parks may benefit the poor, but since it is generally commercial and high-income residential areas that are best served, the benefits to the poor are small.

The huge resources used by Cebu for the South Reclamation Project will have little direct benefit for the poor. However, it is possible to justify such an investment if, as is claimed, it will generate substantial financial returns that can then be used for pro-poor expenditures. Other cities such as Bangalore, Ahmedabad and Johannesburg have all undertaken major loan-financed projects, some of which are of questionable benefit to the urban poor. Whether or not large-scale infrastructure improvements aimed at enhancing local economic growth prospects ultimately benefit the poor is open to debate. But there are clearly risks that such 'mega-projects' actively disadvantage the poor, by pre-empting available land, expelling the poor from valuable locations and upsetting fragile trading relationships. This is demonstrated clearly in the case of major road and market projects in Bangalore (Benjamin, 2000). Loan financing for bulk water supplies and sewerage projects can be justified, so long as costs are recovered from consumers, particularly high-income and commercial consumers. But there are risks that heavy debt-service obligations may pre-empt resources which might otherwise be used to address the needs of the poor. One of the over-riding considerations in the restructuring of the Greater Johannesburg Metropolitan Council after the fiscal crisis of 1997 was to re-establish the city's credit-worthiness with lending agencies. In order to do that, cherished anti-poverty initiatives were abandoned or put on hold.

What all this shows is that, unless there is a clear policy of redirecting expenditures towards the poor, which is followed through into actual service and infrastructure delivery, the normal, 'budgeting-as-usual' pattern of city government expenditure will have only incidental benefits for the poor – and in some cases could actually disadvantage them.

It should also be noted that much of the public spending which relates to the urban poor bypasses city government altogether. In most of our case cities, the bulk of funding for health and education comes from central ministries. Even where such functions are formally decentralized, funding – and therefore control – may remain with central ministries, as in Ghana. In several cases, water supply is the responsibility of state enterprises, and, in Kumasi, this has now been privatized. In South Africa, funding for housing and related infrastructure – probably the most significant public spending on urban poverty – flows through provincial rather than municipal governments. In Bangalore, there has been a perceptible shift in responsibilities from the municipal government to state boards, remote from the urban poor. The Karnataka Slum Clearance Board, for example, appears to have delivered virtually nothing of benefit for Bangalore's poor residents. Meanwhile, the housing and land-banking projects of the Bangalore Development Authority (BDA) have pre-empted land resources for the benefit of higher-income groups and for revenue generating activities. Ironically, however, the poor have at times benefited by illegally occupying land owned by BDA.

Processes of budgeting and expenditure management

A central question for this research is how decisions are made by city governments, including decisions about the use of financial resources. Another is how far citizens – especially the poor – are able to have any influence on these decisions. What emerges is that even where the poor are able to exert some influence on the formal budget process, outcomes in terms of actual expenditures depend more on informal processes. These informal processes are often under the control of a small executive group.

All the cities have formal systems by which the elected members of the city government as a whole approve the annual budget. In cities with directly elected mayors (Cebu, Recife, Santiago), responsibility for preparation of the budget is in the hands of the executive, ie the mayor and his/her cabinet, with the council or legislature having power only to reject or amend the budget. In the executive council system, councillors have – in principle at least – a greater opportunity to influence what goes into the budget. But since the locus of executive power is more diffuse, paid officials (chief administrator/clerk and treasurer/finance director) tend to play a greater executive role. Whatever the system, there is much negotiation over the final shape of the budget. The ability of individual councillors to influence the outcome in the interests of their constituents (or, indeed, in their own interests) depends on their position, power and negotiating skills.

Whatever the formal arrangements, the executive (taken here to mean those at the centre of the processes, whether the mayor and cabinet or senior officials) have considerable scope to influence the outcome, through their control of both the process and the information. Their construction of the draft budget generally allows little scope for ordinary elected representatives to suggest changes, even if the latter had the information and technical skills to do so. More significantly, formally approved budgets often bear little relationship to what is actually implemented. In the Philippines and in much of Latin America, the budget represents only an authorization to spend if funds are available. In Cebu, budget approval is followed by a process of 'allotments', which is mainly in the hands of the executive. These allotments depend on the resources actually available and are generally much smaller than the allocations in the approved budget. In Recife, while participatory budgeting has shifted budgetary priorities in favour of the poor, it has had less impact on actual expenditures because resources have not been available to implement all the agreed projects. At the same time, the mayor is empowered to spend up to 30 per cent beyond the budget if resources permit – potentially a huge area of discretion. In Mombasa, and quite commonly in Africa, local budgets are based on unrealistic projections of revenues. This is done in order to satisfy the demands of councillors while at the same time meeting the legal requirement for a balanced budget. Since the projected revenues do not materialize, budget cuts have to be made during the year. Because of the difficulty of cutting staff or other overhead costs, cuts fall mainly on maintenance, service operations and capital projects – including the pet projects of local councillors. The executive effectively operates a 'shadow budget' which determines how resources are actually used and protects those areas deemed to be essential, notably salaries and councillor allowances.

There are other devices at the executive's disposal. The power to bring forward or postpone expenditure gives the executive considerable discretion. Supplementary budgets, which are usually subject to less rigorous scrutiny than the main budget, can provide some room for manoeuvre. Extra-budgetary funds, too, offer considerable scope for discretion. In Cebu, the Mayor controls a number of such funds, with little accountability to the elected legislature. The largest of these relates to the revenue share from gambling (PAGCOR), the accounts for which show all manner of uses, from water pumps and dental supplies to training and contributions for celebrations. Other extra-budgetary funds include a Special Education Fund and the unspent balances from previous years' budgets. All these offer scope for mayoral patronage.

Of course, it is not only the executive that seeks to manipulate decisions during budget implementation. Councillors, civil society organizations and individual citizens continue to lobby for particular projects during the course of the year. Since the budget may be regarded by those responsible as little more than a general guide, or even just a wish list, there is nothing to stop councillors or others from lobbying at any stage. The mechanisms noted above provide the executive with considerable scope to respond to such lobbying. The result is that effective decisions about resource use differ markedly from those approved during the formal budget process.[10]

All this is not to say that control by the executive is necessarily bad for the poor. The poor, and organizations representing the poor, may be able to take advantage of executive discretion, by virtue of their persistence in pressing their demands. There are also situations where executive discretion may produce a more rational use of resources for the city as a whole than responding to numerous demands from local communities or councillors for small, unrelated projects. For example, investment in bulk water supply capacity may be required before local water taps can deliver any water. But the opportunities the executive has to manipulate financial resources concentrates power, reinforces clientelistic relationships and undermines the democratic link between poor communities and formal decision-making through local councillors.

Explaining city government financial performance

Why do some city governments manage to perform better than others in terms of mobilizing and managing their financial resources? The most obvious factor is the economic position of the country concerned: cities in richer countries find it easier to generate resources and to recruit skilled personnel to manage their finances. Then the national political and institutional context clearly plays a large part, in terms of defining the freedom which cities have to mobilize and manage their resources, and the checks that are applied to prevent local excesses. But it is important to look at the reality, which is often shaped more by informal processes than formal ones. Thus, while revenue systems may be designed (whether at national or local level) to be equitable and to protect the poor, the way these are administered may render the system very inequitable in practice, through tax evasion, rent seeking and unofficial charges.

The engagement of civil society may also explain some differences between cities, although probably less so in relation to finance than some other aspects (for example access to land or infrastructure), not least because of limited access to information about finance. Again, in terms of the influence of civil society, there may be a large gap between perceptions and reality. This may occur where the formal budget process in which civil society has engaged is overtaken by other, unofficial processes, and where democratically agreed and published budgets are not implemented. As a result, while organizations of the poor may appear to make gains through their engagement with city government, what is eventually delivered may be much less than what had been agreed.

Fiscal crises and resource shortfalls are often the reason for non-delivery. These crises may, under certain circumstances, provoke far-reaching reforms to improve the fiscal situation, albeit at a cost to some, as in Ahmedabad and Johannesburg. More often, they reinforce the informal processes of decision-making and the position of those with power over resources, as in Kumasi and Mombasa. In the end, much depends on the attitude and capability of the local leadership – mayor, senior elected representatives and senior officials, and how this cascades down to junior officials charged with implementing revenue and expenditure policies. This aspect of civic leadership is one to which we will return at the end of the chapter.

Responsive city government: Mechanisms of participation and accountability

Even if city governments manage to overcome the many constraints they face, what chance is there that they will be responsive to their citizens, particularly those who live in poverty? From the discussion in Chapter 5, it is clear that the conventional model of representative democracy has many limitations in terms of responsiveness to poor people. Periodic elections are a crude mechanism for ascertaining citizens' preferences and priorities about services, infrastructure investment and public expenditure, and are often dominated by élite groups. Representative democracy needs to be complemented by a range of mechanisms of participation and accountability that can ensure that decisions made reflect the interests of ordinary citizens including the poor. Of course, élite groups may not wish to open up decision-making in any way and may use their power to prevent other voices from being heard. Nevertheless, our case studies show that a number of city governments are seeking to be more responsive, and others are being forced by pressures from civil society to become more responsive and accountable. Many of these initiatives can be criticized in terms of: which voices the city governments are responding to, how far those voices are representative of the poor, and whether the initiatives reinforce rather than challenge dependent and clientelistic relationships. In this section, we will look at six aspects of a more responsive and pro-poor city government which emerge from the ten city case studies.

Developing a pro-poor agenda

A pro-poor agenda only emerges, and that agenda only turns into reality, if there is political commitment to it at the city level. That political commitment may emerge as a result of pressure from civil society, but it requires an institutional context that is capable of responding to that pressure. In a number of cities, a more pro-poor agenda emerged as a result of a national struggle for democracy that galvanized civil society. In South Africa, the commitment of the post-apartheid government to poverty reduction was apparent in both the discourse and the range of anti-poverty initiatives being pursued throughout government, national and local. Local governments were required to identify Land Development Objectives (LDOs) and prepare Integrated Development Plans (IDPs), in consultation with local citizens, in order to address the inequalities of the past. But here, as elsewhere, there are tensions between the demands of those in poverty and the need to promote economic growth within a market economy. In Johannesburg, this was exemplified by the competing claims on the one hand for a radical redistribution of resources and, on the other hand, for economic modernization and high-tech growth. Following the city's fiscal crisis in 1997, the adoption of *iGoli 2002* as the development strategy for the city was seen by many as the triumph of the neoliberal agenda, but this is to underestimate the extent to which the city's agenda had already shifted in favour of those disadvantaged by the previous system.

Cebu, too, faced tension between promoting economic growth and more specific policies to address the needs of the poor. Economic growth from the mid-1980s to the mid-1990s succeeded in raising living standards for the majority, but made little impact on poverty. NGOs played a key role in keeping poverty on the national and local agenda. Local governments throughout the Philippines were made responsible for formulating and implementing the national anti-poverty agenda in their jurisdictions. Cebu City adopted the Urban Basic Services Programme (UBSP) as the centrepiece of its poverty alleviation strategy, and was the first city government in the Philippines to establish a specific department concerned with urban poverty. Commitment to poverty reduction has been a major issue in every recent mayoral election. But as in any city, there are competing centres of power and wealth which resist significant redistribution, and vested interests which promote major projects that disadvantage the poor.

In Santiago, rapid economic growth combined with national systems of targeted welfare payments enabled the worst problems of absolute poverty to be addressed. The discourse has now shifted to issues of inequality and exclusion, over which there is much less political agreement. In Brazil, (re-) democratization and decentralization, combined with the increased resources available to the municipal governments, enabled Recife to embark on a number of initiatives to address the needs of the poor, including recognition of the rights of favela dwellers, the integration of squatter settlements into the city and the adoption of participatory budgeting.

Other cities have yet to take the pro-poor agenda seriously. In India there is much pro-poor rhetoric, as well as a number of legal obligations to the poor such as the special treatment for Scheduled Castes and Tribes. But these do not seem to have had much impact on the practices of municipal governments. In Visakhapatnam, more or less the only poverty-focused initiative was the externally-driven slum-upgrading project funded by DFID (Department for International Development). In Bangalore, the principle pro-poor programme,

UBSP, was funded mainly from the centre, while a number of municipal initiatives have been decidedly anti-poor. In Mombasa and Kumasi, poverty reduction has barely made it into political rhetoric, never mind into any effective programmes of action.

Avenues for citizen participation

The case cities provide a number of instructive examples of attempts to broaden participation and engage citizens in decision-making, but few have been sustained. Some have been externally driven as part of a donor-funded programme, as in Visakhapatnam, rather than being based on local political commitment.

The role that Community Development Councils (CDCs) played in the Million Houses Programme in Colombo illustrates the potential for increased citizen participation in identifying priorities and preparing plans for their area. However, that case also illustrates how such participation can wither once immediate needs have been met and political support is withdrawn (see Box 5.4). In South Africa, despite the good intentions of enabling the citizens to engage in identifying priorities and plans, the IDP process was effectively taken over by professional consultants and the voice of the poor marginalized. In Johannesburg, the IDP process also became sidelined by the city's fiscal crisis. By contrast, the case study of a low-income informal settlement on the periphery of Johannesburg illustrates how a local organization like the Diepsloot Community Development Forum (CDF) can be effective in negotiating on behalf of poor residents (see Box 7.2). But this case also illustrates how the municipal government can become reliant on a community organization as the sole means of communication with local residents, thereby according that organization a monopoly role in allocating housing resources.

In the Philippines, citizen participation relies heavily on the privileged position of NGOs within both national and local government. Etemadi (2001, p153) estimates that between 50 and 70 per cent of Cebu's urban poor households are organized, and alliances of NGOs and CBOs have played a key role in shaping mayoral elections. Even so, Etemadi concludes that formal participation by NGOs in planning has been more in form than substance, with the consultative body between the city and NGOs rarely meeting (Etemadi, 1999, p42). In Santiago, there is an elaborate, participatory process for producing local development plans. However, such plans are rarely put into effect, either because of the lack of resources, or because of a lack of commitment by the mayor. Similarly, legislation in Ghana established an elaborate system for participatory planning through institutions below the metropolitan government, yet in Kumasi these institutions were never allowed to function. In Mombasa, contacts between Municipal Council staff and local residents were said to be 'infrequent and antagonistic' (Gatabaki-Kamau et al, 1999, p90).

The most systematic form of citizen participation amongst the case cities is the participatory budgeting programme (PB) in Recife. As Box 6.3 shows, whatever the weaknesses of the process, PB has greatly enlarged the number of people, including the poor, who engage with the municipal government over budgetary choices.

BOX 6.3 RECIFE: PARTICIPATORY BUDGETING

Participatory budgeting (PB) is an approach that has been adopted in a number of municipalities in Brazil. The stated purpose is to widen participation in budgetary decisions to include the poor majority who have hitherto been excluded or kept in a state of clientelistic dependence by the political system. An unstated objective is to strengthen the position of the mayor in pushing through his priorities, with community support, against the resistance of the local legislative chamber (the elected councillors).

In Recife, PB started in 1993, but grew out of earlier initiatives (eg *Prefeitura nos Bairros*). It is organized through 6 regions and 15 micro-regions of the city. Public meetings are held in each micro-region to discuss the statement of broad budgetary options and resource availability, as prepared by city officials. Five hundred delegates are then elected at the micro-region level (roughly one per 4000 citizens), through a combination of individual votes and votes of community associations. These delegates prioritize the expenditure options. Around 30 of these delegates are then selected to participate in supra-regional meetings which consolidate the priorities in the light of technical feasibility, citywide needs and resource availability. CBOs and civil society organizations are also represented in the forums responsible for coordination, oversight and technical assistance to the process. From this, the budget is prepared and sent to the legislative chamber for approval.

The impact of PB has been more limited than the above description might suggest. The executive remains firmly in control, setting the initial agenda and budget priorities and restricting the PB process to a subset of capital investments. The executive also tends to pack the list so that delegates are obliged to propose cuts in order to prioritize other expenditures. Moreover, the executive is not bound to implement everything in the budget, since the budget only provides the authorization, and cost overruns mean that resources are insufficient to fund everything. Typically, only 80 per cent of the budget is actually implemented within a given year. Ultimate decision-making power rests with the mayor, who is not obliged to implement the decisions taken in micro-regional and regional meetings. In practice the political costs of failing to fund agreed projects ensure that most are implemented. However, they have to be juggled with other priorities, including large-scale infrastructure, identified by councillors and the mayor himself.

Around 5 per cent of the city's budget is subject to PB (or 9 per cent if related programmes are included) – essentially that part which relates to local level capital projects. This represents between 15 and 25 per cent of the municipality's capital expenditure (depending on definitions). Nevertheless, PB has resulted in a shift in expenditure towards social programmes and local infrastructure benefiting the poor. More importantly, the process has extended participation considerably to include the poor – although probably not the poorest. Although the proportion of the population voting for delegates has been very low (2.3 per cent), and only one-third of those elected are women, many thousands of citizens participate in meetings that elect delegates and establish spending priorities (over 28,000 meetings in 1998).

The relatively small number voting leaves the process open to challenge by elected councillors who consider that they have a much more substantial mandate. Also, unlike in Porto Alegre where delegates are elected on a mandate only after priorities have been agreed in the public forum, the delegates in Recife are elected to make choices using their own judgement. Thus, the Recife PB delegates operate more like councillors. As a result, councillors, who are effectively excluded from the process, perceive PB as a threat and have periodically tried to reduce the scope of the exercise. They have also sponsored candidates for election as delegates and colluded with them to secure municipal resources for the areas in which their support is concentrated. Delegates are very conscious that their lack of a specific local mandate limits their ability to influence decisions, and that the large projects are outside the scope of PB. Many regard themselves as scapegoats, forced to take the blame for local government's poor performance or failure to implement agreed projects. Research shows that residents regard the representative political system as corrupt and clientelistic, and that their awareness of the PB process is limited.

The system of PB is less well entrenched in Recife than in some other Brazilian cities such as Porto Alegre and Belo Horizonte. This is partly because, despite a history of left-wing activism in Recife, the city's contemporary politics is fragmented, bringing frequent threats to the process. In Belo Horizonte, PB has been incorporated into local law, giving it a degree of protection, and elected councillors are formally involved in the process, unlike in Recife.

Despite its limitations, the PB process has made budgetary choices more transparent, especially since the executive is required to publish information both about the budgetary options and about implementation. Above all, community level participants have gained new, more institutionalized opportunities to participate in rule-based rather than clientelistic decision-making.

Source: Melo et al, 2001 and Souza, 2001

It cannot, of course, be assumed that greater citizen participation and an active civil society always benefit the poor. The most articulate voices, with the best connections to city government, are usually those of the better off. Business interests are generally well organized, and partnerships with the city government to promote economic growth may adversely affect the poor. NGOs claiming to serve the poor may instead promote their own, élite interests and create dependency. In Johannesburg, the most powerful CBO is the Sandton Ratepayers Association, representing the residents of the richest district of the city, whose rates boycott had a crippling effect on the city's finances.

Mechanisms of accountability

Responsive city government also requires accountability to citizens for the decisions made. Yet mechanisms of accountability are seriously weak in virtually all the case cities. In most systems, meetings of the full council or legislature are open to the public, but in reality decisions are taken beforehand in closed sessions. There may be forums for consultation with 'stakeholder groups' but these may have more to do with public relations than real accountability. In Colombo, the mayor holds 'Division days' and 'public day interviews' with electors and tax-payers, as well as dialogues with professional groups. In Cebu, the mayor holds meetings with various organized groups, but such meetings tend to reinforce patron–client relationships rather than achieving real accountability. More significant are the independent studies carried out by NGOs on the performance of the municipal government, such as the efforts by the federations of civil society organizations in Cebu to monitor the performance of the mayor against a poverty-reduction agenda. In Recife, one of the most significant achievements of PB has been to bring budgetary choices into the open and to oblige the executive to report on implementation.

Information is typically seen as something to be withheld rather than distributed. At the most basic level, plans, budgets and audited accounts should be public documents which are easily accessible. This is not generally the case in practice. Nor do accounts, where they are available, necessarily give an accurate picture of the city's financial position.[11] In Mombasa, accounts have not been produced, let alone audited, for some years. Cebu does publish monthly revenue and expenditure figures in the press, but these do not tell the complete picture (omitting, for example, the extra-budgetary funds). The format of the budgets and accounts may also be extremely difficult for ordinary people, and even elected representatives to understand or engage with. It is often difficult to see from these how resources are actually being used, or to identify the extent of subsidy for a particular activity or client group.

Responsiveness though informal mechanisms and traditional authorities

Much of city governance happens through informal processes. This reflects the fractured nature of the administrative system and the clientelistic nature of politics in many cities. The poor may, however, be able to make use of these informal mechanisms, through persistence, to assert their claims. In Bangalore, Benjamin and Bhuvaneswari (2001, p35) describe what they call the 'porous bureaucracy', in which councillors or community leaders are able to achieve results through their informal networks with lower level bureaucrats. Such arrangements may enable the poor to consolidate their land claims, protect themselves against enforcement action and obtain essential services, but may also reinforce their dependent position.

In Kumasi, traditional authorities such as tribal chiefs offer an alternative avenue for the poor, at least for those of the indigenous Asante population. Local traditional leaders have some voice within the formal system of city government, and they have a central role in land allocation. They are accessible to, and understood by, ordinary people, who are therefore more likely to bring their claims to them than to the municipal government. This is not to say that such authorities are necessarily benign: they may also be unresponsive, corrupt and interested mainly in maintaining power and patronage. Nevertheless, traditional authorities have provided something of a countervailing influence to the remote and unresponsive municipal government in Kumasi.

Sub-city levels of government

The conventional argument for decentralization is that decisions made at the local level will more accurately reflect the needs and priorities of citizens. But where the 'local' jurisdiction covers a population of a million people or more, it is hard to see how this can happen without sophisticated mechanisms of citizen participation on specific issues. Decentralization below the city level to, say, a settlement or neighbourhood, can give ordinary citizens, including the poor, a greater chance of having their voice heard and influencing the spending choices which affect them. This is not to say that very local level decision-making will necessarily be more responsive: indeed it may still be dominated by local élites who maintain a feudal control over their locality. But decision-making at such a level is more accessible to the poor, and there may be greater scope for the poor to organize collectively than at the metropolitan level. Nor is it to say that the metropolitan level is not required: there are many matters which need to be decided at that level, for example about planning, transportation and bulk infrastructure. But the metropolitan level needs to be supplemented by something much more local. Yet few of the case study cities have any elected level below the city, and for those that do, the arrangement is mostly unsatisfactory.

In Colombo and the three Indian cities (serving between 1 and 6 million people), there is nothing apart from administrative subdivisions below the municipal level, although Ahmedabad has started to decentralize its administration and budget allocations to the zonal level and even to wards (Dutta with Batley, 1999, p80). For a while, the Community Development Councils in Colombo operated somewhat like a lower tier of local government in the parts of the city occupied by the poor. But in the absence of any statutory basis, their role greatly diminished with a change of government. While the metropolitan area of Santiago is divided into 34 municipalities, these are still very large, with an average population of 150,000, and their resource base is very unequal. Similarly, the metropolitan area of Recife is divided into 14 municipalities (of which Recife municipality is the largest), each with varying financial capacities. In Johannesburg, the abolition of the four metropolitan local councils (MLCs) means that there is now a single metropolitan authority for nearly 4 million people.

In Ghana, the 1988 local government law established an elaborate structure of local governance below the metropolitan level. In Kumasi, there are officially 4 sub-metropolitan councils, 24 town councils and 1020 unit committees. This would mean one unit committee for every 500 or so residents – truly a local-level institution. Unfortunately, most of this exists on paper only. The sub-metros operate but are deprived of the resources they are entitled to and so do virtually nothing. The town councils have never been inaugurated, and only a few unit committees function at all. This is largely the result of the opposition of the previous metropolitan chief executive – and members of the Metropolitan Assembly – to any alternative locus of power in the city.

Of all the case cities, only Cebu has an effective system of sub-city local governance, called *barangays*. These are small scale and hence accessible, having a statutory basis (unlike CDCs in Colombo), and receive an equitable distribution of resources (unlike Johannesburg's MLCs). As a result, they do enable local citizens, including the poor, to have an influence over at least some spending in their locality. It could be argued that such an arrangement offers a more secure institutional framework for local-level decision-making about resource use than does Recife's version of participatory budgeting, which ultimately depends on the political commitment of the mayor.

BOX 6.4 CEBU: SUB-CITY LEVEL GOVERNANCE – *BARANGAYS*

Barangays are the sub-municipal level of governance in the Philippines. In the past, they were part of the system of state control, with *barangay* captains appointed by the ruling party. But with the democratization and decentralization of government from the late 1980s, they have become part of the local democratic system. *Barangay* captains and council members are elected by local citizens. *Barangay* assembly meetings, which are open to all adults, are supposed to be held twice a year.

In Cebu there are 80 *barangays*, with an average population of around 8000 each. *Barangays* receive a share of national tax revenue plus one-third of the city's property tax with which to fund their activities. These include local security and certain local services such as sanitation, drainage and waste collection. A large proportion of their revenue is spent on honoraria for elected officials and security staff, but some is available for development. *Barangay* leaders have become adept at negotiating for additional resources from the mayor and congressmen.

The proximity of the *barangay* to citizens (an average of one *barangay* councillor per 1000 citizens) helps to ensure responsiveness to the needs of the area. In low-income areas, the poor are able to exert influence through the electoral process, and through standing for election themselves. The Cebu case study identifies a number of ways in which the *barangay* leadership is approachable and responsive to the poor, including allowing *trisikads* (cycle taxis) and informal traders to operate in their areas, improving basic services and providing emergency relief for the poorest. However, where the poor are only a minority in a better-off *barangay*, their needs may be neglected. The study also shows how *barangays* provide an avenue for issues of concern to the poor to be put to the city government. The fact that the *barangay* has some funds for local development projects brings decision-making over those resources closer to the poor. While this does not guarantee responsiveness or accountability, it certainly helps.

Conclusions: City government and the poor

In an era of decentralization and democratization, much is expected of city governments, especially in terms of responding to the needs for the urban poor. Yet, as this chapter has sought to show, city governments are heavily constrained in what they can do – legally, administratively and financially. Some city governments appear to be more successful in overcoming these constraints than others. Some cities have made progress in developing pro-poor strategies, widening citizen participation and becoming more responsive and accountable. Others have made little if any progress on these scores.

What, do we conclude, can explain these differences? As already noted, one obvious factor is economic: cities in relatively richer countries find it easier to generate resources and to retain the skilled staff to manage those resources properly. Greater resources can permit many other initiatives to take place. Another key factor is the national legal and institutional framework within which cities have to operate, together with the national political environment which shapes the political and administrative processes at city level. A third factor is civil society – the extent to which there is an active civil society, working effectively on behalf of the poor. However, as the next chapter will argue, the role of civil society in the case study cities appears to be rather less significant than is sometimes claimed, certainly in terms of negotiating with city government.

Finally, and perhaps most importantly, there is the role of civic leadership. From the case study cities, it is clear that civic leadership can make a difference to city governance and to the outcomes for the poor. City governments may be highly constrained, but there is always some room for manoeuvre. How cities make use of that depends to a large extent on the qualities of the civic leadership. In most systems, civic leadership is focused on the mayor, but it also includes other senior elected representatives and senior paid officials. It may also include some outside the formal structures of city government whose voice is influential. Clearly, some civic leaders are more responsive to the poor and have more vision, more integrity, more dynamism, and a greater capacity to make the system deliver than do others. Recent mayors of Colombo, Cebu and Recife, although open to criticism on various counts, have all been able to achieve results that have been of benefit to the poor. Other mayors have been more concerned with maintaining their hold on power and lining their pockets than with the interests of the poor, or have been too ineffectual to achieve anything of lasting value.

Moving beyond pro-poor rhetoric into policy and practice depends – in large part – on the commitment and dynamism of the mayor and other civic leaders. It also depends on the ability of the leadership to build and sustain supporting coalitions around such issues. This is a challenge where political allegiances are fluid and where, as in much of Latin America, there is a tradition of abandoning all previous initiatives whenever a new administration comes into power. In this context, the role of externally appointed leadership can be significant. In Ahmedabad, it was a particularly dynamic municipal commissioner – an appointed not an elected official – who is credited with turning around the fortunes of that city. By contrast, the appointed metropolitan chief executive in Kumasi – dynamic but ill-motivated – seems to have done much to discredit that organization in the eyes of its citizens.

While individual leadership qualities are important, they must be exercised within an adequate framework of public accountability, to avoid the emergence of personal fiefdoms. An institutional framework is required which allows dynamic, responsible and responsive leadership to emerge, and which obliges leaders to deliver results for the poor, not just as favours but as a matter of routine. While such a framework seems to be lacking in most of the case study cities, there are signs of movement in the right direction in a number of places.

In the end, though, what matters for the poor is what happens in practice: how policies and official processes are translated into actual practices and outcomes. This chapter has highlighted the distinction between the rhetoric and the formal systems on the one hand, and the informal processes and decision-making that determine what actually happens, on the other. Even apparently benign policies towards informal sector businesses, land development and service provision may be degraded in the process of execution, or have unintended negative consequences for poor people. These are issues to which we will return in later chapters of this book.

Notes

1   In 1999, Mombasa Municipal Council, already overstaffed and financially insolvent, took on 2000 additional junior staff through political patronage.
2   The Kumasi study records how the Chief Executive made key decisions, including dictating the budget, in the car park of the Metropolitan Assembly offices or at his home (King et al, 2001, p43).
3   There are, of course, circumstances in which some of the poor may benefit, at least temporarily, from certain forms of corruption: illegal electricity and water connections and non-enforcement of trading regulations, for example. But the impact of such arrangements is at best uncertain and uneven, and at worst imposes greater costs on the poor and increases their vulnerability.
4   It was the attempt by Mayor Balala to resist one such land-grab that led to him being ousted as Mayor of Mombasa (Rakodi et al, 2000, p161).
5   An exception is Ahmedabad, which seems to have remarkably high revenues. These come mainly from *octroi*, a local tax on goods entering the city. This tax is noted for its buoyant revenues but also for its negative impact on the economy.
6   This is somewhat surprising since in many other cities in the South, restrictions on transfers limit local discretion considerably.
7   Exempting low value rented properties may, in practice, benefit the owner (through the higher rents that can be charged) more than the (poor) tenant.
8   It is estimated that, for a family of five each using the toilet once a day, the cost would absorb 10 per cent of the basic wage (Devas and Korboe, 2000, p130).
9   Johannesburg, in common with other local governments in South Africa, has now introduced a progressive tariff structure for water which provides the first 6000 litres per month free of charge. It remains to be seen whether this arrangement can be self-financing without external subsidy.
10 This supports Grindle's contention that, in developing countries, policy making occurs mainly at the stage of implementation (Grindle, 1980; Grindle and Thomas, 1990).
11 For example, an analysis of budget implementation in Bangalore for 1997/98 suggested that, in order to show a positive balance at the end of year (as required by law), figures had been adjusted even though there was actually no surplus. More seriously, it appeared that capital expenditures had fallen short of capital receipts – in other words, the Corporation appeared to have been using loan funds to cover revenue shortfalls. In Mombasa, deficits are routinely disguised by postponing payments, leading to serious problems of indebtedness and inter-agency arrears.

Chapter 7

Civil Society Organizations: Do They Make a Difference to Urban Poverty?

Diana Mitlin

Introduction

Civic action, the coordinated activities of urban dwellers, has been recognized as an important feature in urban development by a number of urban theorists (Castells, 1983; Douglass and Friedmann, 1998). The significance of collective (rather than individual) action was popularized by Putman's (1993) study of Italy and his analysis of the role of social capital within economic development. For urban theorists, the ongoing role of social movements in influencing the governance of cities has long been recognized, as has the significant role of socially motivated agents such as non-governmental organizations (NGOs).

More specifically, many have noted the significance of civil society in reducing poverty (see for example Gorman, 1984; Carroll, 1992). Civil society groups have long been considered to be a means to poverty reduction through lobbying for improved policies, pressurizing to ensure policies and practices reflect laws and regulations, and through offering direct support for those in need (see, for example, Hirschman, 1984; Turner, 1988). At the same time, civil society groups have been recognized as an end in themselves, providing a political voice and supporting a collective identity – cultural, ethnic, class or otherwise (see for example, Bebbington's (2002, p6) description of the impact of ethnic organizations on the composition of local municipal councils in Ecuador).

But what does civil society offer to the urban poor and, particularly, to their efforts to reduce poverty and achieve development? This chapter examines what we have learnt about the role of civil society in regard to poverty reduction and, more specifically, the contribution of grassroots organizations (GROs) and NGOs to addressing the development needs of the urban poor in the ten selected cities. It is an opportunity to look at some critical questions facing civil society in the 21st century. First and foremost, what are the ways in which civil society contributes to poverty reduction? Second, does civil society unambiguously contribute to reducing poverty and inequality? Do all groups within the urban poor benefit equally from the actions of civil society groups? Is there exclusion within civil society and, if so, what are the social processes involved: co-option, oligarchy, élitism or market? Third, what are the trends within civil society, its social processes and institutional relationships? What can we understand about how its role might develop in the short to medium term? Finally, how are the actions of civil society influencing the shape and nature of urban development? This study offers an opportunity to extend our understanding of civil society at the level of the city – to understand how citizens and their social organizations (be they formal or informal) are shaping and changing the nature of urban opportunities and challenges.

It may be helpful, at the outset, to define the terms as they will be used here. 'Civil society' is used as an all-embracing term for voluntary associations between the state and individual citizens and their families (Salamon and Anheier, 1992).[1] As such, the definition includes non-government organizations, non-profit associations, informal organizations addressing public interest issues, and self-help groups and associations. The discussion here concentrates on two categories of organizations within this broad umbrella. First, grassroots organizations (GROs) are membership organizations that are (or are considered to be) independent of the state.[2] As membership organizations, the risks, costs and benefits are shared among the members, and the leadership may be called to account by members. Most are non-profit, although some operate as cooperative commercial enterprises. Many are informal and operate as loose networks of social relations rather than as regulated organizations. Trade associations of informal and self-employed workers and residents' associations are the two most important groups of grassroots organizations in the discussion that follows. Second, non-governmental organizations (NGOs) are defined as professional, non-profit intermediary organizations (often without a membership) that are independent of the state and which undertake a range of activities in order to further developmental objectives. In general, they are also charitable institutions, belonging to a larger family of organizations providing welfare and addressing public interest issues for a wide range of beneficiaries.

The significance of civil society's contribution to development practice and policy has been recognized by authors such as Gorman (1984) and Hirschman (1984). The popularity of civil society organizations (CSOs) grew during the 1980s and 1990s with an increasing number of bilateral agencies creating and extending co-financing programmes to NGOs. Multilateral agencies such as the World Bank and the United Nations Development Programme (UNDP) established consultation arrangements in addition to direct funding and programme collaboration. The major emphasis of development agencies has been on the contribution of NGOs and GROs rather than other civil society organizations.

Growing support for civil society from official development assistance agencies continued in the 1990s. However, there was also a more detailed consideration of the potential role of NGOs (and self-help organizations) and of their emerging development experiences, both in traditional small-scale projects and in the more ambitious scaled-up roles that were now being required of them. Edwards and Hulme (1992, 1995) and Hulme and Edwards (1997) reviewed some aspects of programme experiences in their edited volumes and highlighted issues of scale, accountability and relations with the state. At a similar time, Carroll (1992) suggested that the commitment of NGOs and GROs to participation and accountability could not be taken for granted.

The next section briefly summarizes some of the issues that emerge in the literature considering the role of NGOs and GROs in urban poverty reduction and urban development. This is followed by a description of the extent of the NGO and grassroots sectors found in the case study cities, from which we identify the contribution of these agencies to urban poverty reduction. Broadly speaking, their contribution was disappointing. Finally, we analyse some reasons for this poor performance, with a focus on those internal to the sector, such as participation, accountability, representativeness, responsiveness and engagement with city government.

Civil society and urban development: A background

In the context of urban development, there has been a widespread acceptance of the potential role of grassroots organizations. Arrossi et al (1994), Moser (1998, p13), Choguill (1996, p393) and Evans (1996, p1121) emphasize the importance of organized squatter communities in securing services and, in many cases, the supporting role of NGOs.

However, others, especially those who have completed detailed neighbourhood studies, highlight some of the complexities involved. In particular, they draw a picture of relationships with the state that are characterized by clientelism and patronage (Scheper-Hughes, 1992; Burgwal, 1995; Rashid, 1998; van der Linden, 1997; Hardoy et al, 1991; Klaarhamer, 1989; Desai, 1995; Pornchokchai, 1992; and Wood, 2003). Politicians and/or state officials work with community leaders to secure financial and political advantage for both parties. The ability of politicians and/or officials to control access to land tenure, infrastructure and services is used to reinforce the dependency of the urban poor on more powerful structures and processes. Women may have little influence on the grassroots organizations that may or may not address their needs.[3]

The literature on NGOs is comprehensive and has been growing substantially during the last two decades. One of the most widely used distinctions is that of Korten (1987, pp147–149), who distinguishes between relief and welfare, small-scale, self-reliant development and sustainable systems development (in which they extend activities from their own organization into relationships with public and private agencies including advocacy). Carroll (1992, p10) makes a five-fold distinction between NGO purposes: charity, relief, development (subdivided into business development, social development and social business), political action and advocacy of special interests (which may be combined with other assistance). Fowler (1997, p32) summarizes a growing concern throughout the 1990s with a table of NGO 'pretenders'; these include NGOs set up to have a commercial advantage, those for illegal purposes, those created by official donors, those created by governments and those created by politicians. Perhaps more significantly, Fowler (1997, p31) emphasizes that NGOs generally have to mix 'sustained poverty alleviation and social justice' while 'functioning as businesses to provide public services'.

While a relatively small proportion of this literature focuses on the work of NGOs with the urban poor, there is sufficient to develop an understanding of the range and scale of NGO activities. Housing improvements are encouraged through a number of strategies including loan finance, technical assistance and community mobilization. Although many micro-finance initiatives have been associated with rural development (most notably the Grameen Bank in Bangladesh), others are located in urban areas (Hurley, 1990). Some emphasis has also been placed on NGOs' role in policy-making and advocacy. Perhaps critically, and as exemplified by Karaos et al (1995) in the context of the Philippines, policy success can be difficult to achieve and once achieved may not be easily translated into changes in practice. INTRAC recently reported on a study of 141 NGOs working on urban issues that offers an understanding of the balance of these activities in five southern cities. One-third of the NGOs in their sample have a primary focus on income generation with the second and third categories being education and health respectively (Sahley and Pratt, 2003, p39). Most NGOs were working in four to six sectors. While 61 per cent of NGOs noted they were engaged in service delivery, the agencies put more stress on capacity-building activities (such as training and awareness raising). Drawing on this literature, many NGOs would fall within the 'developmental' category, with some addressing issues of relief and charity as well. However, there is also evidence of alternative approaches and some NGOs place considerable emphasis on partnership with organizations of the urban poor (see, for example, the approach of members of the international network Shack/Slum Dwellers International, *Environment and Urbanization*, 2001).

One particular issue is that of relationships within civil society and specifically between grassroots organizations and the NGOs that are seeking to support them. A number of earlier studies suggest that their relations are neither simple nor uncontentious (Desai, 1995; Mitlin, 1999). Tensions exist between NGOs that are seeking to control the development process and the urban poor who want greater power over decision-making and activities in development programmes and projects. This is just one of the themes that we will consider below.

The extent of civil society organizations in the ten cities

The cities studied illustrate the breadth and diversity of grassroots organizations in the towns and cities of the South. Local neighbourhood organizations are abundant and include those undertaking social activities (such as religious organizations) and those more concerned with the specifics of the urbanization process (such as infrastructure and services).

The city studies confirmed the prevalence of GROs. In each of the neighbourhoods surveyed, some form of organization was present, and NGOs were found to be working on issues related to urban poverty in all but one of the cities. Box 7.1 summarizes the breath and diversity of CSOs.

Given the emphasis placed on the autonomy of CSOs from the state by the numerous authors defining such organizations, it was surprising to note that in six of the ten cities state agencies were instigating some form of grassroots organization, either for the purposes of general administration and consultation or to enable participation in some specific poverty reduction programme. While the practice of state sponsored organizations has been discussed elsewhere, other studies of grassroots organizations have not suggested state involvement on this scale (Carroll, 1992; Verhagan, 1987).

In the context of this study of governance and the ways in which the urban poor bring their agenda to the government, it is notable how concerned the state is to create and support local organization. Even the most basic reading of community politics gives us reason to believe that these new organizations will draw on existing leaders and decision-making processes to embed themselves in the existing network of formal and informal association. For this reason, Howes (1997) and Christian Aid (1993) both argue that it may be more effective for activities to be developed within existing organizations. At the same time, we can expect the interests and potentially the practices of the state to be embedded in these newly created agencies.

Three possible reasons account for state intervention in local grassroots organizations. First, community organizations are created to form the lowest level of government. In Mombasa, for example, chiefs are appointed by the administration and they in turn appoint elders (community leaders). Second, in other cities such as Johannesburg and Bangalore, community forums or groups are encouraged in order to enable local participation in national government programmes for housing and poverty reduction respectively. Third, in Cebu and Recife, groups have specific functions; in these cases, water management and

Box 7.1 Civil society in the case cities

Ahmedabad: There are reported to be more than 1200 GROs in Ahmedabad. One of the most significant civil society organizations is SEWA (Self-Employed Women's Association) with almost 90,000 members. SEWA was set up in 1972 as a trade association working to improve the status of self-employed women, including providing credit. There are some 21 NGOs working on urban issues. For those with an urban focus, women, credit and the development of low-income settlements are the main areas of work.

Bangalore: There are estimated to be hundreds (even thousands) of community organizations in the city.

Cebu: In low-income communities, there have long been associations for social activities and religious festivals; however, exact numbers are unknown. There are 164 NGOs with government accreditation, 20 per cent of which are development NGOs.

Colombo: Over 600 Community Development Councils (CDCs – government sponsored GROs) have been registered in the city; however, many are no longer operational. In two neighbourhoods more intensively studied, there are other community-based organizations (CBOs) including traditional funeral societies, youth and sports groups, and savings and credit groups for micro-enterprise development. There are 26 NGOs working in the city, primarily in urban basic services.

Johannesburg: There are no city-based estimates of CBOs, but the indicative scale of activity can be understood through figures from Alexandra, a low-income area close to the city centre. In this formal township, 46 per cent of the population belong to church groups, 13 per cent to political parties, and 7 per cent to street communities. No figures for NGOs are available but a large number are operating, including housing service organizations, specialist agencies such as those concerned with urban violence, and local welfare charities.

Kumasi: With respect to GROs, in the 1990s there was a revival of mutual aid including rotating savings schemes in order to cope with economic hardship. Neighbourhood chiefs and elders continue to operate a system of dual administration alongside modern local government structures. Nineteen NGOs were identified as being active within the city, of which half were concerned (not always exclusively) with income generation.

Mombasa: In 1997, 15 per cent of households had access to credit from a voluntary association, either a cooperative or rotating savings and credit association (ROSCA). Neighbourhood organizations do exist, but it is not known how many there are, nor what they do. There are an estimated 30 NGOs, together with a few service organizations and religious organizations (although many are not concerned with urban poverty).

Santiago: There are a growing number of organizations of indigenous people with more than 35 such groups in the metropolitan region. With respect more generally to CBOs, an estimated 42 per cent of families belong to at least one organization. There are 89 NGOs in Santiago (although many are concerned with general issues such as human rights rather than urban poverty).

Visakhapatnam: In almost all localities, from the better off to the poorest slums, there are some sort of loosely held caste-based organizations. There are thought to be no NGOs working on urban poverty in the city. However, service organizations and charitable trusts, along with concerned citizens, carry out activities such as basic health and nutrition programmes.

Note: * Recife was not included in the first phase of the research and hence information was not collected on this aspect.

mothers' clubs respectively. However, grander ambitions are also noted. The creation of mothers' clubs in low-income neighbourhoods in Recife is linked to a desire in the city administration to influence (and possibly control) community politics.

Civil society and poverty reduction

What contribution have GROs and NGOs made to reducing poverty and securing development? There are a number of possible ways in which GROs might assist the needs of their members, including contributing to political voice and providing access to material benefits. Such material benefits include any resources that they secure from the state (and/or other potential benefactors) as well as resources that GROs provide directly to their members. This section summarizes the findings under three headings: resources GROs provide directly to their members; resources they secure from the state (and other resource-rich agencies); and benefits gained in regard to representation and political voice. A fourth subsection looks at the specific contribution of NGOs.

Grassroots organizations and the benefits they provide to their members

Although modest in scale and extent, there is evidence that GROs provide direct benefits to their members. In Kumasi, GROs and their networks may be important in providing moral support and welfare assistance – even if (as argued below) they are not able to influence important figures in authority. In Mombasa, increases in urban poverty have been associated with the creation of support groups with common interests; for example, hawkers working together to help pay bribes and fines. At the same time, in some low-income settlements, residents have organized vigilante groups in an effort to reduce crime and violence. In Bangalore, associations help hawkers to manage the bribes to the police and officials that enable them to continue trading. Their contribution is assessed as being significant: 'the power relationship that emerges between hawkers acting individually and hawkers organized as associations to ensure that pressure can be generated via political contacts is one that seems to make a difference' (Benjamin and Bhuvaneswari, 2001, p140). In Cebu, there are examples of clean-up activities undertaken by local residents' associations. However, in at least one case, the collected waste was dumped in an area immediately adjacent to the settlement and hence the initiative may be of limited value.

This focus on the value of micro-level support reinforces the finding of Moser (1998, p8) about the social capital that appears to be useful to low-income urban dwellers. However, despite the benefits of such programmes, few schemes to support self-help initiatives emerged from the city case studies. Reflecting on Korten's (1987) assessment of NGO strategies, this may be because such programmes were seen by NGOs to be limited in approach. SEWA, and its programme of micro-finance for women informal entrepreneurs in Ahmedabad is one of the few examples of larger scale self-help activities. In this case, micro-enterprise support has been extended to include a more comprehensive programme of upgrading in selected low-income settlements (Biswas, 2003). This experience highlights some of the challenges involved for GROs and support agencies in providing self-help. While they can provide moral support and small assistance to the urban poor, more substantive support to provide essential services and/or to increase informal entrepreneurship requires collaboration with state agencies especially local authorities.

Grassroots organizations and the benefits secured from the state

Relations between the state (and other external groups) and the members of GROs are mediated by community leaders. In some cases, this is in conjunction with professional individuals and groups such as NGOs.

Community leaders aim to achieve both collective development benefits for their members and personal benefits for themselves. There is an emerging emphasis on the personal benefits that are often secured in exchange for votes or other resources requested by more powerful groups. In Santiago, for example, community leaders receive 'rewards' (generally public sector jobs, access to public grants and subsidies, and social investment funds) in return for managing votes at election time. 'The political relation in the *comunas* establishes a reciprocity model – that has an implicit character – based on a mutual favour policy' (Rodríguez and Winchester, 1999, p61). In both Colombo and Visakhapatnam there was evidence of local community leaders securing benefits from politicians without the interests of other local residents being taken into account.

At the same time, it should not be assumed that members are passively dependent on their leaders, nor are leaders solely concerned with benefits for themselves. There is a process of active negotiation between leaders and agents or powerful individuals outside the community that control or influence access to essentials resources. Whether or not leaders retain their positions depends in large part on what they manage to secure for their supporters through these negotiations. Box 7.3 illustrates the gains made by grassroots organizations with respect to informal trading in Cebu. While informal traders still face many difficulties in finding space in which to trade, city authorities now respond more positively to their activities and have come to recognize the legitimacy of their needs.

In the case of Bangalore, GROs have been able to secure land and services for their members despite a political system that does not appear, at first sight, to be receptive. However, local democracy does provide opportunities for political and institutional access by poor groups, as illustrated in Box 5.2 in Chapter 5. Benjamin and Bhuvaneswari (2001) have termed this process 'politics by stealth', in which the poor (often in diverse and complex alliances with richer groups) use multiple strategies to obtain access to state resources and to influence regulatory processes. One avenue is through 'porous bureaucracy': lower-level bureaucratic channels that are amenable to influence by local groups in non-transparent ways. Another is 'vote banks' which can be used to secure investments for poor wards. While some vote banks can rightly be criticized for being simple party-based affairs centred on liquor distribution with the poor groups being bussed to party rallies, others can also be used by poor groups to secure genuine gains from candidates in local elections. Vote bank politics can facilitate access to land and services, protect poor groups from demolition by richer ones, resolve local disputes over property boundaries, and help ensure the bureaucracy is responsive to local needs. Councillors (and their competitors from other political parties) have party workers operating as their representatives. These party workers are generally local community leaders who link to street leaders, more formal office bearers of residential associations (the 'community') and the party political representatives. Street leaders may approach several party workers to test out their responsiveness to their demands, and may approach the councillors directly (Benjamin and Bhuvaneswari, 2001). There is active and rigorous competition as to who can offer what to the organized urban poor. Ethnicity, income and occupation create and fracture groups and alliances. Often such links work vertically as well as horizontally, drawing the poor together with more powerful groups. However, the processes explored in the study of Bangalore are limited in the extent to which they are really pro-poor.

In a very different context, mixed benefits also emerge from a donor (United Nations Children's Fund, UNICEF) project to improve health services in Mombasa through community pharmacies run by village health committees. The most successful example was the Mtongwe Bamako project, which secured real benefits for those living in that low-income settlement, but in other areas the leaders have used the health facilities for their own private benefit. Thus, the organizational capacity of a community and its internal politics influence the extent to which projects benefit all residents and are sustainable.

Grassroots organizations, political representation and the voice of the poor

One of the underlying issues for GROs appears to be that of competition. Who or what is a legitimate body to represent the interests of the poor? In Colombo, a hostile political environment is one reason given to explain the failure of the community development councils (CDCs): 'Some politicians ... actively seek to weaken CDCs... They don't want a competitor taking credit for improvements', Russell (1999, p104). Similar problems emerge in Recife where there has been a tense interface between local councillors and the elected community delegates for the participatory budgeting (PB) process (see Box 6.3). In 1999, councillors moved to abolish the scheme, criticizing the local participatory process and arguing that allocation decisions should be taken in the legislature. Their proposal for abolition received widespread councillor support and failed only because of the position taken by the mayor. Both councillors and delegates feel responsible for their constituencies; as a result, councillors started competing with the delegates and, in some cases, began to sponsor delegates.

A lack of political voice is also highlighted in Santiago, although the perceived problem is not competition between GROs and political interests but rather, residents' associations competing for inclusion in the state poverty programme, FOSIS, with little apparent interest in collaborating to challenge the shortcomings of the programme. A particular explanation emerges in the case of organizations established by the state. In Colombo and Santiago, it is suggested that such GROs tend to present projects to the state and implement state programmes, rather than taking on a broader and autonomous agenda.

In Kumasi, low-income groups have little capacity to influence decisions of the Assembly. The powerlessness of the poor is reflected in their own perception of their difficulties. As one woman in the low-income community of Anloga argued 'the KMA [Kumasi Metropolitan Assembly] does not care so much for us because we are poor and we are not Ashanti' (King et al, 2001). Their lack of political connections and lack of skills in English are further reasons put forward by the urban poor in Kumasi to explain their exclusion from the political process.

The contribution of NGOs

There are diverse but largely pessimistic experiences with the NGO sector across the cities in this study. While a large number of projects are noted in the cities, many appear to be small, involving less than 100 families. In Kumasi, Korboe et al (1999, p143) conclude that: 'many of the NGOs have programmes only on paper', and that, even for those bona fide NGO programmes that really exist, the numbers involved are very small. A further problem within the city is that NGOs find it difficult to translate their grand visions into actual projects, in part due to limited resources. A somewhat more positive perspective on NGO activities in Kumasi is given by King et al (2001, p52), who note the growing recognition and role given to NGOs in Kumasi especially 'in areas such as urban waste management and the collection of market levies'.

In Mombasa, Gatabaki-Kamau et al (1999, p88) draw on an earlier study by AMREF and OVP/MPND (1997) that argues 'many poor residents have not benefited from ... NGO poverty reduction projects, because of their small scale in relation to the extent of the problem'. In Ahmedabad, SEWA has a wide range of activities to support self-employed women. Together with SAATH (a local NGO) they have been involved in an innovative 'slum networking' programme to improve living conditions in one area of the city. However, the programme has helped only a small proportion of the urban poor and it may be difficult for the project to increase in scale.[4] In Bangalore, Benjamin and Bhuvaneswari (1999, p107) conclude that 'in general the argument that NGOs play a substantive role in Bangalore in poverty alleviation is not easily justified'. In general, the assessment in this city is profoundly pessimistic about the potential contribution of the NGO sector. 'We find that at a very fundamental level, there is very little attempt by both NGOs and official programmes to even understand the economic, political and institutional context within which poor groups operate... On the contrary, the alliance of interest that emerges from this approach has a regressive impact on existing pro-poor processes' (ibid, 1999, p17). In Recife, different challenges can be observed for the NGO sector. Non-governmental organizations became less significant as the grassroots organizations became involved in collaborative projects with city officials, local residents developed their own technical capacity, or required assistance in areas in which the NGOs did not have skills.

In Cebu City, NGOs enjoy a particularly good working relationship with local government and state agencies; this involves both service delivery and advocacy. As discussed in Box 7.3, there has been considerable collaboration between CSOs in the city with emerging benefits for the poor. The success of NGOs in influencing government practices has been through a more practical engagement in social issues of common concern, rather than at higher-level municipal policy-making. In part, this opportunity for collaborative programmes may be due to a high level of institutionalized participation by civil society in local government within the Philippines.

Some of the contradictions in the assessments (including the diverse perspectives on Kumasi) can be resolved through the understanding that NGOs may have successful programmes at the micro-level in specific areas that are not seen as controversial. However, larger-scale success appears to be harder to achieve. It also appears that a two-stage assessment occurs with regards to advocacy and lobbying. When NGOs secure inclusion and are invited to meetings, there is often a sense of success and achievement. However, in the longer term there is scepticism about the value of such inclusion.

Conclusion on the contribution of GROs and NGOs in the case study cities

Generally speaking, the discussion in this section suggests we should be pessimistic about the contribution of GROs to addressing the development needs of their members. While many GROs seek to address these development needs, and some have achieved success, they are often immersed in relationships of dependency, clientelism and patronage. Gains have been secured, particularly through the process of elections and the securing of votes, but there remain questions as to the effectiveness of civil society contribution. In regard to NGOs, serious questions are raised about their capacity and sometimes about their commitment to achieve significant poverty reduction.

The following section examines some reasons for this low level of success of civil society in addressing urban poverty. Three particular issues will be explored: GROs that are not really inclusive of the poor; limitations of NGOs; and civil society's lack of participation in citywide political structures and debates.

The constraints facing civil society

Grassroots organizations: Issues of participation and representativeness

In seeking to understand the strengths and limitations of GROs, issues of participation and representativeness immediately come to the fore. There are repeated concerns about low levels of participation across the studies. While low levels of participation might not necessarily be problematic, in situations of widespread poverty a lack of participation suggests that residents do not see such organizations as contributing to their needs. In two cities in which grassroots action has been recognized to be successful, Cebu and Bangalore, a related issue arises that, even when communities and groups have managed to organize and unite for specific objectives, they find it hard to maintain that unity once their goals have been secured. Over time, participation slips away. This suggests that even when participation in GROs is recognized to be a successful strategy, other activities are also important. There are also concerns about how representative leaders are of the interests and characteristics of members. Such a lack of representativeness combined with limited accountability may help to explain the significance of the personal agendas of community leaders.

In Cebu, Kumasi and Recife the picture emerging from the studies is that there are commonly low levels of participation by residents and a reluctance of some potential members to be involved. Although there are 60 registered associations at Kumasi Central Market, less than 20 are active; 'The records are poorly kept and some members exist only in name. They rarely attend meetings or pay membership dues' (King et al, 2001, p143). It appears to be relatively easy for organizations to be formed but when problems arise, they stagnate and may die. Such a process is illustrated in the case of one organization for drivers of *trisikads* (cycle taxis) in the port of Cebu. The committee is divided and no activities are happening following an internal conflict, with members disputing the financial transactions of the treasurer. Etemadi (2001, p69) concludes 'unless and until the internal conflict is resolved the organization would remain divided'. Similar problems are noted in the provision of water in the city. There is a possibility for communities without water to have subsidized communal taps. However, take-up is low with less than 10 per cent of urban poor families using water from such taps. Etemadi (2001, p118) suggests that this is because of a 'lack of active participation by members, undemocratic if not oppressive management style, irregular or no annual election resulting in a monopoly of leadership and lack of financial transparency and accountability'. As a consequence, water vendors are widely used despite prices that are three times those of the municipal water company.

A number of reasons are put forward to account for low levels of participation. In Cebu, it is suggested that the poor are so preoccupied by their immediate needs that further activities are not possible. Another explanation is offered in Santiago, a city in which significant removals took place during the 1970s and 1980s. The poor were relocated into peripheral areas with considerable disruption to existing social networks and solidarity. In the context of state-sponsored GROs in Bangalore and Colombo, membership is thought to be short-lived due to a lack of ownership on the part of local residents. However, Mtongwe Bamako, the UNICEF project in Mombasa, while limited in some areas, did succeed in others and continued after UNICEF's withdrawal because of the strength of local support.

One of the implications of low participation is that even when there are elections within GROs (rather than less explicit processes), leaders may emerge with a relatively low degree of member involvement. In Recife, for example, delegates for the participatory budgeting process may be elected with as few as 25 votes due to an apparent lack of interest in the elections. As a result, leadership may be unable to represent the needs of members or be uninterested in doing so. In Kumasi, persuading individuals to take on leadership is itself problematic as, unlike the situation in rural areas, there are no traditional mechanisms to allocate such roles. The young people living in the low-income community of Mossi Zongo identified the following 'desired leadership qualities': educational background; maturity; God-fearing; permanent residence in the community; eloquence; and social standing. This suggests that it is unlikely that one of the poorest members would be selected as a leader. This concern is reinforced by findings from Johannesburg and Visakhapatnam in which low-income and low-status residents were the least likely to take part in leadership roles.

With respect to gender, there appears to be relatively low participation by women in leadership positions. In Kumasi, for example, leadership structures in the community are male-dominated and there is little real consultation of the ordinary membership, especially the women. This finding is consistent with earlier literature which also reports that a male élite within the settlement often dominates leadership positions (Harrison and McVey, 1997; Hardoy et al, 1991; Pornchokchai, 1992; Thorbek, 1991; van der Linden, 1997).

Some of the consequences of a low degree of representativeness are indicated in the studies. In Mombasa, 'Chiefs and elders are used to exercising power by filtering information and directing communities, and residents are used to them dominating community decision-making' (Gatabaki-Kamau et al, 1999, p89). As has been found elsewhere, the emerging picture is of poor accountability with low membership participation, little membership involvement in decision-making and no process to enable a common agenda to be set (Klaarhamer, 1989; Magutu, 1997; Moser and McIlwaine, 1997; Moser and Holland, 1997; Peattie, 1990).

The case study of the Diepsloot community in Johannesburg (Box 7.2) illustrates how the poorest and most vulnerable may be disadvantaged when interests compete within GROs. In this case, existing residents opposed squatters joining their community. The most significant GRO in Diepsloot is the Community Development Forum (CDF), an umbrella organization that 'assumes sole responsibility for liaising with outside actors in the development processes unleashed by the findings of the Land Development Objective (LDO) (Beall et al, 2001, p68). The Forum's contribution to local development is widely acknowledged and it has clearly been successful in addressing some development needs within the community. However, its hegemony has been challenged and there has been violent conflict especially in relation to the housing allocation process. Furthermore, while valuable development work has been done by the Forum, three groups do not appear to have their interests well served: women, who are more concerned with the risk of rape and flooding and with the problems of securing a livelihood than with the concerns of the CDF; children, who have no play or recreational facilities and who may be having to work; and illegal immigrants, who are being prevented from squatting in the river bed (adjacent to the site) by CDF members.

BOX 7.2 ISSUES ON THE TABLE: DIEPSLOOT, JOHANNESBURG

Post-apartheid reconstruction of South African cities is intended to be based on new local planning processes, including the production of Land Development Objectives, now superseded by Integrated Development Plans (IDP). These processes are intended to involve local residents, so that the programmes reflect the priorities of underprivileged communities. Consultation is undertaken through the local development forum, the members of which are organizations, including, for example, ratepayers' associations, youth groups and the old civics.[5]

Diepsloot is a low-income settlement located on the farm of Zevenfontein on the northern fringe of the Greater Johannesburg Metropolitan Area. It has 30,000 residents, many living in shacks and in urgent need of improved shelter and job opportunities. The settlement has benefited from a substantial government subsidy programme for improved tenure security, infrastructure, services and housing. Nevertheless, it is typical of the peripheral form of low-income post-apartheid urban settlement, where squatting and in-situ upgrading merge with new mass housing construction to accommodate an often unskilled and unemployed or under-employed population. Initial consultations with residents were undertaken in 1996/7.

To facilitate the process and increase their influence, a number of GROs formed a Community Development Forum, which has subsequently assumed sole responsibility for liaising with outside organizations with respect to the development of the area. It has mediated the allocation of housing and basic services, the definition of the settlement's size and layout and its long-term status within the metropolitan area. It is accountable to residents and GROs and has developed a sophisticated structure of sub-committees. It has good relationships with the local councillor and the provincial government. The settlement's needs were initially taken up by the Provincial Premier, in part to provide himself with a popular support base. He facilitated a housing development for 3800 families, funded by provincial resources.

The organizational power of the Diepsloot CDF is legendary in Johannesburg. Local government officials, private sector developers and local NGOs are all quick to assert the solidity of community organization in this informal settlement. Although it is not the sole community organization operating in Diepsloot, the CDF has established itself as the voice of the people and the coordinating forum for small, sectoral or issue-based GROs. However, two emerging issues raise questions about the deals that have been negotiated and how well the interests of the community have been served.

First, the ability of the CDF to deliver land, housing and services to its constituency hinges on the management of government funds. The new houses being constructed have a floor area of just 25 square metres. Since the contract was agreed, protests from GROs nationwide about the poor quality of subsidy-financed housing has resulted in the government requiring a minimum size of 27 square metres. Those Diepsloot residents who receive the new houses will have a product that is 'substandard' by current norms. This suggests that community organizations are likely to experience problems when working with technical planning processes.

Second, Diepsloot has been excluded from the Spatial Development Framework for the Province of Gauteng and will be treated as a stand-alone town rather than integrated into the metropolitan urban development structure. The CDF has agreed with this proposal, but it is not clear why. Ostensibly, consolidation and containment of the existing settlement is necessary because of capacity constraints on bulk water supply, its peripheral location and to protect nearby open areas of environmental value. The CDF seems to have accepted the first argument. However, less explicit reasons for the planning proposal include the desire of nearby high-income residents to limit the growth of a low-income settlement and maintain an undeveloped area between them and

Diepsloot. As a consequence of the CDF's agreement to limit the growth of the settlement, it is now actively preventing new shack development, thus closing off an important reception area for poor in-migrants.

All concerned with planning and service delivery in Diepsloot regard the CDF as the legitimate voice of the residents and the key to meaningful participatory democracy. Gradually, infrastructure has been installed in the settlement and houses have been consolidated. However, the Forum's ability to engage ordinary citizens in influencing the development process has been limited by both the wider context and internal political contests. It has not succeeded in changing the priorities of service-providing agencies where the latter have professional blind spots regarding the priorities of low-income residents. In addition, acceptance of its leadership is not universal, it neglects some concerns of residents in its responses to consultative processes, and it does not represent dissenting voices or new residents. Monopoly of community organization and consultative processes by a single channel is, therefore, neither stable nor desirable.

Similar issues of contested interests arise in the other two neighbourhood studies in Johannesburg. One of the emerging explanations is a leadership which may be democratically elected but which may not be representative. For example, in Meadowlands (another low-income area in Johannesburg), the African National Congress (ANC) is led by the Veteran's League which for the most part involves the home owners, even though nearly a quarter of the residents are tenants. Hence 'community organization, to the extent that it engages with local government, is firmly the terrain of the more established, respectable older working class' (Beall et al, 2001, p113).[6]

Even without the active intervention of the state creating conditions for dependency, GROs face many difficulties. Box 7.3 discusses trade associations of informal vendors in Cebu and describes issues related to the representative nature of leaders, the interests of the poorest groups and the capacities of the organizations themselves. Also considered is the continuing need to negotiate with the relevant authorities to increase the opportunities and reduce the oppression facing the poor. While successes have been achieved by the traders' association, generally the more politically successful organizations are those that represent the higher-income traders.

NGOs – a role in poverty reduction?

The role of NGOs in influencing state policy and practice is potentially significant. However, the findings from this study are mixed with, on balance, a somewhat pessimistic conclusion about the contribution of NGOs to poverty reduction. This subsection seeks to understand why this is. Although NGOs appear to be gaining in 'policy space', in many cases it is not evident that there are benefits for the poor. In some cities, issues have been raised about NGOs' willingness and capacity to act for the poor. For example, despite NGO claims to be active in advocacy in Kumasi, there is little evidence to show that they are undertaking such work and few NGOs are known to the city government. Even when advocacy is undertaken, it is through reports that are rarely read by policy-makers. However, this criticism is tempered by the acknowledged lack of interest

BOX 7.3 ORGANIZATION OF STREET VENDORS IN CEBU

The informal sector is important to the poor in Cebu, with a large proportion of the labour force securing their livelihood in this way. One of the most important areas of activity is informal trading, generally on the streets. During the early to mid-1980s, the situation of street vendors in Cebu was very difficult. The administration of Mayor Duterte was hostile to their activities and stalls were regularly demolished.

In 1984, one of the vendors' associations proposed that the existing groups work together, particularly to provide a united front against demolitions. The Cebu City United Vendors Association was formed from 13 existing groups. In the following years, the Association became experienced in resisting demolitions (often unsuccessfully), and its leadership began to recognize the need to strategize and negotiate rather than simply resist. By the time that Mayor Osmeña took up office in 1988 (following the fall of the Marcos government), the Association already had several years of proactive negotiation behind them. The Association has continued its work and currently has about 5000 members (some 5 per cent of those working in the sector), 75 per cent of whom are women.

Mayor Osmeña began his term proposing the complete phasing out of street vending in the city. The vendors responded by strengthening their lobbying of the administration. They made some progress and, in the early 1990s, a vendors' management study committee was established by the city authorities. The committee concluded that activities should be legalized in some areas of the city. When the Supreme Court did not agree, the city authorities shifted to a policy that demolitions would not be considered unless a complaint was made by other road users – an approach which was known as 'maximum tolerance'.

Street vending has become more acceptable over the last ten years. Traders are able to find niches in the city from which to make a living without, or with only low levels of, harassment. The negotiation and lobbying skills of the organizations are stronger than was previously the case. However, the situation remains far from easy. Demolitions have continued, creating immense difficulties for a group of the urban poor who have few alternative sources of livelihood. While SPEED (the city's Squatter Prevention Encroachment Elimination Division) seeks to provide some support to keep areas tidy and acceptable to other users, vendors find their attitudes patronizing and disrespectful. On the whole, the relationship between the vendors and SPEED has remained distant but cordial, although in some cases the vendors have complained about the lack of due process. As a result of the continuing difficulties and trade association lobbying (supported by an NGO in recent years), the city authorities agreed in 2000 to establish a technical working committee to recommend new practices.

Within the vendors' organizations themselves, there has been a mixed experience in organizational development. Leadership struggles mean that groups come together, in some cases affiliating to the citywide federation, only to break up and/or leave some years later. While successful organization and subsequent negotiations have offered greater security to groups such as the Tobacco Vendors Association and Lahug Vendors Association, problems remain. In the case of the Cebu Port Authority Trisikad Drivers' Association (CPATODA) a trade association for *trisikad* drivers operating at the port, leaders are vulnerable to pressure from local politicians, making agreements that provoke divisions within their membership and a weakening of their unity and capacity. Despite this, the association had some success in resisting repressive enforcement and in winning certain concessions from the Port Authority.

Source: Etemadi (2001)

on the part of the local authority. The role of NGOs in advocacy is particularly difficult in Kumasi, in part because the Ghanaian culture is one in which criticism is taken to mean opposition.

A more complex picture emerges in the three cities in countries where radical political changes have led to recognition being given to the potential role of civil society. In Santiago, Johannesburg and Cebu, there are concerns about NGOs' over-involvement with service delivery roles. This debate suggests that NGOs have taken up opportunities to engage with state programmes. In part, this is understandable, as many of these NGOs have been actively involved in the struggle for democracy, and in each of these countries staff have moved from the NGO to the state sector following democratization. As new state poverty reduction programmes are created, NGOs are encouraged to participate; in some cases, they may have been responsible for initiating the programme in the first place. However, there are indications that the absorption of NGOs into the state is reducing the ability of NGOs to remain a critical commentator on state practice and policy.

Turning to governance within the civil society sector itself, there is a concern about relationships between NGOs and GROs. More specifically, there are fears that NGO staff may be reluctant to delegate power and responsibility to local residents. In Colombo, for example, there are evident tensions between NGOs and GROs. One reason for the poor participation of low-income residents in NGO programmes is that such programmes do not respond to the needs of the urban poor: 'NGOs have their own objectives and are largely self-interested ventures obtaining funds from government and international donors for their own benefit' (Russell, 1999, p104). NGOs in Colombo are also accused by community leaders of deliberately failing to develop the capacity of CDCs and other GROs in order to enable themselves to dominate local processes, and weakening these Councils by draining human resources away from the community into their own organizations. A further concern is that they dominate financial and project-level decision-making.

In other cities, NGOs are also treated with suspicion by the poor. King et al (2001, p57) reinforce concerns that 'beneficiaries do not have a sense of ownership of the projects and therefore take no responsibility for their sustainability'. It is argued that NGOs have done little to support self-reliant interventions for communities, partly because they are more concerned with their own survival. This situation is also repeated in Bangalore. Benjamin and Bhuvaneswari (2001, p17) suggest that NGOs participate in the formalization (and 'techno-managerial zeal') of urban development processes with adverse consequences for the poor. For example, one NGO scheme to create 'hawking zones' had a disastrous effect on the income of hawkers (as discussed in Chapter 8). 'If one were conventional, we would argue that the NGOs have been co-opted by the system. A more radical perspective could hypothesize that the élite NGO groups are now one of the main players in shaping the system to be increasingly repressive to poor groups' (ibid, 2001, p194). As a result, 'It is hardly surprising in the above context that local communities are usually suspicious and sceptical of NGOs and official programmes aimed to improve their lot' (ibid, p218). Such worries echo some of the reservations previously expressed by Thurman (1994), Desai (1995) and Gazzoli (1996).

There are fewer concerns in Cebu, where NGOs claim high levels of involvement by local beneficiaries in their projects. The relationships are positively assessed by Etemadi (2001, p92): 'Their direct relationship is founded on trust and support'. However, the success has brought challenges and NGOs face a growing pressure to respond to a deeper relationship with GROs. Demands for financial transparency, while indicative of a degree of empowerment of the poor, are considered to be adding to the pressures on NGOs as they seek to manage funds in ways that they consider to be equitable and effective.

Civil society and city-level decision-making

In the cities studied, there appears to be little evidence of the poor influencing the agenda of the city with respect to city-level plans and strategies. There are few citywide lobbying activities and, more profoundly, apparently little ambition within the NGO and community sectors to determine city policies in favour of the poor. One exception to this situation is Cebu where an alliance between civil society groups that was formed in 1987 for the mayoral elections in 1988 has provided a platform for GROs and NGOs to work together in defining their joint priorities (Box 7.4).

Such lack of citywide perspectives and activities can be illustrated, at both the macro and micro scale, for the city of Johannesburg. Considerable financial problems have led to a new strategic plan for the development of the city. While it is evident that the plans should be of concern to the poor, there has been little involvement of civil society. Officially the city favours consultation, both through stakeholder involvement in the Integrated Development Plan that local authorities are now legally required to prepare and through the consultation commitments in *iGoli 2002* (GJMC, 1999), the city's own plan. However, there has been little actual involvement of ratepayers, civil organizations and other civil society groups. As discussed in Box 7.2, it is evident that the lack of a 'broad picture' affects the choices being made by community groups, potentially to the detriment of their longer-term interests. Communities tend to have a local perspective and a reluctance to challenge broader urban policies.

The lack of information and knowledge about, and engagement in, broader city plans also occur in other cities. In Kumasi, leaders often lack the knowledge to represent their communities in the broader political arena and their perspectives are invariably focused within their own communities.

There are other reasons for lack of involvement by civil society. In Bangalore, the decisions are increasingly being made at the state level (and dominated by private corporate interests) rather than at the local level (see Box 5.2). As a consequence, urban renewal programmes for the city appear to have had a regressive impact. In Recife, one problem is the low ambition of those involved in participatory budgeting. Melo et al (2001, p91) quote a councillor from the Workers Party in Recife who argues that one shortcoming with participatory budgeting in the city is that 'the city as a whole is not discussed.

Delegates do not debate structural projects... Participatory budgeting ... was restricted to the discussion of containment walls, staircases in sloping areas, paving, improvements in schools and health posts and so on'.

In Cebu, despite the recognized strengths of civil society, citywide consultation by local authorities may be concerned with a specific area of local government responsibility (for example, hawking and vending) or with citywide planning processes. Local politicians, even the Mayor of Cebu, make clear their preference for dealing with a single representative or group of representatives in such consultative processes. Nevertheless, the situation of civil society in Cebu appears to be somewhat different from that in the other case cities. Box 7.4 describes citywide approaches that seek to move forward the agenda of the poor in that city. Why is Cebu different? There appear to be three related factors: the relatively high degree to which civil society in the Philippines has been formally included in local government process; the fact that Cebu is not a capital or primary city (and hence subject to fewer political interests and less contesting); and finally the relatively strong personal ties between the political and NGO élites.[7]

BOX 7.4 CEBU: WHO PARTICIPATES IN WHOSE PROCESS?

For the 2001 municipal election in Cebu, NGOs and urban poor groups together organized a series of meetings with contenders for election as Mayor and councillors. Over 300 participants representing 94 urban poor organizations attended meetings in order to learn from and influence candidates.

Civil society in Cebu has more than a decade of experience in city-level planning. With increased engagement with the authorities, their strategies have changed. Non-governmental organizations and people's organizations have adopted a policy of critical collaboration. At the end of the Marcos dictatorship, their tactics were very confrontational. Rethinking among NGOs and people's organizations (POs) led to a change of paradigm in dealing with the authorities. They shifted their strategy from 'expose–oppose' to 'expose–oppose–propose'. Confrontational politics was replaced by a politics of engagement characterized by negotiation, compromise and (hopefully) 'win–win' resolution of conflict.

The ability of the urban poor to make favourable changes in the political process of the city has depended particularly on their ability to work together, build networks and ensure that they 'police their own ranks'. Groups have been able to negotiate to achieve compromises while putting pressure on the city government to secure their demands. In part, their success may be due to their scale – 50–70 per cent of the urban poor are organized through some kind of social organization for housing and land. About 30 per cent of members of community-based organizations participate in activities, and 20 per cent have acquired housing through the Community Mortgage Programme (CMP) or other socialized housing schemes. Another 10 per cent are involved in NGO supported livelihood programmes. There are consequences for both local residents and local authorities. For example, vendors who used to evade the law are now working for the enactment of a new regulatory ordinance. And, virtually all *barangays* have, as required, allocated 10 per cent of their budget to gender and development.

A virtuous cycle has been created as urban poor groups recognize that they have to participate in the political process to advance their cause and that government is responsive to the needs of the poor because of such advocacy. Patron–client relationships remain, but city government has become more inclusive and pro-poor.

Source: Etemadi (2001)

Despite the generally favourable account in Box 7.4, not all the problems have been resolved. As noted above, it is often hard to secure high levels of participation and many are simply reliant on authority without questioning decisions or challenging direction. In 1999, only 5 per cent of the budget in Cebu went on capital projects potentially benefiting the poor. The budgeting system encourages the '... clientelistic political system that pervades Cebu, like the rest of the Philippines' (Devas, in Etemadi, 2001). Devas argues that while the political system is delivering resources to the poor, it is also reinforcing dependency: 'It also puts a premium on the ability of groups (or individuals) to lobby; clearly some are in a better position to do this than others. Each individual project has to be separately negotiated, preventing proper comparison between competing uses for the resources.' Despite such reservations, the balance of power and resources appear to be substantively different in Cebu from that in the other cities discussed here.

Conclusion

Is the picture really so pessimistic? Is there any evidence that democratization and decentralization have increased the capacity of civil society to secure benefits for the poor? From the city case studies, it is clear that some civil society groups are seeking more inclusive and pro-poor urban development approaches. At times, as shown above, such approaches have secured some limited success. What is evident is that success cannot be taken for granted. It may be short-lived as more powerful forces seek to use the urban development process to their own advantage. It may also exclude some of the poorest and most vulnerable among settlements of the urban poor.

The emerging picture is, for the most part, of isolated communities whose leadership is anxious to use urban development processes and structures to further their own individual interests and is able to address some immediate development needs, but which has little ambition to substantively address issues of inequity and discriminatory development. As Abers (1998) and Evans (1996) argue, the way in which the state interacts with citizens appears to influence the way in which CSOs operate and hence their capacity to represent themselves and their members. A potentially unrepresentative and often unaccountable grassroots leadership appears to reflect, at least in part, an urban development process that is itself exclusionary. The interests that are served by this process seek to create and maintain a grassroots leadership that meets their needs.

The conclusion is that, for the most part, the experiences in the ten cities substantiate the existing findings that relationships between grassroots organizations and the state are characterized by clientelism and patronage. Unable to provide comprehensive services and legal land tenure to everyone, city governments control access to such benefits as a way of influencing votes and, in some circumstances, securing other resources, especially land. Some politicians and/or state officials appear to work with community leaders to secure financial and political advantage for both parties. The ability of politicians and/or officials to control access to land tenure, infrastructure and services is used at best to influence communities in the choices that they make and at worst may reinforce the dependency of the urban poor on more powerful structures and processes. While vote bank politics have helped to address the needs of the poor and have secured real benefits in some areas, other neighbourhoods remain neglected.

The discussion has suggested that three factors in particular have restricted the ability of civil society to act in the interests of the poor. First, the leaders of grassroots organizations may not represent the interests of the poorest or most vulnerable groups. Moreover, that leadership may have only limited accountability to their members. Second, NGOs may be failing to support grassroots activities effectively. In some cases, they may actually compete with GROs for power and other resources, or they may dominate decision-making, reducing the effectiveness of project interventions. Third, civil society may simply not operate at the level of the city and may therefore not be able to take a sufficiently broad perspective. Planning and economic development issues may be ignored in favour of short-term advantage. Politicians and officials may seek to isolate community groups so that they can address their own interests.

Looking ahead, it is potentially significant to note that, in Cebu, despite the limited NGO influence on policy-making at the highest level, it is the institutionalization of partnership at a project level that has created space for innovation. NGOs and CBOs may maximize their effectiveness through negotiations around social policies and social provision in a number of groupings (commissions, committees and task forces) that are outside of mainstream government policy-making. This argument reinforces some of the conclusions of Boonyabancha (1998) and Khan (1997). These two authors, writing about Thailand and India respectively, suggest that NGOs and CBOs may be most successful when they are able to work alongside local government in operationally focused activities rather than lobbying from 'outside'. Hence, in addition to the three arguments above, the strategies used by civil society are also important in explaining success.

Finally, we should also note that the studies may be limited (and unduly pessimistic) because of the specific focus on *city* governance. In several of the countries (including Chile, the Philippines and South Africa), NGOs and GROs have sought policy changes at the level of national governments rather than the city. In each of these three countries, significantly large, national programmes to assist the poor, improve access to secure tenure, housing and basic services have been introduced.

Notes

1   The issue of definitions is considered in more detail in Mitlin (1999, pp4–5).
2   Although, as explored below, this characteristic is considerably more complicated than first appears.
3   Looking specifically at gender issues, Thorbek (1991, pp79–80) summarizes the contrasting experiences of women in residents' associations in Bangkok and Colombo. In one, women and men participate equally in addressing infrastructure

and livelihood issues; in the other, a local 'strong man' dominates, women are seen (at best) as passive beneficiaries and their needs are not considered.

4   A more recent report suggests that up-scaling has been achieved (Biswas, 2003, p55) – see Box 9.4.

5   See footnote 2 of Chapter 5 for an explanation of civics.

6   At the same time, we should recognize that some grassroots organizations have been established specifically to represent the interests of high-income groups within the city: one such case in Johannesburg is the Sandton Ratepayers Association.

7   In regard to this final point, it is harder to explain why strong personal ties should have a beneficial impact in Cebu and a regressive impact in Bangalore.

Chapter 8

Regulating the Informal Sector: Voice and Bad Governance

Philip Amis

Street hawkers and informal sector traders are among the strongest visual images of any urban area in the South. Their activities provide the principal source of income of many of those living in poverty in these cities. Their position is often fragile, dependent not only on the uncertainties of passing trade but also vulnerable to the exploitative behaviour of those with power to enforce oppressive regulations. This chapter is concerned with the relationship between city governance and those engaged in informal sector trading. One of the main arguments of this chapter is that it is easier for city governments – through 'bad governance' – to destroy the livelihoods of the poor than it is to create, sustain or enhance them.

The following sections provide brief overviews, first, of the scope and scale of the informal sector in the ten case study cities, second, of the development of the concept of the informal sector and third, of the role of municipal government in relation to this sector, together with some examples from the case study cities. From this analysis we will develop the argument that the regulation of the informal sector is often determined at the local level – and often through informal processes – because of the difficulty and inappropriateness of applying the relevant legislation. In this situation, it is the extent to which those in the informal sector have 'voice' that determines whether or not city government is constrained from applying detrimental policies. This notion of 'voice' – the influence that the poor can exert – is intimately connected to the nature and practices of democracy at the local level, and is an essential constraint on 'bad governance'.

The importance of the informal sector

Table 8.1 gives some information about the importance and characteristics of the informal sector in the case study cities.

Two points are worth making. First, the data are very incomplete for most of the case cities, so that most of the figures in Table 8.1 are little more than rough estimates. Second, there is no standard definition of the informal sector, so that the term is often used to refer to different categories in each city. In many cases, the categories of 'unemployed', informal sector and service sector overlap. It is worth noting that, as a classification, the informal sector is used less in India than elsewhere: rather, the emphasis is on the small-scale enterprise sector. Benjamin (2000), in his study of Bangalore, argues that the use of the term 'informal sector' is misleading as it implies a linear development path. Furthermore, he argues, it misses the critical importance of the clustering of local firms that are often able to achieve synergies by subcontracting with each other. Benjamin prefers to use the term 'local economies': 'Local economies form the economic base of urban areas in India. Drawing on studies of similar local economies, one could argue that the bulk of employment generation happens from a much more diffused set of services and small-scale manufacturing-centred local economies' (Benjamin, 2000, p41).

Despite the limitations of terminology and data, it is possible to make the following broad observations. First, with the possible exception of Santiago in Chile, the informal sector is crucial as a survival strategy for the urban poor. However, it is important to appreciate that not all the poor work in the informal sector: in Santiago, the majority of those below the poverty line work in the formal sector. The converse is also true: not all of those working in the informal sector are poor. The Bangalore case shows that many informal entrepreneurs have been able to earn substantial incomes.

Second, as one would expect, the importance of the informal sector is inversely related to the level of economic development; thus, among our case cities, the sector is largest in Kumasi, Mombasa and the cities in India. But its importance is also related to other characteristics of the labour market and, as noted elsewhere, the sector is often counter-cyclical – that is, it tends to absorb more labour as the rest of the economy contracts (Thomas, 1992).

While the size of the informal sector is important, so too is its spatial distribution within urban areas. Informal traders, like all retailers, usually prefer

Table 8.1 *Labour market characteristics of the informal sector*

City	Labour market characteristics: Informal sector	Comment
Kumasi	Estimated at 75% of the labour force (1999)	Major market and trading centre
Mombasa	Approx. 30% of city's population work in informal sector (1995). (Nationally, in urban Kenya, 38% work in informal sector, 1993.)	General decline of formal sector employment, especially manufacturing
Johannesburg	Unemployment rate in Gauteng province is 30% (1997). Working in informal sector important as survival strategy for urban Africans	Absolute and relative decline in formal employment, especially manufacturing and mining; increase in service sector. Easing of restrictions on informal sector in 1990s
Cebu	Unemployment rate 13.9%, while 3.0% 'visibly underemployed' (1999). Most of 73,000 self-employed and 12,000 unpaid family workers are in informal sector (1995). 13,000 street food vendors (1993)	Growing export processing economy alongside increased inequality. Hawkers and street traders partly organized into Cebu City United Vendors Assoc. with 4078 members
Visakhapatnam	Critical importance of daily casual labour as a major source of employment	Increase in number of industrial workers: 36,342 in 1984/5 to 53,534 in 1993/1994
Bangalore	20,000 registered small-scale units employing 189,000 people (1985)	Despite the hype of the city as the 'silicon valley' of India, the small-scale sector dominates
Ahmedabad	Informal sector increased from 50% of the labour market in 1981 to 64% in 1991 due to closure of textile mills	Major changes in labour market associated with restructuring of the textile industry. Self-employment increased from 712,000 in 1987 to 795,000 in 1993; the main increase was in female self-employment
Santiago	No figures but informal sector is small. Evidence of outsourcing and increasing informalization	The majority of those below the poverty line work in the formal sector

busy pedestrian sites in central business districts, even though these are often areas of conflict. Some parts of the informal sector seek very marginal locations – river banks or adjacent to railway tracks – often hazardous sites with almost no economic value. Many informal businesses, however, are located in the homes of their operators, resulting in mixed uses in primarily residential areas. The location of the informal sector is one of the key issues in relation to its regulation.

Background to the informal sector

The informal sector is a much disputed concept and there have been many debates about its definition. It is not our intention to rehearse these in any detail here. Nevertheless it is worth briefly outlining the way the concept has evolved in the literature. Keith Hart is generally credited with first conceptualizing the informal sector in relation to Ghana in 1970 (Hart, 1973). But the concept was popularized by the famous report by the International Labour Organization on Kenya (ILO, 1972). The most commonly used definition of the sector is from that report, which identifies the informal sector as being characterized by (ILO, 1972, Table 2):

- ease of entry;
- reliance on indigenous resources;
- family ownership of enterprise;
- small scale of operation;
- labour-intensive methods of production and adapted technology;
- skills acquired outside the formal school system;
- unregulated and competitive markets.

In contrast to this enterprise approach, Hart defined the informal sector in terms of whether individuals were wage earning (formal sector) or self-employed (informal sector). He makes the important point that individuals can reside and work within both sectors and move between them (Hart, 1973). Other writers have sought to define the informal sector in terms of its relationship to the state and government. Thus Roberts (1995), following the lead of Portes et al (1989), defines 'the informal sector as those enterprises, which avoid state regulation, such as fiscal obligations and labour standards, in contexts where similar activities are so regulated. In practice, the informal sector is mainly constituted of small-scale enterprises and the self-employed' (Roberts, 1995, p116–117).

Other work has sought to identify the dynamics within the informal sector. The original position of 'marginality' in the Latin American literature was posited by Quijano in terms of the informal sector as an area which was forever deemed to be marginal and where capital accumulation was not possible (Quijano, 1974). This seemed a particularly depressing interpretation, and one that has been challenged by empirical research that has shown a high level of differentiation within the informal sector. House's research distinguished between an 'intermediate sector' where capital accumulation was possible and one where the basic activity merely enabled survival (House et al, 1993). Work in Kenya suggests that constraints on expansion are often more to do with the extent of the market for the output of the informal sector than a shortage of capital (House et al, 1993).

The profitable sections of the informal sector are often controlled by particular groups, frequently reinforced by caste, ethnicity or other social norms that make them difficult to enter. Illegal drug dealing is the clearest case but informal shelter, transport and some metalworking have similar characteristics. Ultimately the sanction that supports this control is violence. Veena Das' work on the riots in New Delhi associated with Mrs Gandhi's assassination in 1984 are revealing about the nature of the informal sector: 'the fencing mechanisms and regulation of entry into most sectors of the informal economy were a product of several factors – caste and kinship networks, defined spheres of influence by politicians and local Big Men, and the constant threat of violence to regulate behaviour. The informal sector does not consist only of those who live on the disaster threshold. Enormous differences in wealth may be found in the resettlement colonies' (Das, 1996, p188).

To conclude, a working definition of the informal sector needs to contain four notions, namely: an idea of the contested relationship with the state regulation; the small size of the enterprise; the idea of a self-employed or survivalist livelihood strategy; and finally the notion of a dynamic and moving frontier between the three first notions. This is the working definition that we shall use for the rest of the chapter.

The role of city government in enhancing and protecting the assets of the poor in the informal sector

In order to consider the role of city government in relation to the informal sector, it is helpful to adopt the livelihoods framework of the assets of the poor (Moser, 1998). The four main assets are labour, human capital, social capital and productive assets (such as housing). The following suggests the ways in which actions by city governments can potentially enhance or protect these assets of the poor.

Labour

- providing a framework which encourages economic growth generally (but the city government's scope for action may be quite limited – see Chapter 3);
- providing and maintaining infrastructure needed for industrial growth (but responsibilities for major infrastructure may lie outside city government);
- using planning and regulatory powers to encourage rather than restrict the development of informal and small and medium enterprise (SME) activity.

Human capital

- provision of primary education;
- provision of health services;
- provision of residential infrastructure and services (water, sanitation, etc).

However, much of the responsibility, and many of the resources, for these may lie outside the city government.

Social capital

- setting the scene and providing the environment and funds which enable community organizations to operate, and for inclusive participation by citizens;
- maintaining law and order (critical for social capital);
- provision of street lighting, which can enhance social capital by extending the time for social interaction.

Productive assets

- regulation (eg planning and zoning) can influence the extent to which housing and land can be used as an asset, including for urban agriculture.

The potential contribution of city government in relation to labour relates both to promoting economic and industrial growth generally and to enabling the development of small and medium enterprises. This involves both providing an appropriate and supportive environment and ensuring that essential infrastructure is provided – even where that is outside the direct responsibility of city government. Raj (1993) observes that industrial development in urban areas suffers from a lack of infrastructure. This will also be the case with SMEs even if their dependence on water, power and roads may be less than that of large industries. But the most significant impact of municipal government in relation to labour and employment comes through the application of planning controls and other regulatory activities. Inappropriate application of these can substantially destroy employment opportunities.[1] Benjamin (1993) shows the negative impact of restrictive regulations and bylaws in the case of New Delhi in India. The removal of informal traders often as the result of 'city beautification' schemes can have a similar impact. The damaging consequences of repressive regulation of the informal sector will be discussed further in the next section.

Box 8.1 illustrates the way in which restrictive 'master planning', in this case in Bangalore, can stifle and undermine local economic activity. This is contrasted with the mixed land-use settings in non-planned areas that lead to diverse economic activity and offer far greater opportunities for the poor to participate. This box also illustrates the critical importance to the informal sector both of land as a productive asset and of location, and the impact of city government (or other agencies of the state) on these.

The case of South Africa provides a contrasting example, with the relaxation of a restrictive planning and regulatory system following the end of apartheid in the early 1990s. In the early 1980s there were estimated to be only 300 hawkers functioning in Johannesburg's inner core, whereas the estimate for the mid-1990s was 4000, with a total of 15,000 in the Greater Johannesburg area. While this growth is partly explained by an influx of migrants from elsewhere in Africa, the main explanation is the change in official policy from repression to one of greater tolerance (Tomlinson, 1996, pp188–189).[2]

The impact of the changed policy was also noted in the inner city area of Yeoville: 'There are informal businesses springing up all over ... ranging from barbers, to car repairers, to vendors of various kinds. There also has been a

---

BOX 8.1 BANGALORE: ACCESS TO LAND AND
SMALL BUSINESS DEVELOPMENT

Bangalore, the capital of the state of Karnataka, has become known as the 'silicon valley' of India with the development of its software and high-tech industries. The city also illustrates the processes of settlement planning and the relationship of these processes to the growth of small- and medium-size businesses. Land is a critical resource in urban development, and one which can be used either to enable the poor to enhance their livelihood opportunities, or to increase their vulnerability.

In large parts of south Bangalore, the 'master planning' approach, with its 'top-down' emphasis on public land acquisition, has been dominant. This approach restricts mixed land use and so allows a very narrow spectrum of economic activities to emerge. Land use is dominated by high-class residential neighbourhoods, with relatively few unserviced plots and intense competition over available land. Often the only way in which the poor can benefit from this process is by squatting on publicly acquired land prior to its development.

By contrast, in Mysore Road in west Bangalore and Yashwantur in the northwest, there are highly diversified employment nodes for local economic activity. This includes mechanical repair and fabrication, plastics and recycling, weaving, auto repair and electroplating units. These areas have important local political interests associated with the land market, which have been able to resist master planning. Successful local economic business development, both informal and formal, has been facilitated by a land tenure system that is flexible, diverse, and allows for mixed uses. Sites can be developed incrementally as and when businesses expand. In many cases, sub-contractors and suppliers live and work close together. Such land settings allow poor groups to establish themselves on central sites, giving them access to employment opportunities and creating a diverse economic structure with a variety of income groups. Furthermore, this allows for a form of politics which is based on local land ownership but which cuts across party lines, and to a certain extent, class and ethnic lines, and involves complex, reciprocal relationships. In this situation, small enterprises are integrated into local politics and so have some protection from developments that might force them out.

The Bangalore case study highlights the role of planning in both a negative and a positive sense, the importance of land as a scarce resource in an urban setting, and how competition for land is a critical element in urban politics and governance.

Source: Benjamin and Bhuvaneswari, 2001

---

proliferation of *spaza* [informal kiosks on the street], shops and mini-businesses ... located randomly around Yeoville, selling sweets and foodstuff'. (Beall et al, 2001, p122).

In relation to social capital as an asset for the informal sector, the critical issue for city government is maintaining law and order and preventing violence and insecurity that can so easily undermine economic activities. Moser and Holland (1995) have shown the devastating effect crime, violence and insecurity have on social capital formation in Jamaica. Similar problems were noted in the Johannesburg case study: 'The 1990–1993 violence ... was directed against gatherings of people engaged in their day-to-day routines, such as funeral vigils, parties, shebeens and stokvels (savings clubs). As a result trains, buses and taxis came to be commonly used for peaceful social activities, ... until they too became sites of political attack.' (Beall et al, 2001, p101). In the Yeoville area, the negative impact of crime upon commercial activity was also noted; in particular, the withdrawal of banks and major commercial outlets from the area (Beall et al, 2001, p121).

Regulation of the informal sector

The livelihoods framework outlined above indicates the ways in which city governments can potentially enhance or protect the assets of the poor. However, what emerges from the preceding section is that it is more likely that the actions of city government will damage rather than enhance the position of the informal sector. The main way in which this happens is through inappropriate or repressive regulation. There are, of course, valid reasons for regulation – orderly development, public safety, consumer protection, and so on (Kelly and Devas, 2001). However, the objectives of regulation are often contested, and tend to reflect the interests of the dominant class, often to the disadvantage of the poor. As much as the purpose and content of regulations, it is the way that they are implemented that is often the critical issue for the informal sector.

The concept of the informal sector, as we noted earlier, implies a contested relationship with state regulation. Regulation is, therefore, a critical issue in relation to the informal sector, since it ultimately implies legality and hence, in some sense, formality. But legality is itself multi-dimensional. Tokman (1991, p143) identifies three types of legality that are relevant to the distinction between formal and informal enterprises:

- legal recognition as a business activity, involving registration and possible subjection to health and security inspections;
- legality concerning the payment of taxes;
- legality vis-à-vis labour matters, such as compliance with official guidelines on working hours, social security and other benefits (Chant, 2002, p209).

The above aspects of regulation are concerned with the informal sector as an enterprise. In addition, there are aspects of regulation which are more likely to be of concern to municipal government. These include the following:

- planning and development control;
- building bylaws;
- business licensing or permits;
- local taxation;
- public health and safety.

As we shall see in the examples presented below, it is unusual for municipal governments to be concerned with all of these aspects of regulation at the same time. Legality should not to be conceptualized along a single dimension (yes or no, black or white). As we shall see, there are many situations where informal enterprises may be illegal on one dimension (for example health and safety or social security legislation) but may be paying local tax. Given the inherent difficulties in implementing diverse legislation, municipal (and national) governments tend to be selective – or perhaps arbitrary – in what they implement. An important theme that emerges is that actual implementation of regulation is substantially affected by the behaviour of bureaucrats at the local level. This is consistent with the observation, frequently made, that where policies may have contradictory elements these are usually resolved by lower level officials in the process of implementation (Grindle, 1980).

From the viewpoint of the informal sector, regulation can have negative consequences in terms of the ability of entrepreneurs to survive and to earn a living. In the worst cases, it can involve destruction of assets, eviction and/or resettlement. Informal activity is highly dependent upon both location and the nature of the local urban economy. Informal traders are acutely aware that relocation is harmful to them. They know that what is suggested or imposed on them by municipal government, such as relocation from pitches in the city centre to a peripheral location, is likely to spell economic disaster.

The question we are concerned with is: what are the circumstances that determine these actions by city government? The city studies suggest that it is the informal sector's ability to protest ('voice' – through democratic processes, whether formally or informally) and/or to divert regulatory activity (eg through 'politics by stealth') that determines whether municipal governments are able to implement repressive regulatory policies. In other words, the 'voice' of the informal sector acts as a significant restraint on repressive actions by city government.

The stories from the cities

In this section we briefly summarize the experience of the case cities in relation to regulating the informal sector. We focus upon the key episodes, many of which exemplify conflict. There are, as we shall see, substantial differences in approach, from outright harassment to de facto acceptance. In all the cases we seek to understand the rationale of the actors involved and the nature of the political processes.

There were two interesting episodes in Mombasa. First, in 1997, informal traders in the Likoni district south of Mombasa were subject to violent raids as part of an attempt by the then political ruling party (KANU) to win the national elections. This process was part of a wider scheme to win political support within a local context of resentment by the inhabitants of coastal Kenya toward those from upcountry. These evictions lead to violent 'tribal clashes' during which neither the government nor the security forces were willing or able to restore order. The result was major losses to both large and small-scale business, especially tourism, all along the coast. Bed occupancy at hotels declined from 53 per cent in 1993 to 26 per cent in 1998, and a large tuna-processing factory had to suspend operations, affecting 1000 semi-skilled jobs. Yet there was no organized opposition to this onslaught (Rakodi et al, 2000, p161).

BOX 8.2 'MAXIMUM TOLERANCE' POLICY IN CEBU

This box summarizes the informal policy of 'maximum tolerance' towards the street, sidewalk and ambulant vendors in Cebu:

One site vending

- Vending on one side of the street only, permitting the vendors to sell in designated areas

Zero growth

- No new vendors are allowed after the master list is finalized by 9 February 2001
- Each vendor family is limited to one stall/structure

Time

- 6.00 pm to 6.00 am in some areas

Stall/structure

- Light and temporary structure
- Uniform colour
- Size of table 2×3 or 3×2 or 3×6m, depending upon area
- Edges of tables should not extend beyond allowable distance
- No new structures or extension

Distance from the street

- 1.5 metres from the gutter of the street

'Clearing of the area' or 'demolition'

- No demolition unless there is a formal complaint filed at the Office of the Mayor, City Attorney, or other agencies
- Specified consultation procedures before clearing the street/public places of illegal vending

Cleanliness/sanitation

- Keep surroundings clean, arrange structures orderly
- Dispose of garbage properly
- Stalls/structures not to be used as sleeping quarters

Fees

- Arcabala: Peso 2–15 (average P5) (Arcabala is a fee, which represents a combination of entrance fee and space rent; the amount is legislated by the City Council; an increase in the fee is done through a public hearing, in which the vendors bargain for the amount.)

Penalties

- P500 for violating anti-loitering ordinance; P300–350 for redemption of confiscated goods.

Source: adapted from Etemadi, 2001, pp123–126

The next episode took place after the election of the mayor following the 1997 election. The newly elected mayor, Najib Balala, came to office with an ambitious programme of improving municipal governance, reducing corruption and 'beautifying' the city. The last of these involved denying licences to curio traders and demolishing kiosks in the city centre, on the basis that tourists who visit Mombasa do not like being hassled by street traders. Balala, who was also chairman of the Coast Tourist Association, was more concerned to protect the interests of large tourist operators and formal retailers than the interests of the street traders (Rakodi et al, 2000, pp161–162).

Kumasi, which has a very high proportion of local employment in the informal sector, has a similar story. The number of informal sector traders had grown, partly as a consequence of structural adjustment and retrenchment, and far exceeded the number which could be accommodated within the city's central market. The Metropolitan Chief Executive (MCE) (at the time of our study) adopted a ruthless policy toward unofficial traders in the central business district and regularly led raids to destroy such sites. As a result, traders, who are amongst the city's poorest, regularly lost both stock and premises. The Chief Executive was effectively protected from any democratic repercussions from such idiosyncratic and repressive behaviour because of his direct appointment by the President. Meanwhile, in 1998, licence fees for traders were increased by a factor of three, provoking a major dispute between the municipal government and the market traders. This issue was exacerbated as the collection of the licence fees was assigned to a traders' association widely perceived to be in the hands of the national ruling party rather than representing the interest of traders (Devas and Korboe, 2000, p130). The overall judgement on the Kumasi Metropolitan Assembly is that: 'KMA does not have any specific pro-poor interventions, it also stifles the attempts by the poor themselves to earn a decent living through trading activities, for instance, through the seizure of items being sold at unauthorised places' (King et al, 2001, p104).

In Ahmedabad, a voluntary association, SEWA (Self-Employed Women's Association) has campaigned to protect the rights of vendors and those who work in the unprotected sectors. In particular, it has worked with the families of jobless former textile workers. A study in 1995 estimated that there were 72,500 workers engaged in home-based (but also informal) trades. SEWA has fought a legal battle for these local vendors to protect their rights and has helped them organize into a national alliance for vendors. At the local level, SEWA has assisted those involved in rolling out incense sticks (*argabatis*) to increase their piece rate from Rs 1 to Rs 5 per 1000 sticks. However their earnings are still below the minimum day wage of Rs 35–40 prevailing in other states (Dutta with Batley, 1999, pp50–51).

The Cebu study provides perhaps the most interesting and complex series of episodes in relation to the informal sector. As noted elsewhere, Cebu has a fast growing local economy, but street vending remains an important survival strategy for the urban poor. During the 1980s the situation of vendors was described as 'dreadful', with demolitions a daily event. At this time it was the Mayor's wife who was active in the programme, claiming that she was 'sweeping and/or cleaning up the area!' (Etemadi, 2001, p48). The previous chapter (Box

7.3) has already outlined the process by which street vendors got together to form the Cebu United Vendors Association in order to protect their livelihoods, first through confrontation and then through negotiation with the city government. Despite many setbacks, they were able to bring about a change of policy. According to Etemadi, 'the plight of the informal street traders and sidewalk vendors has gained recognition. Despite the city ordinance against illegal vending, Mayor Garcia and the … Working Committee on the street vendors regard the issue as one of regulation rather than outright eviction and demolition. As pragmatic politicians seeking office or re-election, they cannot ignore the interests and demands of the urban poor who constitute over 60 percent of the city's residents' (Etemadi, 2001, p89).

This was to result in a new policy: 'Street vending is [still] illegal by law … [and this was supported by the Supreme Court and other local level ordinances.]… In practice however, Cebu City has implemented a policy of 'maximum tolerance' towards the street vendor, in terms of unwritten regulations or guidelines that must be followed instead of outright demolition and/or eviction. City officials have come to accept the reality that this sub-sector of the informal sector provides an alternative livelihood for the unskilled labour force' (Etemadi, 2001, p120). Box 8.2 provides some details of these informal rules.

In summary, the story of Cebu is one of a degree of openness by the municipal government and an appreciation of where its political support comes from, but also a change in tactics by those lobbying government. The vendors' organizations moved from 'confrontational politics' to a strategy characterized by lobbying and engagement (Etemadi, 2001, p142).

The story from Bangalore is also complex. It is concerned ultimately with local democracy and how that does or does not provide political and institutional access resulting in pro-poor and inclusive decisions. While Benjamin makes this argument in general terms, it also applies to the informal sector. As already noted, Benjamin rejects the concept of the informal sector due to its 'inherent ideological assumptions of linear development trajectories' (Benjamin and Bhuvaneswari, 2001, p19), focusing instead on concepts of economic clustering. He also argues that it is only possible to understand local economic activity at a finer grain. In particular, areas of mixed land use allow for a diversity of economic activities, which can mutually benefit local traders in complex trading relations. Such areas allow for entry points for newcomers and for poor households. Drawing on earlier work in east Delhi, the concept that captures this is that of the 'neighbourhood as a factory' (Benjamin, 1993). A related issue is the way such areas allow for an incredibly diverse range of local financial mechanisms to operate. This includes chits and other local, indigenous financial arrangements, which support and are intimately tied up with the development of individual businesses and the local economy. There is much in common here with Rutherford's discussion of local indigenous financial arrangements (Rutherford, 2000).

In all this, questions of access to land, and the location of that land, are critical. As such, the role of municipal planning is highly significant. Large parts of Bangalore fall under the Bangalore Development Authority's (BDA) 'Master

Plan'. The rigid zoning of these areas results in homogeneous land-use patterns, making it difficult for the poor to establish claims. By contrast, in the 'unplanned' areas where local economies flourish, there is a more flexible and incremental process at the local level, involving councillors and officials in allocating or legitimizing claims to land in ways that are accessible to the poor and to small-scale enterprises (SSEs). A key factor in explaining the difference between these two approaches is the accountability of those involved. In the latter case, local politicians have to be responsive – at least to some extent – to their local, ward-based electorate, and must be seen to be delivering some tangible benefits. In the case of the master planned areas, decisions are made at higher levels, remote from those immediately affected, whether at the state level or through an appointed body such as the Development Authority with minimal accountability to citizens.

Box 8.3 illustrates the complex relationship between traders and the processes of urban renewal, but also illustrates the way in which money – and bribery – are necessary to secure an appropriate urban location.

The experience of hawkers in the implementation of 'hawking zones' in two different areas of Bangalore further illustrates the argument. Ironically, the threat to hawkers came from an apparently progressive source. The idea of 'hawking zones' was one supported by a lobby group of academics and concerned NGOs across India. In Bangalore, this group advocated that Bangalore City Corporation (BCC) should demarcate 'hawking zones'. In 1999, the courts directed BCC to declare such zones – a judgement that was bound by the Indian Supreme Court 1989 ruling on pavement dwellers in Mumbai. This judgement 'recognised hawking as a fundamental right *but allowed* for eviction by state agencies provided allotment for alternative places was made' (Benjamin and Bhuvaneswari, 2001, p158).

What is interesting is how this policy was implemented in different areas of Bangalore. Hawking zones were to be identified jointly by the BCC and the traffic police. Recognized hawkers were allocated space and given licences. Almost without exception the zones identified were in areas with minimal pedestrian traffic and so were not suitable for hawking business. 'This had a drastic impact on the hawkers with one exception. This relates to hawkers in Central West Bangalore, who were able through their councillor to organize the licensing system on an 'as is where is' basis. The result was that rather than being displaced as in other cases, these hawkers were able to consolidate and 'regularize' their claims' (Benjamin and Bhuvaneswari, 2001, p159). The difference was that, in Central West Bangalore, leaders were able to negotiate on behalf of their members, and local politicians were responsive to the demands of their constituents.

Benjamin and Bhuvaneswari (2001) refer to such forms of incremental negotiation as 'politics by stealth', in which poor groups and their alliances operate in low key and non-visible but persistent ways to achieve their objectives. This has emerged as a strategy to subvert a fundamentally inappropriate planning system, to achieve security of land tenure or to protect traders from harassment. The key to 'politics by stealth' is local councillors who find ways to accommodate the demands from their constituents in conjunction with low-

---

BOX 8.3 REDEVELOPMENT IN BANGALORE: DISRUPTING PATRONAGE POLITICS IN THE KR MARKET

KR Market was a major market and trading node in West Bangalore. It has recently been redeveloped on the same site as part of a major redevelopment scheme that includes a new concrete market, revised street layout, parking space and an elevated expressway. This new infrastructure is all designed to support the idea of Bangalore as a modern city. This redevelopment significantly altered the relationship between the municipal officials and street traders.

Only those traders with good links to retailers and wholesalers were able to establish themselves inside the new complex. A large number of traders were forced to move and re-establish themselves on the pavements nearby. These pavement traders formed themselves into associations in order to enter into agreements with the staff of Bangalore City Corporation (BCC) and the traffic police to protect them from removal. Traders had to bribe a whole range of government officials: there was a well-organized system of bribes that went right up to the top. The level of bribes were determined by the number of stone slabs occupied, with each hawker being allowed to occupy a site the size of a *gunny* bag. For an individual hawker, the total bribe worked out at Rs 22 per day or Rs 100 weekly, composed of separate bribes to the traffic police, corporation officials, sweepers and local *dadas* (strongmen). Some hawkers have organized themselves into groups to facilitate the payment of such bribes, with a member of the group collecting the money and handing it over directly. This reduced the level of bribe closer to Rs 50 a week per trader for a group of 100 traders. This amount covered payments to municipal officials and various types of police (traffic, crime and local), including payments to morning, afternoon and evening shifts.

Unfortunately, the move to the new site resulted in a decline in earnings for the traders from an estimated Rs 150–200 a day to Rs 50–80 a day. The creation of the new market has disrupted the complex system of interaction between local traders, wholesalers and officials. Furthermore the new bribery system is much greater – three times greater – than the previous system. It is also, from the traders' perspective, dangerously unstable, with increasingly random raids leading to arrest of hawkers and confiscation of their produce.

There are two lessons from this case. First, traders have to maintain their claims through bribery of local officials. Second, urban renewal has disrupted the livelihoods of the traders and the complex patronage networks that enabled them to operate, resulting in a much more unstable form of patronage politics.

Source: Benjamin and Bhuvaneswari, 2001, pp130–138

---

level officials (the 'porous bureaucracy'). Problems are resolved in unofficial and non-transparent ways, outside the formal, legal system. Paradoxically, as we saw in the case of the 'hawking zones', moves towards a formal, legal system and greater transparency can undermine the informal political arrangements that enable the poor and their local economies to survive. Thus, the current system of local politics, which may seem to many to be corrupt, can sometimes work to the advantage of the poor, whereas simplistic reforms may worsen their position.

The relationship of the informal sector to municipal government in Johannesburg has a somewhat different dynamic. One of the key issues emerging there is the tension between the local African population and the new

– often illegal – immigrants from other regions of Africa. An example of this was the sudden explosion of hawkers and traders on the streets of Yeoville, an inner area of the city. Given the structure of South Africa's housing market, these inner city areas are the only places where recent migrants can live and trade. The most controversial issue was the erection in 1999 of the Yeoville market and the relocation of hawkers from the streets into the market. While local residents seem to have approved of this action, the hawkers felt that their business had suffered from the lack of passing trade. There was a dispute about allocation of stalls in the new market, particularly over whether foreigners had been over-represented. What is interesting about the dispute is that the traders and their association, the Rockey Street Traders Association, did not appear – unlike their counterparts in Cebu and Bangalore – to have good connections into local politics. Instead, they were seen 'in terms of community politics more generally' as 'a lot of hot air' (Beall et al, 2001, p135).

Emerging themes

In this section we discuss a number of particular themes that emerge from the city case studies, leading on to a more general discussion of the role of voice in the relationship between the informal sector and city government.

The importance of private sector patronage at the micro level

The first theme concerns the importance of patronage by the private sector at the micro level. These patronage networks are often very important for the poorest. There were interesting examples from both Cebu and Bangalore of private shop or property owners allowing informal traders to occupy the edges of their property in return for the protection they provided. In Cebu, the municipal policy of 'maximum tolerance' has also been adopted by a number of local businesses, including the local hamburger chain and the city's main shopping mall, which permit informal traders to operate adjacent to their premises.[3] One of the shopping malls has designated an area for a market where farmers and small-scale vegetable growers can sell their produce at weekends. The existence of a degree of mutual interest suggests that the possibility of cross-class alliances improves the position of informal sector businesses.

New markets as key episodes

It is noteworthy that in Johannesburg (Yeoville), Kumasi and Bangalore, the construction and operation of new markets were major points of conflict with the informal sector. These conflicts were about who gets access to the new markets, especially where these cannot accommodate all those who wish to trade in them, and the extent to which traders' livelihoods are adversely affected by forced relocation. In none of the cases were those representing the informal sector traders sufficiently well organized or politically well connected to be able to prevent them being disadvantaged in the process.

Licensing: harassment or legitimation

Attempts to license informal sector enterprises have been a major source of conflict in many of the case cities. Whatever the legitimate objectives of licensing may be in terms of regulation or revenue raising, in practice it frequently becomes an opportunity for those in authority to extract bribes. Because of the multiplicity of regulations, and the lack of transparent information about those regulations, those charged with their enforcement are in a position to extract protection money. Nevertheless, the payment of licence fees is sometimes seen as according a business some form of legitimacy.

The role for the legal system

The informal sector exists with a degree of legal ambiguity. In both Cebu and Bangalore activist lobby groups put a substantial amount of effort and faith into trying to get legal rulings in favour of the informal sector. In both cases, the rulings of the respective Supreme Courts were unhelpful.[4] In both countries, the legal system is increasingly being used by middle-income groups to protect their position and in some cases to oblige municipal governments to enforce legislation against the informal sector. Thus, in India, there is a growing phenomenon whereby middle-income and/or élite groups seek to use public interest litigation to require municipal governments to remove informal or non-conforming land uses. It seems that there is increasingly a conflict over the implementation of legislation concerning the informal sector.

Recent research in New Delhi highlights an interesting relationship between the 'rule of law' and the informal sector. It is a common phenomenon for those living in low-income lanes (or *galis*) to form collective organizations to provide themselves with illegal water connections from the public water mains. These organizations collect contributions that are used to provide the illegal pipe connections, including any necessary bribes to the local officials of the water board. The entire operation is illegal but successfully provides water for low-income groups in a situation where the formal public system is unable to do so. The role of the police is particularly interesting in that while they appreciate the illegality of this process, they are unwilling to take enforcement action. In their view, enforcing the law would destabilize and politicize the situation, with the risk of civil disorder. For the police, maintenance of peace and order represents a higher objective (Tovey, 2002).

In many cases, informal sector businesses are, by their actions, practices and location, technically illegal. It is therefore problematic to defend the practices of the informal sector simply in terms of 'the rule of law'. The only legal defence could be in terms of a principle of equity, derived from common law, rather than in terms of statutory legislation. However, while there may be philosophical problems with the legal status of the informal sector, what actually happens is usually determined at the local level, and at the stage of implementation, through the resolution of competing interests and claims. As a result, there is often substantial de facto 'room for manoeuvre' in managing the informal sector at the local level. There are often surprising differences in attitude and practices towards the informal sector between municipalities within the same country. This was the case in Ghana in the 1990s: while Kumasi was involved in a policy of harassment of informal sector traders in the central business district (CBD), Accra was developing a more tolerant policy.

It is therefore relevant to observe that the relationship is always 'mediated' and the outcome is the result of some form of compromise between those involved. The question is: how is this compromise arrived at? The outcome obviously depends on the parties concerned, principally the municipality and those in the informal sector, but also involves a range of elected and paid officials, community leaders and organizations representing informal sector businesses. The result depends on the relative bargaining strength of those involved, their tactics, and the nature and responsiveness of the political processes, informal as well as formal, through which the negotiations are conducted.

Local-level political processes: politicians, bureaucrats and 'politics by stealth'

One of the main conclusions from the case studies is the importance of local level politicians and bureaucrats in mediating the problems of the informal sector during implementation. This is the central argument from the Bangalore case study, which conceptualized the issue in terms of 'politics by stealth', in which local politicians and bureaucrats, together with community leaders and organizations of the informal sector, are able to resolve issues through local compromises. These compromises can work to the advantage of the urban poor. In Cebu, the policy of 'maximum tolerance' unofficially codifies a new relationship with the informal sector, effectively circumventing the ruling of the Supreme Court and local government ordinances. This new policy is more likely to be successful if it is carried out discreetly, since the city government cannot advertise that they have a policy that effectively undermines its own bylaws. However, the Indian case shows how the use by the middle class of public interest litigation is directly challenging this dualistic approach.

The argument we want to develop here is that it is the extent to which the informal sector, and the individuals involved in that sector, have a 'voice' that determines how such mediation takes place. This is clearly related to the processes and operation of democracy in the country concerned, which have been discussed in Chapter 5.

An example that illustrates this comes from the riots that occurred in Delhi in December 2000. These followed a ruling by the Supreme Court that the city government of Delhi should shut down all polluting industrial units in the city's residential areas, as required by its master plan. Environmental problems are a major issue in New Delhi but research had shown that the main sources of air pollution were large industrial units, power stations and motor vehicles rather than the small industrial units located in residential areas. Many of these units had been in the same location for 50 years and between them employed 200,000 workers. Not surprisingly, the workers objected and started to riot. The owners of these units and the local politicians – who saw these locations as their 'vote banks' – effectively encouraged the riot. After three days of rioting, the city government had to back down and allow the units to remain (Roy, 2001, pp206–207). The conclusion from this is that it is simply not possible to enforce a planning regime that, at a stroke, makes 200,000 individuals unemployed – certainly not in a democratic system which allows citizens a 'voice'.

The recent work by Amartya Sen on *Development as Freedom* (2000) is relevant here. In this analysis, Sen makes a strong case for the idea that development ultimately is about securing five distinct freedoms: political freedoms; economic facilities; social opportunities; transparency guarantees; and protective security (Sen, 2000, p10). These five freedoms are inter-related but ultimately advance the capability of the individual in relation to the state. Developing his now familiar argument concerning the importance of democracy in the prevention of famine, he goes on to discuss the role of democracy in other circumstances, thus:

> '*The preventive role of democracy fits well into the demand for what was called 'protective security' in the listing of different types of instrumental freedoms. Democratic governance, including multi-party elections and an open media, makes it very likely that some arrangements for basic protective security will be instituted... The positive role of political and civil rights applies to the prevention of economic and social disasters in general. When things are routinely good and smooth, this instrumental role of democracy may not be particularly missed. But it comes into its own when things get fouled up, for one reason or another. And then the political incentives provided by democratic governance acquire great practical significance.*' (Sen, 2000, p184)

Concluding remarks

From this review of the city case studies in relation to the informal sector, what can be said to be the key factors which determine the relationship between that sector and city government?

The first is the nature of illegality. The activities of informal sector enterprises may transgress any of a number of laws and regulations, but the ability of city government to take action – and the extent of public support for that action – depends on how serious those transgressions are considered to be. Some activities, like street vending and informal settlements, while they may be technically illegal, have a high degree of public acceptability. Even the illegal tapping of water pipes may have wide acceptance, at least within a particular community, especially where this is the only way for the poor to access public water. Meanwhile activities like dealing in hard drugs and robbery are socially unacceptable as well as illegal. There is likely to be much greater political support for repressive policies towards the latter than the former.

Second, the scale of the problem will influence the ability of city government to take action. Where, as in the example from Delhi, huge numbers of people are affected by a planning policy, it is likely to prove difficult for the authorities to enforce that policy.

Third, the ability of those affected to organize and to oppose or lobby effectively is critical. Effective, organized opposition greatly increases the costs to city government of taking action. The success of the street vendors in Cebu – although far from total – was the direct result of organizing to oppose oppressive policies, and then moving to constructive engagement with the city government in developing more appropriate policies.

Fourth, there is the matter of the accountability of those making decisions, not just to citizens in general but to the poor in particular, including those in the informal sector. An elected mayor cannot afford to alienate a very large section of the electorate. Local councillors, at least those representing low-income wards, must demonstrate responsiveness to their constituents. On the whole, the closer the elected representative is to the electors, the greater the chances of accountability. Thus, in Cebu, when the city government sought to ban the use of trisikads (cycle taxis), elected leaders at the local *barangay* level continued to permit them to operate within their areas. By contrast, in Bangalore, the Development Authority, which is not directly accountable to citizens, can impose policies that effectively exclude the poor majority of the population.

In this chapter we have sought to discuss issues associated with the regulation of the informal sector. We have argued that the way this regulation operates is largely determined at the very local level, and at the stage of implementation. Whilst, in practice, much of this regulatory activity is repressive and burdensome for those in the informal sector, there may be scope for those involved, especially where they are able to organize, to negotiate less damaging arrangements. Their ability to do so depends, we have argued, on their 'voice', which in turn depends on the nature of the local-level democratic processes and the accountability of those elected to their constituents. In the end though, it often easier for municipal governments, in their dealings with the informal sector, to undermine or destroy the livelihoods of the poor, through relocation or repressive regulation, than it is to enhance those livelihoods.

Notes

1   This is of course a familiar criticism of the planning process in the North. The earliest and still a classic text is Jane Jacobs (1961) *The Life and Death of Great American Cities*.

2   A senior official from the city government of Durban claimed that the city had created 30,000 jobs without using any capital, simply by changing the policy towards hawkers. As with any job creation estimate, it is difficult to know the accuracy of the figures or the extent to which jobs were created rather than simply relocated.

3   This is, however, very much a local policy: when the Manila-based owners of the shopping mall are expected to visit the Cebu branch, the street vendors are asked to disappear; once the executives have left, the vendors can return and reclaim their sites (Etemadi, 2001, p95).

4   There are parallels with the movement against the Narmada dams in India, in which the Indian Supreme Court eventually ruled by 2 to 1 in favour of the dams (Roy, 2001).

Chapter 9

Accessing Land and Services: Exclusion or Entitlement?

Fiona Nunan and Nick Devas[1]

The challenge

Urban poverty is inextricably linked to people's access to land and basic services. Those living below the income poverty line almost invariably suffer also from insecure and over-crowded housing, inadequate access to water and sanitation, and environmentally hazardous living conditions (Hardoy et al, 1992; UNCHS 1996; UN-Habitat, 2001a; McGranahan and Satterthwaite, 2002). The economic and social costs of the disease, injury and premature death associated with poor quality housing, infrastructure and services are often underestimated in analyses of poverty. These burdens fall most heavily on vulnerable groups such as women, children and the elderly. Even where basic services like water are available, they are often located far away, operate only intermittently, and are costly. Quite apart from the direct effects on physical well-being, the inadequacy of such basic services increases the costs to the poor and undermines their ability to earn a livelihood.

One of the most direct influences city governments have on the scale and nature of poverty is in what they do – or do not do – in regard to provision of basic services and in supporting housing construction and improvement. City governments' influence on land markets is also important since the possibilities for lower-income groups to obtain housing with infrastructure and services usually depends on the opportunities available to them to obtain land. Yet the potential contribution of city and municipal authorities to poverty reduction is often underestimated, as discussions usually focus on inadequate incomes or consumption, and on the role of national government and international agencies in addressing these. Meanwhile, primary responsibility for the provision of basic environmental services – so critical for the life-chances of the poor – usually rests with city or municipal government, even if delivery of such services may be delegated to private or non-governmental agencies.

Ensuring access by poor people to adequate environmental services and shelter is not simply a technical, engineering matter, but is conditioned by a range of economic, social and political factors. It is bound up with local power structures, including the extent to which low-income groups can influence local government policies and resource allocation, and by the relationships between local government, higher levels of government and other institutions of urban governance.

The central theme of this chapter is how the nature of urban governance affects the quality and extent of provision of basic environmental services, housing and access to land for the poor. The chapter outlines the inadequacies of provision in the case cities, and reviews how the poor obtain access when the formal system fails to provide. It then examines a number of key governance issues that impinge on provision of environmental services and shelter: the national policy framework; the responsiveness of city government; political accountability; and the roles of the private sector, community organizations, non-governmental organizations (NGOs) and external funding agencies in strengthening, or at times undermining, access by the poor.

Inadequacies in provision

The city studies highlight the inadequacies in infrastructure provision, even in some of the more economically successful cities such as Cebu and Bangalore. In general, the wealthier the city or nation, the greater the proportion of the population adequately served with environmental infrastructure and services. However, the quality and capacity of local governance also influence this (Satterthwaite, 1997).

In relation to water, Santiago is the only case study city where nearly all of the population are adequately served. A high proportion of Johannesburg's population is also well served, although there are still considerable numbers lacking adequate provision. There is also a major issue over the ability of the poor to pay for the relatively high standard of services in Johannesburg, a city characterized by vast inequalities in income. In the other cities, large sections of the population have no access to piped supplies, while for many more, access is difficult, supplies are erratic and the water supplied is contaminated. For instance, in Bangalore, more than half the population depends on public fountains, many of which supply contaminated water because of poor maintenance or broken pipes. In virtually all cities, those inhabitants lacking formal provision often have to pay high prices to informal providers. In most cities, official statistics understate the inadequacies in water supply by classifying all those with 'access to piped supplies' as adequately served, even if the water supply in the pipes is irregular and of poor quality, or access is through public standpipes shared with hundreds of others. In Mombasa, a large section of the population with water pipes has seen no water in their pipes for several years because the supply as a whole is insufficient to meet demand.

With regard to sanitation, most of the low-income population in all but Santiago and Johannesburg has inadequate provision. Official statistics again underestimate the scale of the problem because they assume that if a household has access to a latrine, it has adequate sanitation. Large sections of the population whose only access to sanitation is through poorly maintained communal latrines where queues are common are classified as having 'adequate sanitation'. The case studies of Ahmedabad, Bangalore and Cebu highlight how a significant proportion of the population lack sanitation facilities and defecate in the open or into plastic bags (what is termed 'wrap-and-throw' in Cebu). In Kumasi, nearly 40 per cent of the population depend on 240 poorly maintained public toilets (see Box 9.2).

In most of the cities, large sections of the population have no regular garbage collection services. The inadequacies are particularly notable in Kumasi, where only high-income areas are served by (highly subsidized) house-to-house collection. Low-income areas are served by skips, which are emptied infrequently, and not all areas are included. In Mombasa, attempts to privatize garbage collection resulted in increased charges that the poor were unwilling or unable to pay, with the result that the private contractor abandoned the service in the areas concerned.

Most urban governments have some influence over who obtains land for housing (and under what terms), its quality and location, and the likelihood of it being provided with infrastructure and services. The ways in which they allocate the land they own or control, define land uses and implement zoning and planning controls influence whether and where low-income households can legally acquire land on which to build their homes. In most of the case study cities, the supply of housing, or of land for housing, falls far short of the need, so that most poor people are forced into over-crowded and insecure slum housing, squat on public land or obtain plots on illegally subdivided private land.

Only in Santiago is public and private housing construction on a scale that approaches the level of need. Even here the poor quality and adverse location of housing for low-income groups reinforce the inequalities in society. In Johannesburg, the massive, publicly-funded Reconstruction and Development Programme (RDP) housing schemes still fall far below the level of need of the growing population. A particular issue in these more prosperous cities is that rising land prices and opposition from higher income groups have limited the ability of city governments to provide housing for low-income groups in appropriate locations, such as close to the centre.

In most of the other cities, city governments have made little attempt to provide housing or even to ensure access to land for low-income groups. Indeed, land-use controls and building regulations often impede the efforts of the poor to provide their own shelter. The most positive contributions made by city governments have generally been through ex post regularization and provision of services to informal settlements. But this often occurs many years after the initial settlement and is dependent on the ability of the residents to negotiate with the city authorities – in turn often dependent on clientelistic political relationships or ethnic connections.

Gaining access: Ways and means

How, in practice, do people in poverty achieve whatever limited access they have to land, housing and basic services? In some cases it is through formal public programmes, usually financed from central funds or by donors, and often accessed through informal contacts and networks involving ethnic, caste or political affiliations. In some cases, NGOs may play a role in facilitating access. The formal private sector plays only a limited role in most of the cities, mainly in relation to rental housing, although the private sector is increasingly being contracted to provide urban environmental services such as waste collection. The informal private sector is important in terms of provision of water in poorly served neighbourhoods, but often at considerable cost in relation to residents' income. In terms of accessing land for housing, informal mechanisms are generally the main route for poor people, but as these mechanisms become increasingly commercialized, the options are reduced. In the following sections, we consider how the poor obtain access to water, as perhaps the most critical of environmental services, and to land and housing.

Gaining access to water

Most of the low-income communities studied lacked proper access to water supplies. Inadequate access may be in terms of any of a number of indicators: the distance to a standpipe or well; the time involved in queuing; the limited number of hours for which water is supplied to an area each day; inadequate water pressure; the poor quality of the water supplied; and the high costs, particularly in the case of water supplied by informal vendors. Inadequate access to water affects incomes and livelihoods as well as health. This is particularly true for women, not only because of their domestic responsibilities, but also because their livelihoods tend to be neighbourhood-based and often involve the use of water, such as for food processing.

In Cebu, around half of all households in 'poor' *barangays* (districts) have individual water connections. For others, access to water is via wells, communal taps and water sellers. The municipal water company will provide a communal tap where the community establishes a Communal Water Association (CWA) with elected officers to manage the tap. However, less than 10 per cent of urban poor families in Cebu make use of water from communal taps. Etemadi (2001, p118) observes that many CWAs are beset by problems, including lack of participation by members, irregular elections, undemocratic management and lack of financial transparency and accountability. Meanwhile, a large proportion of the urban poor in Cebu purchase water from water sellers, paying at least three times the rate from the municipal water company. In one area, residents reportedly pay almost ten times as much because water sellers transport water from a distance of 400–500 metres, and in another, the rate was 17 times the charge for a formal water supply. Small-scale water sellers are not monitored or regulated. On the other hand, water vending is a significant source of income for some low-income households.

The quality of the water reaching low-income areas can be very low. In Bangalore, 10–20 per cent of the city's water demand is met by groundwater via 80,000–120,000 bore-wells and open wells. The quality of the water is very poor and often contaminated. Even piped water needs to be boiled or filtered via ultraviolet light – an unrealistic requirement for most poor people. The poor in central Bangalore depend upon public fountains. Although these are free of charge they often have broken taps and pipes or damaged platforms. Poor groups frequently dig pits to collect water, but the lack of drainage and sanitation results in contamination. Private tankers supply a vast population in the intermediate and peripheral zones of the city. The supply of water therefore depends on a range of delivery mechanisms, resulting in varying levels of access to, and quality of, water. Political influence plays a key role in determining whether and when infrastructure and services are provided or improved. Maintaining a reliable water supply is viewed as being of utmost importance in low-income communities. A survey of slums in Bangalore found that, in many cases where the hand-pump needed to be repaired, women had collected together money to pay for the repairs. In other cases, the leader of the *sanga* (local community organization) approached the local councillor to ask for the repairs to be done.

Limited availability of water during the day was found in all the South Asian cities. Certain areas of Colombo, notably those occupied by low-income groups, suffer from low water pressure and therefore limited access to water. People are obliged to collect water at night for use during the day. Storage brings problems of hygiene and increased risk of disease. In Visakhapatnam, while 48 per cent of residents have domestic pipe connections, 42 per cent rely on public fountains. As there is only one such fountain for every 150 residents and water is available only twice a day (for one and a half hours in the morning and an hour in the evening), collecting water implies queuing and hence opportunity costs. Although it is possible for a slum area to receive a water supply once the area has been notified by the Urban Development Authority (ie once the slum has received official recognition), notification can take three to four years from first settlement, and usually requires political patronage.

In Kumasi, about three-quarters of the city is served with piped water by the Ghana Water Company (a public corporation until 1999, when it was converted into a limited liability company). The remaining parts of the city, notably the peri-urban areas, are served by private water vendors, boreholes, wells and streams. Many of these boreholes and wells are highly contaminated, while many of the streams used for water collection are also used for defecation. Within the areas served with piped water, around 6 per cent of the city's population depend on public taps, but the water company views these as problematic and is not proposing to increase the number of such taps. Another 27 per cent buy water either from private taps or from neighbours (Rakodi, 1996). Because of the high initial cost of a water connection, many residents resort to making unauthorized connections. The proliferation of such unauthorized connections results in leakage and risks of contamination, rendering the supply less reliable and the whole system less financially viable. In order to obtain a connection or a repair, residents often make contact with the company's technicians, paying them directly. The payment is generally below the official charges and receipts are not issued. This route is faster and more accessible than going through the formal application process. Those who do not have the resources for such payments may make their own illegal and unmetered connections, or else continue to depend on vended water or contaminated sources.

In Mombasa, a particular issue is the inadequacy of the bulk supply. Although official statistics (the 1989 census) indicated that 92 per cent of households had access to piped water, very few parts of the city have a continuous supply, and some areas have had no water for several years. In a survey of local residents, water was identified as the top priority in terms of problems affecting their community (AMREF and OVP/MPND, 1997). In response to the inadequacy of the public provision, many residents have had to cut back on water use or have resorted to obtaining water from wells, boreholes or vendors.

Gaining access to land and housing

Urban poor people gain access to land and shelter in a great variety of ways, but most commonly by renting or by occupying space in some sort of informal settlement. Virtually all the case cities have informal settlements of some form or another, although the scale varies markedly. Informal settlements – variously referred to as slums, squatter settlements, shanties, *barrios* or *favelas* – involve differing degrees of illegality in terms of occupation of publicly or privately owned land and nonconformity with official regulations. The reasons for the existence of such informal settlements vary between cities, but reflect a lack of formal provision of housing (whether by the state or the private sector), unaffordable rents, inadequate formal access to land and the need for low-income dwellers to live near sources of income and employment.

Access to land is shaped by complex social and political processes, rather than being purely a market transaction. In Bangalore, some of the poorest citizens reside on the pavements, alleyways and shop terraces where they work. Shop owners may allow them to stay because of the security they offer for the premises, but their position is just about as vulnerable as it is possible to be.

Gaining any firmer foothold in terms of land and shelter often requires ethnic or political connections, and may require group negotiation to lower prices and reduce risks of accessing private land.

Around the KR Market area of Bangalore, low levels of infrastructure and relatively insecure tenure make plots affordable for the poor. Land is transformed incrementally, giving the poor the chance to remain and to consolidate their position. The variety and flexibility of tenure arrangements outside the 'master planned' areas of the city also enable the poor to establish themselves. Shelter tends to be constructed incrementally, using a variety of materials. Provision of infrastructure and services in these areas is incremental, influenced by politics, particularly through the consolidation of vote banks.

Benjamin and Bhuvaneswari (2001, pp61–62) describe a common access route in one ward, Azadnagar:

> *'The poorest groups may move into a locality as renters in a squatter settlement in a thatch house. For this, they would initially borrow an amount from the private financiers to pay the required advance. This may be helped by seeking support from one of the local leaders (using ethnic, employment-based or class linkages) to gain a foothold in the political system. This move can help them squat on the land. Once settled in close proximity to employment opportunities, access to various social circuits helps them consolidate their social and economic contacts. With greater stability, they move on to other tenure forms or to more productive locations. Those groups who manage to accumulate surplus seek to invest in the private layouts.'*

Access to land is not just important in relation to shelter but also in terms of economic activity. Benjamin and Bhuvaneswari note that land is 'an active ingredient for the economic strategy of poor groups' (2001, p4). Land, they suggest, interfaces with the economy in three ways:

1 access to productive locations: those areas that provide access to multiple employment opportunities are more advantageous for the poor;
2 diversity of tenure regimes that allow for the poorer (among other groups) to consolidate their claims on contested locations;
3 upgrading of infrastructure and services (the quality of land) which both influences the productive potential and reinforces tenure claims (2001, p4).

They also note that land plays a critical role in the expansion and diversification of local economies. This is illustrated in Azadnagar, west Bangalore, where many small enterprises are based. The range of infrastructure and services available in different locations affects the types of economic activities that can take place there. Although the forms of tenure are heavily influenced by institutional and political factors, the diversity of tenure allows a range of income groups to access space, with different combinations of space size, cost and land use (economic, commercial, residential) to suit different needs, including those of the poor. The same building may be used for both productive activities at the front and accommodation at the back, with multiple rented rooms (*vattarams*) with a range of rental options. This contrasts with the high costs, uniform layout and inflexible tenure in formal schemes, such as those developed by the Bangalore Development Authority (BDA), which provide few opportunities for the poor.

In Kumasi, most low-income households live in rented housing in single or multi-storied compounds. These are often over-crowded with minimal facilities: 30 per cent of those living in 'indigenous' compound housing lack toilets, water and electricity. Overcrowding is exacerbated by the tradition that 'homeless' family members can expect to be housed by other members of their family – a crucial means of support for the poorest. There has been an increase in the number of squatter settlements located on the marginal lands around the city, as well as a growing number of people with no roof over their heads, occupying abandoned buildings or paying on a daily basis for a place to spread their mats (Abugre and Holland, 1998). These people are often young, mostly migrants, and are often organized according to village or kinship lines.

The allocation of land in Kumasi (except for state land) is the responsibility of the traditional authorities, that is, chiefs and queen mothers. The level of access depends on whether the applicant is a 'stranger' or 'indigene'. For the indigenous poor, access is determined by family landholdings, family membership and the position of the family and the individual in relation to stool (traditional) lands. While the official cost of obtaining land is relatively modest ('drink money' for the ancestors), the process has become increasingly commercialized. Thus, while the traditional system of land allocation does enable low-income groups (at least those who are native Asantes) to gain access to land, rising demand for land has resulted in prices that increasingly reflect market conditions, thereby excluding the poor.

This observation confirms Jenkins' (2001, p630) view that 'in general, in urban areas traditional and customary rights begin to enter the commodification system', and informal markets 'may not be as effective when exchange values grow more important'. While traditional systems of authority and land allocation may provide some scope for the poor to access housing and land, with increasing pressure on urban areas and the subsequent emergence of land markets, such routes are diminishing.

Access and the nature of urban governance

The nature of urban governance is critical to the extent and quality of both environmental services provision and access to land and shelter. While government agencies play a pivotal role in this provision, the private sector, non-governmental and community organizations and donor agencies are also instrumental in facilitating access, as well as in direct provision. It is, however, a government responsibility to ensure that the poor have appropriate services and access. This section focuses on six themes of urban governance that impact on the quality and extent of provision, and on access to that provision, for the poor, as illustrated from the city case studies. These are: the national policy framework; the responsiveness of city government; accountability through elections; the consequences of formal private sector involvement in service delivery; the role of community organizations and NGOs; and the role of external funding agencies.

The national policy framework

National governments play a central role in relation to urban environmental services and housing, through setting the policy framework and by transferring resources to local government for policy implementation. They also determine the level of autonomy of local government in terms of raising local revenue and making spending decisions. One issue which runs through several of the city case studies is that of incomplete decentralization, which leaves uncertainty and conflict over which levels of government, and which agencies, are responsible for what services – a topic already discussed in Chapter 6.

The delivery of appropriate environmental services and housing requires the right policy framework for local governments to work effectively and to enable local communities to participate in decision-making. This policy framework must be shaped by clear poverty reduction objectives if the needs of the poor are to be addressed. In addition to setting out clear technical guidance on the quality and extent of service provision, national policy can promote empowerment of the poor. One example is South Africa's 1994 White Paper on Water Supply and Sanitation (South Africa: Department of Water Affairs and Forestry, 1994), which emphasized community participation as the foundation of water delivery. There have, as a result, been a number of discussions and experiments in pricing structures for services in order to make them accessible to the poor. Subsequent national legislation guaranteed the free provision of a basic needs amount of water to each household, cross-subsidized from high volume consumers.

In other countries, attempts have been made to address poverty through national pricing policies for water. However, these have had only limited impact since the poorest people rarely have direct access to publicly provided piped water. The Ghana Water Corporation, for example, adopts progressive tariffs according to the volume of water consumed, on the assumption that the rich will consume higher volumes of water. However, the low tariff rates for low-volume consumers is of little benefit to most of the poor who are not connected to the system. Meanwhile, the higher tariffs penalize those low-income households living in compound houses served by one tap. In Cebu, by contrast, lower tariffs are applied to all water supplied through communal connections. National policy in the Philippines also establishes the mechanism of Communal Water Associations to enable low-income communities to obtain a connection. However, extensive subsidies may adversely affect the capacity of the water provider to maintain the system, let alone extend it to those not currently served. While free standpipe water in Indian cities directly benefits the poor, when combined with under-pricing of the supply to higher-income users the result is that water undertakings are unable to cover their costs, never mind having the resources to extend the system to under-served areas.

In the provision of housing for the poor, national policy has had a critical influence on access in many cities, even though the policies may not always have been ideal. In the Philippines, the responsibility for the provision of housing was devolved to local government through the 1991 Local Government Code. The 1992 Urban Development and Housing Act provided the impetus for the implementation of a social housing programme. In Cebu, this became one of the functions of the Cebu City Commission for the Urban Poor (CCUP), which was set up following the creation of the Presidential Commission for the Urban Poor at the national level. One national programme, the Community Mortgage Program (CMP), has been particularly effective in facilitating access to housing for the poor – see Box 9.1.

In South Africa, the chronic housing shortage was a visible legacy of the previous regime, so providing housing has been a major issue for the post-apartheid government. During the apartheid years, housing for black people was provided either through standardized public housing in townships or through 'site-and-service' schemes, where people were expected to build their own houses on serviced land. From the mid-1970s, there was a trend for people to build shacks in the backyards of government-owned houses, and, from the 1980s, shanty-towns emerged on land adjacent to the formal African townships.

Huchzermeyer (2001, p305) notes that 'current housing policy in South Africa is based on a fundamental understanding that housing is a basic need'. This policy is articulated in the 1994 Housing White Paper, with a commitment to deliver 1 million houses in five years. Huchzermeyer reports that the most common form of subsidy used to promote house building has been the project-linked subsidy, channelled through private developers, which has led to the development of 'uniform, free-standing, mostly one-roomed houses with individual freehold title in standardized township layouts, located on the urban peripheries' (ibid, p306). It has been suggested that these segregated dormitory developments are themselves poverty traps and do not represent a route out of poverty. The target set in the White Paper was not reached and, subsequently, there has been a shift in thinking away from a blanket solution of free-standing houses on individual plots with freehold tenure. Part of the housing problem now is of beneficiaries leaving their new houses to return to squatting, in part due to the cost of travelling to and from employment opportunities. This illustrates how a better understanding of the socio-political and socio-economic environment of the poor is needed to develop more appropriate solutions to the housing crisis.

In South Africa, then, housing is seen as critical to poverty reduction and the national housing policy provides those involved with a framework in which to respond to need. Although the policy framework may not be entirely appropriate, without it urban governance agencies would have had less direction and fewer resources than they have to address the acute housing need.

National housing policy has also played a crucial role in Chile. Rodríguez and Winchester (1999) suggest that Chile's housing policy since the early 1990s has been successful in significantly increasing house construction. Diverse housing subsidies are available for homeless families, managed by the Housing and Urban Development Ministry. These include *Progressive Housing*, a

BOX 9.1 CEBU: COMMUNITY MORTGAGE PROGRAM

The scale of housing need in the Philippines is immense. In Cebu, more than half the population is either homeless or landless. The CMP provides subsidized loan finance to regularize and improve low-income squatter settlements. It is a nationally financed programme that is implemented through a wide range of different institutions. In the Philippines as a whole, it has assisted 100,000 families (up to 2000) to legalize their land tenure. Although this is modest in relation to the scale of need, it is nevertheless substantial for a government intervention.

In Cebu, the CMP has been nurtured due to the strength of the local economy, a political alliance between the mayor and the urban poor, capable local NGOs, and the local presence of one of the designers of the programme who is a long-standing resident and NGO activist in the city. A number of positive steps have been taken including a shortening of the time required to process CMP applications from two years to six months. By mid-2000, over 4000 families in the city had benefited from CMP loans in 65 different improvement projects, with a further 18,000 benefiting from related social housing schemes (Etemadi, 2001, Table 12). CMP sites are also eligible for basic services (footpaths, electrical posts, artesian wells, drainage and roads), with the government providing materials and the community completing the works.

The low-income community in Inayawan is one of those which has benefited from the CMP. Residents first occupied the privately owned land in the 1960s. In 1985, the owner sought a court order to evict them, and this was eventually granted in 1988. Residents had to make repeated appeals to the demolition team to prevent their homes being destroyed. They then lobbied the Mayor, Thomas Osmeña, at his home, very early one Sunday morning. He agreed to seek a court order to prevent demolition and referred their case to the Cebu Commission for the Urban Poor. As a result, and with the help of a local NGO, the Pagtambayayong Foundation, the residents organized themselves into an association (SISARO) and obtained a CMP loan. With this loan, they purchased the land in 1990, with the certificate of title being in the name of the community. Plots range in size from 25 m^2 to 163 m^2. The loan was repayable at 12 per cent over five years (later extended to seven). All except one member have repaid the loan, but because of that one default, it has not yet been possible to individualize the title. The residents have constructed a pathway through the settlement, using collective labour and materials provided by the City. In 2000, the City provided a 6m wide access road, and the Mayor provided materials for the construction of drainage.

Source: Etemadi, 2001

---

programme for low-income families, *Basic Housing*, for families in rented accommodation, PET (Special Programme for Workers) for those belonging to labour unions or guild organizations and *Urban Renovation*, aimed at families who choose to live in zones selected for Urban Renewal programmes in the centre of a city. In these programmes, the role of the municipality is to identify and organize the demand, while implementation is by the private sector (construction companies, housing corporations and housing cooperatives). Although these programmes have been successful in mass-producing housing and in dramatically reducing the number of people living in 'precarious settlements', there has been much dissatisfaction with the type, quality and location of housing created.

By contrast, in both Ghana and Kenya, there is little if anything by way of a coherent national policy framework or dedicated national resources for the delivery of urban services and shelter. Indeed, the absence until recently of any form of inter-governmental transfer in Kenya has meant that Mombasa Municipal Council (MMC) has had virtually no resources with which to tackle the backlog of urban infrastructure. As already noted in Chapter 6, conflicts between levels of government, in Mombasa as well as in several of the other case cities, has tended to undermine whatever capacity there is within city government to address the needs of the poor.

Responsiveness of city government to those in poverty

Chapter 6 discussed in general terms the willingness and the capacity of city governments to respond to the needs of those in poverty. Here we consider the responsiveness of city governments specifically in relation to land, infrastructure and services, with examples from the city studies.

City government attitudes to informal settlements and to the extra-legal ways in which low-income groups can acquire land have much bearing on who gets land for housing. These attitudes range from opposition and eviction at one extreme, via reluctant tolerance of informal settlements, to support for legalization and upgrading. This is not just a matter of what city governments do but also what they permit. For residents of informal settlements, official recognition of their situation is a critical step towards achieving both security and services. As Gilbert (2000, p147) notes, 'most forms of illegality can be removed through the provision of title deeds, the supply of services or the modification of planning regulations'. Yet agencies responsible for infrastructure or services are often reluctant to provide these to illegally occupied or unofficially subdivided land – indeed they may be legally prevented from doing so. Upgrading of informal settlements, through tenure regularization and provision of infrastructure, is now widely accepted as preferable to relocation. Upgrading helps to maintain existing social and economic networks that are vital for the livelihoods of the poor, although there are always risks that rents may increase with the improvement of the physical surroundings, leading to low-income residents being forced out. The evidence from the Indian cities is that slum upgrading has significantly improved environmental conditions for the poor (Amis, 2001).

In Cebu, there are a number of examples of how the city government has been obliged to respond to the urban poor. This has come about in part because of the active civil society (NGOs and community-based organizations (CBOs)) within the city. Institutions such as the Division for the Welfare of the Urban Poor (DWUP – a successor to the Cebu Commission for the Urban Poor) have been quite effective in terms of facilitating access to land for housing, including the transfer of land ownership to low-income communities. Greater protection has been provided to those occupying informal settlements that are faced with demolition, for example for road widening. Residents of such settlements have been given the opportunity to choose from identified relocation sites. Dialogue was initiated in 2000 to improve the relocation process in cases where demolition of informal settlements was necessary. A memorandum of understanding was agreed between FORGE, an NGO housing advocate, together with ANAK (a community-based organization facilitated by FORGE), and the judiciary and police, to ensure that there is adequate consultation and consideration of relocation options prior to demolition.

In Colombo, there was a period when the Million Houses Programme allowed low-income groups a much greater role in improving infrastructure and services through community action planning. It proved difficult, however, to sustain this more participatory model in the face of political changes, as explained in Box 5.4. In Recife, the participatory budgeting (PB) process (described in Box 6.3) has ensured that at least part of the city's budget is spent on infrastructure in low-income neighbourhoods in response to the expressed priorities of the residents.

There are, however, particular difficulties in providing infrastructure and services to some informal settlements. For example, many have developed on steep slopes or flood plains, or have unclear plot boundaries. There are also more general problems of speculation and inefficient use of land (eg vast plots which remain undeveloped), which greatly increase the costs of infrastructure and make access to services by the poor more difficult.

A further issue, given the limited resources available, is how to accommodate the competing demands for bulk infrastructure and local services. The demand from residents of particular neighbourhoods for improved water supplies, for example, may mean that networks are extended and new taps provided despite there being insufficient capacity within the system to enable the water to be delivered. Similar issues arise in relation to extensions to drainage and sanitation, waste collection, electricity and roads: extending local provision may achieve little if there is not the bulk capacity to handle it. The consequence of expansion to serve the poor is often ever greater overloading and failure of the service for everyone. This is exacerbated where under-pricing of services to those who can afford to pay means that there are no resources to fund increases in capacity. A number of the case studies indicate a reluctance on the part of senior technicians (for example, city engineers) to extend services to under-served areas for fear of jeopardizing the supply to those already served. There is, therefore, a dilemma: greater responsiveness to demands from citizens (of whatever income group) for local-level improvements can pre-empt the available resources needed to improve the bulk supply, leaving everyone dissatisfied. This is indeed the position in many of the case study cities.

Accountability through elections

How responsive city government is to the needs of the poor depends greatly on the accountability of its elected representatives. The advantage claimed for local democracy is the ability to hold elected representatives, including mayors, to account through elections. But as discussed in Chapter 5, the mechanisms of local accountability are seriously flawed. The city studies provide examples both of where accountability has contributed to better provision and of where a lack of accountability has had negative consequences.

The Bangalore case provides a contrast between the influence – albeit limited – which low-income residents have on the Municipal Corporation through their elected councillors (see Box 5.2) and the absence of political accountability of major players such as the Bangalore Development Authority (BDA). The appointed BDA Board includes only two locally elected representatives out of 23 members. As a result, it has little interest in prioritizing the infrastructure needs of poorer groups.

Politics plays a role in facilitating access in the Indian cities and in Cebu. In respect of the latter, Etemadi (2001, p138) reports that: 'In the short run, elections are said to be helpful, because it is only during this period that the communities can make their request for basic services which are fast tracked and granted. They can bargain services for votes, and there are no demolitions during the period'. Thus, elections present an opportunity to secure access to services, but this requires vote bargaining, with unequal results for different communities, depending on their degree of organization, the efficacy of their leadership and their political affiliation. Not only do communities vary in their success in obtaining infrastructure, but also elections are too infrequent to deliver adequate access. Furthermore, the process of demand-making, which depends on political patronage, hinders systematic provision.

Kumasi and Recife present contrasting examples in terms of political accountability. The Kumasi Metropolitan Assembly (KMA) is headed by an appointed mayor, officially known as the Metropolitan Chief Executive (MCE).[2] The mayor at the time of this study ruled with an individualistic and autocratic style, allocating resources and services largely on the basis of political patronage. One example was the totally inadequate solid waste service. Although many areas had been provided with a dumping site, waste was only transferred from these to a final dumping ground very infrequently. Up until 2001, approval for the cleaning of areas of the city required approval of the MCE, who tended to refuse to provide services for those areas represented by Assembly members who were not his supporters (King et al, 2001, p85). Another example of political patronage was the 'privatization' of the city's public latrines, described in Box 9.2.

One reason why the mayor in Kumasi could get away with such arbitrary behaviour, so damaging to the poor, was the fact that he was nominated, not elected, and is therefore not politically accountable to the residents of the city. Recife offers a different experience, with an elected mayor bringing in a new programme to formally recognize 'slum' areas and to work in partnership with a range of stakeholders to deliver appropriate tenure, services and infrastructure. This is described in Box 9.3. Although the presence of an elected mayor is certainly not the only factor in improving the services the poor can access, it can be significant. In terms of the title of this chapter, while Kumasi is largely a picture of exclusion, Recife could be said to be moving in the direction of entitlement.

The private sector and service delivery

As already noted, the private sector is a major player in the provision of environmental services such as water, as well as access to land and shelter for

Box 9.2 Kumasi: The politics of public toilets

Sanitation facilities in Kumasi are woefully inadequate. Only a quarter of the population have home-based WCs, most of which are shared, while another quarter depend on the very unhygienic bucket system. Eight per cent use pit latrines, while a further 38 per cent depend on public toilets. The remaining 5 per cent use 'free range' facilities – in other words, the bush. In the late 1980s, the city government (KMA) laid off 400 of the bucket collectors, most of whom continued to operate as freelance contractors without supervision. Most of the buckets are emptied onto rubbish heaps or into streams close to residential areas.

There are some 240 public toilets scattered around the city. In one low-income neighbourhood, Atonsu, there are only two 14-seater public toilets to serve 10,000 people – more than 300 people per squat-hole. Not surprisingly, queues are long, and many resort to using open spaces or streams, with adverse consequences for environmental health, and particular risks for women.

In 1994, in an attempt to improve the maintenance of public toilets, the KMA adopted a policy of privatizing their management, with the revenue from charges being used to pay for operation and maintenance. This worked reasonably well for a while. However, in 1997, the Metropolitan Chief Executive decided to allocate the contracts to those members of the Metropolitan Assembly who supported him. Those who had been allocated contracts were supposed to enter into arrangements with KMA for their operation and maintenance, but many did not pay over the required amount, and the revenues received by KMA were used for other purposes. As a result, the facilities deteriorated.

Charges were also increased, placing a major burden on poor households, especially since there was no longer free access for children. For a family of five, each using the facility only once a day, the cost represented at least 10 per cent of the basic wage. The inevitable consequence was a huge increase in defecation in the bush, in streams and in other unsuitable locations. Privately operated public latrines have also been constructed over local streams which others use for bathing and for drinking water. Thus, rather than improving sanitation, this misuse of the 'public–private partnership' model in Kumasi, with its lack of transparency over contract allocation and its lack of accountability for management of the facilities, has added to environmental problems and burdens for the poor.

Source: Korboe et al, 1999; King et al, 2001

the poor. Most of this is through small-scale, informal and often semi-legal or illegal activities. The formal (or semi-formal) private sector, while a significant provider of rental housing, has a much more limited role in relation to service provision. One area in which this is changing is waste collection, which private contractors in a number of the case cities provide under contract to local government. While in some cases the involvement of the private sector has improved performance, it has often been associated with reduced levels of service and increased costs for the poor.

In part this is because, where services like waste collection are contracted out to the private sector, local governments need new skills in tendering, contracting and supervision – skills that are often lacking. In Santiago, the contracted-out service seems to have worked quite well, with five companies between them collecting the bulk of solid waste in the 32 *comunas* in the late

---

BOX 9.3 RECIFE: RECOGNIZING THE RIGHTS OF
FAVELA DWELLERS

Jarbas Vasconcelos was the first mayor to be elected in Recife after the return to civilian rule. A land-use programme introduced during his first administration (1985–1989) was resurrected during his second term (1993–1996) and was one of the initiatives that led to the development of participatory budgeting (discussed in Box 6.3). The Programme for the Regularization of Zones of Special Social Interest (PREZEIS) involved the recognition of the favela dwellers' right to remain on the land they had occupied, whether private or public. This built on a law enacted in 1983 (the Land Use Plan), which established the concept of zones of special social interest (ZEIS), with the aim of integrating them into the urban structure of the city. PREZEIS further developed this established concept of ZEIS by institutionalizing channels of participation between communities and the local government in the planning and implementation of projects in these areas, through PREZEIS Forums.

In addition to such forums, Local Commissions for Tenure Regularization and Urbanization (COMULs) were established as participatory arrangements in which representatives of local government, communities and NGOs discuss and consider solutions for integrating recognized squatter settlements into the fabric of the city. Integration involves both regularization of land tenure and provision of basic infrastructure and services.

Three implications arise from the granting of ZEIS status: evictions are prohibited and the legal procedures for land regularization are initiated; no physical interventions are permitted without receiving prior approval by the Forum; and there are severe limitations in terms of land use in these areas, mainly to preclude real estate developers from the areas. By 1998, 65 areas had been recognized as ZEIS and 31 were in the process of being integrated into the formal structure of the city through their COMULs. The programme has contributed to a change in attitude of community representatives, from demanding services from government to working in partnership.

Source: Melo et al, 2001

1990s, although the 'precarious settlements' are not covered (Rodríguez and Winchester, 1999, p124). However, in Visakhapatnam, lack of supervision and monitoring of private contractors was cited as an issue, and it is alleged that private contractors have not been collecting as much garbage as they claimed, and are required, to collect. In Ahmedabad, apart from privatizing the cleaning of a couple of important commercial and recreational areas of the city, the main reforms have been to introduce community-based waste collection systems and to subsidize local private societies to clean certain residential areas.

With contracted-out services, low-income communities can easily be disadvantaged, due to a lack of official recognition of 'slum' areas, as well as overcrowding which makes access by collection vehicles difficult. Privatization also makes the conflict between poverty reduction and cost recovery particularly apparent. The Mombasa Municipal Council (MMC) privatized most of the garbage collection service in the late 1990s, partly due to the inadequate rate of collection by the corporation's own staff (only half of the 400 tonnes generated daily was being collected). The private companies introduced higher charges which many people on low incomes were unwilling or unable to pay.

Contractors responded by excluding the low-income neighbourhoods they were contracted to cover. This resulted in dumping along roads, with the MMC forced to collect the dumped garbage. It seems that privatization took place without adequate legislation to force all the parties concerned to meet their obligations. Previously, MMC had cross-subsidized the service to the poorer areas from the wealthier areas, a practice that private contractors were not willing to continue.

Fears are often expressed about the potential effects of increased private sector participation on access to services by the poor. For example, discussions about the possible commercialization or privatization of certain public services in Johannesburg under the *iGoli 2002* strategy provoked protests about the potential impact on the poor as well as about the likely loss of jobs.

In every case city, the private sector plays a major role in the supply of rental housing. Housing types and tenure arrangements in the private sector are often more flexible and more appropriate to the needs of the poor than those provided by the public sector. The informal private sector is often the main supplier of low cost housing. However, without an appropriate policy framework and financial inducements, the private sector (whether formal or informal) cannot be expected to contribute to the goals of poverty reduction. On the other hand, the construction of rental housing can provide an additional source of income to low-income home owners, although this is unlikely to benefit the poorest since it requires access to both land and capital. Even where there are financial inducements, these may not end up benefiting the poor. In South Africa, there is much criticism of the way the housing subsidies under the Reconstruction and Development Programme (RDP) have been monopolized by private developers providing low quality, standardized housing units. There are similar concerns about the quality of housing built by private contractors under the various subsidy programmes in Santiago.

The role of community organizations and NGOs

Community-based organizations (CBOs) and NGOs can play a significant role in the provision of services and land, often through acting as mediators between government and communities. The cities studied exhibit great differences in the scale, nature and effectiveness of CBO and NGO involvement in housing, infrastructure and services.

Cebu is at one extreme, with a privileged position accorded to NGOs in the national constitution, and a city government that has developed a framework to work with a great range of local NGOs in service provision. For instance, many NGOs are active in Cebu's Urban Basic Services Programme (UBSP), which has been in operation since 1988, coordinated by the city's Health Department. Several NGOs (such as FORGE and ANAK discussed earlier) have important roles in official programmes seeking to reach poorer groups with improved housing conditions and to provide services for street children.

Municipal authorities in Colombo and Ahmedabad permit and encourage NGO involvement, but without the kind of framework that has been developed in Cebu to support this. In Ahmedabad, there is a long history of active

---

BOX 9.4 SLUM NETWORKING PILOT PROJECT – SANJAY NAGAR, AHMEDABAD

Sanjay Nagar is located on a plot owned by Ahmedabad Municipal Corporation (AMC) and was earlier earmarked as a garden under the Town Planning Scheme. A pilot project was designed and implemented during 1996–1997, to improve basic infrastructure and provide a water supply and toilets on an individual basis. A unique feature of the project was the partnership of four stakeholders – the slum community, a private textile company (Arvind Mills), the Corporation (AMC) and an NGO (SAATH). Arvind Mills took responsibility for executing the project and set up a trust for this purpose. AMC acted as facilitator, while SAATH looked after community mobilization and development. The project was concerned with community and physical development. Physical infrastructure included water supply, toilets, internal roads and pavements, storm water drainage, street lighting, solid waste management and landscaping. Community development focused on setting up neighbourhood groups, women's groups and youth activities; mobilizing community savings; educational activities for pre-school children and illiterate adults; organizing community health education and mother-and-child care; supporting income-generating activities; and developing linkages with the finance sector to access finance for small businesses and trade.

AMC gave secure tenure for ten years to the slum dwellers. Each household paid Rs 2000 as their share of costs, plus another Rs 100 towards maintenance of services. Two-thirds were able to pay this immediately and the remaining one-third borrowed the money from the SEWA bank. The project was completed within the time allocated, without overrunning on cost. However, at the end of this project, Arvind Mills withdrew its support, citing differences with the Municipal Corporation over work culture and decision-making structures. Despite this setback, the Municipal Corporation has extended the programme, in collaboration with SEWA and SAATH, with work in eight slums being completed by the end of 2000 and in progress in a further nine areas (Biswas, 2003).

Source: Dutta with Batley (1999)

---

voluntary organizations. Various CBOs and NGOs are involved in slum upgrading or other community development initiatives, including measures to improve environmental health among low-income groups. These include: ASAG (Ahmedabad Study Action Group, founded in 1971), SEWA (the Self-Employed Women's Association founded in 1972), St Xaviers Social Service Society (founded in 1976), Vikas (founded in 1978) and SAATH (founded in 1989). The Slum Networking Project (SNP), described in Box 9.4, was developed jointly by the municipal corporation and the private sector, and sought to involve both CBOs and NGOs from the outset.

The city studies illustrate a number of examples where NGOs and CBOs have played a constructive role in mediating between local governments and communities to obtain or improve services and housing. In some cases, they support small-scale initiatives that may act as a pilot and from which lessons can be learnt for broader application. While NGOs and CBOs often strengthen the voice of the poor and can advocate on their behalf, they generally cannot provide infrastructure or services on a large scale. They must, therefore, work closely with local governments and the private sector, as well as with communities and the informal actors involved in service provision. As Chapter 7 has shown, the limitations of such organizations must also be recognized.

For example, in Colombo, among a diverse range of NGOs, there are several whose work centres on improving infrastructure and services or supporting CBOs to improve conditions. However, interviews with community activists found that many disliked both local and international NGOs because of their lack of accountability to low-income groups and community organizations. Similar views were expressed in Bangalore.

There are community organizations in low-income areas of Bangalore, popularly known as *sangas*, which focus on securing land tenure, accessing basic services and upgrading the quality and quantity of services. CBOs and NGOs in the richer areas of the city tend to be concerned with solid waste management, the upkeep and maintenance of roads and parks and anti-encroachment measures. Given the limited resources of the municipality, there is a concern that these groups exert their claims to public investments at the expense of poorer groups.

In the low-income settlement of Diepsloot in Johannesburg, the Community Development Forum (CDF) has been very effective in negotiating for security of tenure and improved services. Box 7.2 describes the role of the CDF, noting the dangers of such an organization becoming the monopoly channel for such negotiations, and the risks of exclusion of other, even poorer, groups.

Although in many of the cities there is a multiplicity of organizations involved, the scale of their activities is still far below what is needed. In addition, where NGOs and CBOs are involved in neighbourhood infrastructure, they are often frustrated by the lack of investment in the trunk infrastructure (water mains and the freshwater sources and treatment plants to serve them, trunk sewers and drains) into which each neighbourhood's network can feed. The costs and complexity of such investments are far beyond the capacity of NGOs or CBOs, but without them neighbourhood schemes to improve water, sanitation and drainage can have little benefit.

In some of the cities, however, there appears to be little involvement by NGOs in relation to urban infrastructure or services. This may be because there are few or no NGOs working on issues of urban poverty (Visakhapatnam) or because most NGO funds are directed to the rural areas. In some cities, for instance Mombasa and Kumasi, it may have more to do with the municipal authorities' unwillingness to work with NGOs and CBOs, or because the NGOs direct their attention to local offices of national agencies rather than to the city government. In many of the cities, there were NGOs at work on environmental issues such as wildlife conservation or the global environment that have little or no relevance to improved environmental health for the city's low-income groups.

The role of external funding agencies

External funding agencies have been involved in providing environmental services to low-income communities in several of the case cities. In Kumasi, for

---

BOX 9.5 VISAKHAPATNAM: POSITIVE IMPACT OF UPGRADING

Visakhapatnam is an important industrial city and one of India's largest ports, but the city's rapid economic growth has been constrained by inadequate investment in its infrastructure. The consequences of this shortfall are felt at all levels of the economy. However, the recent improvement of infrastructure and service provision in low-income areas has had a significant impact on both local economic growth and poverty reduction.

This slum improvement programme, funded by DFID, was implemented by the Municipal Corporation. The results provide clear evidence of the benefits of basic infrastructure provision to the poorest in India's cities. Enhanced water services, drains, communal latrines, paved roads and community halls have all helped to improve the overall environment, reducing problems of flooding, ensuring that roads are passable, and reducing the burden of water collection for women. The infrastructure component had reached an estimated population of 200,000 in 170 slums by the late 1990s, and had had a positive impact on the 'quality of life' of the poor. However, other aspects of the upgrading project, such as primary healthcare, education and community development, were not as successful. Despite some success in providing pre-school centres (*balwadis*), the other project components were not so well implemented and have tended to be usurped by particular groups. The success of the *balwadis* was attributed to staff motivation, strong local ownership over the process, and clear lines of accountability of teachers to communities.

Source: Amis and Kumar (2000)

---

example, the World Bank, the Department for International Development (DFID) and the United Nations Development Programme (UNDP) have each funded projects to improve the provision of basic services such as drinking water, access roads, drainage, sanitation and street lights. However, the sustainability of such measures is open to question in terms of replication and maintenance. Although the KMA was involved in these projects, the Assembly has lacked both the political commitment and the resources to support these initiatives adequately. In such programmes, city governments tend to be involved merely in deciding which areas should benefit rather than in the delivery of the project, which is often assigned to a special project agency.

Slum improvement programmes have been a key element of donor assistance for poverty alleviation in urban centres (Amis, 2001). The UNICEF-sponsored Urban Basic Services Programme (UBSP), for example, involved improving access to basic services through the development of community-based organizations and initiatives in a number of cities. In Ahmedabad, the UBSP was launched in 1985, through a partnership arrangement between the United Nations Children's Fund, the state government and central government. Between the mid-1980s and mid-1990s, the UK's aid agency (the Overseas Development Agency (ODA), now DFID) invested considerable resources in slum upgrading projects in India. One of the most successful, in Visakhapatnam, was estimated to have benefited more than 85 per cent of the city's slum population, and is briefly described in Box 9.5.

Conclusions: Access to land and services: Exclusion or entitlement?

For poor people, access to land, shelter and basic services is not only essential for their physical well-being; it is also vital for their ability to earn a living. Yet in many of the case study cities, access is completely inadequate for those living in poverty – and indeed is one of the reasons why they continue to live in poverty. The poor survive by being able to access land, shelter and services in a variety of ways, usually irregular and often illegal. Attempts, however well intentioned, to standardize and regulate reduce the diversity of options available to the poor and undermine their fragile position. While improving citywide infrastructure and increasing the supply of land for housing can benefit low-income groups, attention needs to be paid to improving access to services and land with secure tenure specifically for the poor. This needs to be done in ways which take proper account of their livelihood systems, their ability to pay, and how they currently gain access.

Although city governments are generally responsible for providing basic services, for the most part they do so quite inadequately, whether because of a lack of political will, resources or capacity. The richer cities among our cases, Santiago and Johannesburg, are able to provide relatively high levels of service, but there remain important issues about coverage, quality, cost and inequality of access. Some city governments, like Kumasi and Mombasa, appear to make little attempt to improve services for the poor.

The provision of environmental services and shelter is far from being a purely technical matter. The political and governance context is paramount, influencing how and where resources are allocated. Lack of resources, while a factor, is not the only explanation for the inadequate provision for the poor. Other explanations include the lack of an adequate national policy framework; the unresponsiveness of city government and the difficulty for the poor in making their voices heard; the lack of accountability of local decision-makers including mayors; and the shortage of effective and accountable CBOs and NGOs to help articulate the needs of the poor and ensure that services are delivered.

A number of the case studies show that external funding agencies can have a positive role in providing resources for improving environmental services, but such initiatives need to work within existing governance arrangements to ensure sustainability, particularly in terms of financing and maintenance. External funding may be the only way to finance the costly bulk infrastructure that is needed to ensure that local service improvements can deliver what is required. The case cities also include examples of NGOs contributing to provision of, or facilitating access to, environmental services, housing and land, but their activities were generally small-scale and not always either appropriate or effective.

For the poor, access to shelter and services is often through informal routes, by using contacts, kinship or political networks to access formal services, or by using informal private sector suppliers. This is not always easy, as poor people lack the resources to purchase services or for bribes, and lack connections and influence, even within local social networks. Regularization of informal settlements is a significant means of delivering services and land for housing to the poor. But for people in poverty the relationships between land tenure, housing services and income opportunities are complex and often fragile. Therefore, interventions need to be based on a proper understanding of how the poor gain access to and make use of the land and services they have. The ability of regularization and upgrading to address the priorities of the poor depends on the nature of the processes involved, the extent of participation by poor people and their representatives, and whether there are safeguards to prevent the poor from being displaced.

In the end, what is needed is a shift in the approach of the institutions of city governance from one of exclusion of the poor to one of entitlement. In some of the cities studied, exclusion from land, shelter and basic services remains the dominant experience of poor people. In several of the other cities, there are positive signs of attempts to extend access and inclusion. To shift to a position where the poor receive services and land for shelter as of right, rather than as a favour, requires a rare combination of an appropriate national policy environment, adequate resources, effective mechanisms of political accountability, and an active civil society articulating the needs of the poor. There were a few examples within the case study cities where such a combination of circumstances existed, but not many.

Notes

1   The authors gratefully acknowledge the contribution of David Satterthwaite to developing the research and many of the ideas on which this chapter is based.
2   See note 4 of Chapter 5.

Chapter 10

Conclusions: Urban Governance, Voice and Poverty

Nick Devas

In this book we have looked at how city governance – in the widest sense – impacts on poor people, and the ways in which poor people can have voice and influence over the institutions of city governance. We have examined these issues on the basis of studies of ten cities in Asia, Africa and Latin America. It is necessary to be highly circumspect in drawing general conclusions from a limited number of specific cases, especially since the experience of each city depends on a host of particular conditions: economic, social, political, historical, cultural and geographic. Nevertheless, there are some common themes that emerge, and some important lessons. Given the limited comparative research so far in this area, we believe that these conclusions can be of value to policy-makers (both elected and appointed), planners, community organizations and non-governmental organizations (NGOs), as well as international agencies. In this chapter, we will summarize the emerging themes and review the conclusions from the previous chapters in terms of the original research questions. We will then present some implications for policy-makers, and conclude with an indication of possible directions for future work. First, though, we make a comparison between the case cities in terms of the issues we have examined in this study.

City comparisons

Table 10.1 presents a very crude ranking of the performance of the ten cities in terms of some key indicators reviewed in this book: economic growth; poverty reduction and inequality; political institutions and processes; participatory mechanisms; the role of civil society; institutional constraints on city government, including finance; access by the poor to land, infrastructure and services; the behaviour of city government towards the informal sector; and specific poverty reduction initiatives. The table seeks to indicate whether the performance in each city is, on balance, positive or negative in relation to the urban poor.

Such comparisons are open to a host of criticisms. They are, inevitably, gross over-simplifications of complex issues, especially since each element in the table is made up of a number of sub-elements, each of which may have both positive or negative features. The rating uses a very limited scale and so can only be the crudest approximation of the differences between cities. Furthermore, given the limitations of the data from the case cities, and the absence of uniform definitions and measures, comparisons between cities remain subject to the perceptions of the researchers involved and are likely to be contested. It is also important to stress that the judgements are essentially relative rather than absolute: although a particular city may perform well against the others in the study, that performance may still be quite poor in an absolute sense. It should also be noted that the judgements made relate to the period leading up to and during the study (roughly early/mid-1990s to 2000/01): conditions may have been different before that and may have changed since then.

Despite all these caveats, the table does give some indication of the relative performance of the cities, and it is clear that some cities perform rather better than others. Since performance appears to be generally correlated with level of development, the cities have been listed in descending order of national income per capita. These assessments will be commented on in the following section, in relation to our research questions.

Some conclusions on the key research questions

We started with three broad research questions:

1 What accounts for whether and how the poor benefit from urban economic growth (or change)?
2 How can the poor bring their influence to bear on the agenda of the various institutions of city governance?

Table 10.1 *Comparative performance of cities*

Aspects: economic and political
1 City economic growth.
2 Equality: evenness of distribution of income and wealth.
3 Poverty reduction: in absolute terms (NB: such measures are often disputed, notably in Cebu).
4 Poverty reduction in relative terms: reduced inequality and greater inclusion of the poor.
5 Formal political institutions and systems which are, potentially at least, inclusive of the poor.
6 Political processes in practice, informal as well as formal, and the extent to which these are inclusive of the poor.
7 The existence of specific participatory mechanisms, including sub-city levels of government, which are inclusive of the poor.
8 An active and effective civil society (notably CBOs/GROs and NGOs) involved with urban poverty issues, engaging with city government.

Aspects: governance and services
9 Institutional ability of city government to respond to the needs of the poor, in terms of: jurisdictional boundaries; range of responsibilities; relations between levels of government; management and staffing capacity.
10 Financial capacity of city government: resources available, improved revenue mobilization, good management of expenditures, autonomy over resource use.
11 Access by the poor to land and/or housing through formal systems, including access via upgrading programmes and traditional authorities.
12 Access by the poor to infrastructure and basic services through the public system, including upgrading programmes.
13 Behaviour of city government towards the informal sector.
14 Significant, specific poverty reduction (or income increasing) programmes, whether national or local.

Performance (early/mid-1990s to 2000/01)
✓✓ positive; ✓ modest; ♦ neutral; ✗ poor; ✗✗ bad. Blank indicates no information available from the city study.

	Santiago	Recife	Jo'burg	Cebu	Colombo	Ahmedabad	Bangalore	Visak	Mombasa	Kumasi
1	✓✓	✓	♦	✓✓	✓✓	✓✓	✓✓	✓✓	✗	♦
2	✗	✗✗	✗✗	✗	✓	♦	♦	♦	♦	✓
3	✓✓	♦	♦	✓ or ✗	✗	✓	♦	✓	✗	✗
4	✗	✗	♦	♦	♦	♦	♦	♦	✗	♦
5	✓	✓	✓	✓	✓	✓	✓	✓	✓	✓
6	✗		✓	✓		✓	✗	✗	✗	✗
7	♦	✓✓	✓✓	✓✓	✓ (1980s)	✗	✗	✗	✗✗	✗✗
8	♦		✗	✓✓	♦	✗	✗	✗	✗	✗
9	✓	✓✓	✓	✓	✓	✓	♦	✓	✗✗	✗✗
10	♦	✓✓	✓	✓		♦	♦	✓	✗✗	✗✗
11	♦	✓	✓	✓	✓✓	♦	♦	✓	✓	✓
12	✓✓	✓	♦	✓	✓✓	♦	✗	✓✓	✗	✗
13			✓				✗		✗	✗✗
14	✓		✓	✓	♦	♦	♦	♦	✗	✗

3   What political and institutional systems, processes and mechanisms, both formal and informal, result in inclusive and pro-poor decisions and outcomes?

Economic change on the poor

On the first question, it is clear that the impact of economic growth (or change) on the poor depends greatly on both the nature of that change and the ability of the poor to adapt to and take advantage of the opportunities offered (or to protect themselves from the adverse consequences). The operation of formal labour markets, including poorly remunerated casual work for formal sector enterprises, is one of the principal mechanisms by which economic change is transmitted to those living in poverty. However, due to limited data and resources, this aspect was not a primary focus of our study. In most of the case cities, it is the informal labour market that provides the main livelihood opportunities for the urban poor (although we acknowledge that 'informal' is an inadequate conceptualization of the diverse network of local economic activities in which the poor are engaged, as illustrated vividly in the study of Bangalore).

The city case studies illustrate both the complexity of the livelihood systems of the poor, and the importance of the networks of relationships that enable the poor to survive. As Chapter 3 makes clear, these networks represent a vital asset for those in poverty, providing both access to income opportunities and a safety net in times of hardship. They are generally location-specific and are highly vulnerable to disruption. Thus, interventions from outside, however well intended, can spell disaster for those whose livelihoods depend on these relationships. In particular, actions intended to benefit the poor in general may disadvantage the poorest. There are examples from the case cities where associations of the urban poor have been scaled up in order to bring influence to bear on city government and to widen the benefits from government actions. However, such networks and influence are difficult to achieve, let alone sustain.

Within the globalized economy, city governments have only limited scope for influencing city economic growth. However, some cities have been more successful than others in positioning themselves and fostering increased economic opportunities, for example through partnerships between city government, the private sector and community organizations. In general terms, city economic growth does benefit the poor in a variety of ways, but it also tends to amplify inequalities, so that while some may benefit, others – and particularly the poorest – may be disadvantaged. In Santiago, economic growth has significantly reduced absolute poverty (not least through generating the resources to fund welfare payments targeted to the poorest), but inequality and social exclusion have increased. What matters for the poor is not the overall rate of economic growth but the nature of that growth, in particular how far it is labour-intensive and based on locally controlled, micro- to medium-scale enterprises. Certain growth strategies, for example those focused on limited, high-tech sectors, or reliant on the attraction of large, externally controlled enterprises may offer little to the poor, while those based on 'mega-projects' are likely to damage the fragile economic position of those in poverty by displacing them from key locations.

For some cities, the story has been one of economic stagnation and even decline, further reducing the economic opportunities for the poor. In such circumstances, labour-intensive public works schemes, such as those adopted by the AGETUR programme in Benin and elsewhere, can provide temporary employment for certain sections of the labour force as well as creating valuable infrastructure. But there are questions about the sustainability of such arrangements in the absence of donor funding, and about the non-involvement of either city government or organizations representing the poor.

For those operating in the local economy or informal sector, secure location is a critical factor. This is an aspect in which city governments can make a difference, by ensuring tenure security and access to essential services. In practice, city governments all too often adopt approaches that are counter-productive: failing to tackle the shortcomings of land tenure and administration systems, and ignoring the informal sector or actively harassing it. There are, of course, valid objectives for regulation of business and trading activity, and conflicts of interest over urban space have to be resolved. But all too often, action by city government reflects the interests of the powerful, as well as corruption on the part of those charged with enforcement. Such 'bad governance' can have a devastating impact on those living on the edges of survival.

The other critical role for city government is in the provision of basic infrastructure and services for enterprises and residents. Although some of the key services may lie outside the responsibility of city government, there is still much that the city authorities can do to ensure access by the poor. This includes extending environmental services (or negotiating with other agencies to extend services) to where the poor live and work. It also involves ensuring that bulk infrastructure capacity is sufficient for local services actually to work (for example, for water to flow through taps in poor neighbourhoods). Furthermore, it requires that pricing policies for urban services provide sufficient resources to maintain and extend the system without preventing access by the poor.

The influence of the poor

In terms of the second question, how the poor can bring their influence to bear, the obvious answer is by organizing so as to make demands through the democratic political system. In all our case cities, recent democratization, or reinvigoration of local democracy, has offered expanded opportunities for this to happen. Yet, as we all know, and as the case studies all demonstrate, this is not a simple or straightforward process. There are huge problems for the poor in organizing and exerting pressure: limited time and resources for those who struggle just to survive; lack of leadership and negotiating skills; conflicting interests among the poor themselves; and limited access to decision-making forums. Even where they do manage to organize successfully, the representative political system may prove to be unresponsive, whether through resistance or incapacity or both. There are, however, some examples from city studies where the poor have been able to organize to bring pressure to bear, with some success.

Notable examples emerged in Cebu (the organization of street vendors and *trisikad* drivers) and in Johannesburg (both the civics prior to the ending of apartheid, and more recently Community Development Forums (CDFs) in places like Diepsloot), but also to some extent in Ahmedabad and Bangalore. Tactics are also important: recent progress in Cebu seems to have come with a shift from confrontation to negotiation, while the Bangalore study highlights the informal and covert tactics used by poor groups to protect or improve their position, characterized as 'politics by stealth'. But the case studies also make clear the fragility of initiatives by organizations of the poor. Community or grassroots organizations are vulnerable to multiple problems: conflicting interests; unrepresentative and unaccountable leadership; co-option or undermining by other political interests; sudden changes in political support; and exhaustion of those in leadership who themselves struggle daily with acute poverty.

NGOs can, in principle, play a valuable role in supporting and articulating the interests of the urban poor. But again the experience is mixed. In Cebu, there are many active and committed NGOs that support poor groups and have at least some influence within city government. A valuable example was the role that a federation of community organizations and NGOs played in scrutinizing and publicizing the policies of mayoral candidates towards the poor. There were also some positive examples from other cities. However, most of the NGOs identified were more concerned with delivering welfare programmes (sometimes with state sponsorship) than with lobbying the institutions of city governance for changed policies towards the poor. NGOs are often regarded by the poor as opportunistic and self-serving, unwilling or unable to offer real solidarity with them, and without much clout within city government. There have, however, been some notable successes by NGOs at the national level in securing programmes that benefit poor people locally.

For the poor to bring their influence to bear, there have to be avenues into decision-making processes. These avenues are more open in some cities than in others, due to variations in political culture and history, as well as the way the representative political system is organized. Ward-level councillors can offer a vital avenue, as indicated most clearly in Bangalore, since those representing poor wards have to demonstrate some responsiveness to their constituents. However, the effectiveness of that avenue depends greatly on the influence that councillors have within city government – not to mention the powers and resources of city government to do anything about their demands. This influence in turn depends on the nature of the political system in that city. Directly elected mayors – unlike appointed city bosses – also have to demonstrate a degree of responsiveness to the poor, who generally comprise the majority of the city's population. The poor may be able to make gains through persistent lobbying and pressure. Persistence is potentially an asset for the poor, where they have a vital interest in the issue at stake. Vote banks and vote bargaining, often perceived as forms of political corruption, can provide ways for the poor to organize to ensure that candidates respond to their needs. But the danger with all these arrangements is clientelism. Clientelistic relationships with those in authority can (and do in several of our case cities) deliver some real benefits for the poor, but they do so on the basis of dependence and the granting of favours rather than on the basis of regular provision and rights.

The case cities also provide some examples of participatory processes which give some voice to the poor: the Community Action Planning system in Colombo in the 1980s; the Integrated Development Planning (IDP) process in Johannesburg; and most notably, participatory budgeting (PB) in Recife. While these arrangements have enabled the poor to have some influence over decisions and resource use, they have serious limitations. They are prone to control by more powerful interests (including professionals in the case of Johannesburg) and are vulnerable to changing political regimes (as in Colombo and Recife) or inadequate financial resources (in Johannesburg and Recife). While PB in Recife has shifted resources somewhat in favour of the poor, and has greatly increased their participation, it remains dependent on the commitment of the mayor. Where PB involves the elected councillors, and where it is incorporated into local legislation, as in some other cities in Brazil, it gives greater assurance to the process and helps to formalize the rights of the poor.

Another possibility for greater voice and access by the poor is through democratically elected sub-city levels of government. Where the sub-city level is truly local (ie neighbourhood based, like the *barangays* in Cebu), has a statutory basis (so that it cannot just be discarded like the Community Development Councils (CDCs) in Colombo) and where it has real resources, then the poor have some prospect of being able to influence decisions that affect them. Alas, in other cities 'local' government is very remote and there is either no provision for a sub-city level or it has not been implemented. For example, in Kumasi, an elaborate structure of sub-city governance was never allowed to function.

The responsiveness of the political and institutional processes

The extent to which any influence the poor have on the institutions of city government results in pro-poor decisions and outcomes depends on the nature of the political and institutional processes and systems within the city. This was our third question. It is clear from our city studies that the political and institutional relationships and processes within any city are complex, and that what happens is often the result of informal processes, often highly opaque, as much as the formal processes of city government.

In terms of the formal systems of political representation and decision-making, the case cities exhibit a variety of arrangements, and it is clear that no one model is necessarily superior to any other. As already noted, ward-based councillors can provide an important avenue for the voice of the poor, but such first-past-the-post electoral systems tend to marginalize women and minorities. Proportional representation (PR) may be more representative overall but puts power into the hands of political parties in selecting candidates, cutting the direct accountability of those elected to their (poor) constituents. The South African model of a combination of PR and ward-based councillors perhaps represents a good compromise. Similarly, as noted in Chapter 7, there are arguments for and against reserved seats for particular groups, as there are in relation to directly elected mayors and indirectly elected mayors. What is clear, though, is that the external appointment of mayors, as in Kumasi, breaks the accountability link to local citizens. Even so, the Indian experience of appointed municipal commissioners can have positive outcomes, including the willingness to take necessary but unpopular measures, as in Ahmedabad. It is clear that the detailed arrangements for representative democracy matter, and must be tailored to the particular political and cultural conditions of that city.

It is also apparent that periodic elections are not sufficient to ensure that decisions reflect the interests of citizens, particularly the poor. Where elections are supplemented by other, more participatory arrangements (some examples of which have just been mentioned), it is possible to produce more nuanced perceptions of citizens' needs and priorities. However, the risk with such arrangements is that the voices of the poor are drowned out by the voices of the more articulate and powerful. In all this, information is critical, both for effective citizen participation and for accountability of elected and appointed officials to those they are supposed to be serving. Yet, in most of the cities, information – particularly about the use of financial resources – seems to be regarded as something to be withheld rather than disseminated. In some cities, the media (and particularly local radio in some places) play an important role in making citizens aware of issues, although all too often the media lack the capacity for investigation or are co-opted by other powerful interests.

However well or badly the democratic decision-making processes work in a city, the outcomes for the poor depend ultimately on the ability of city government and related institutions to deliver on those decisions. In many of the ten cases studied, city governments are heavily constrained: by limited jurisdictions that exclude many of the poor; by fragmentation of responsibilities for infrastructure and services; by conflicts with other levels of government; and by inadequate skills and weak management capacity. Perhaps the greatest constraint is financial. Many of the case cities are in a poor financial condition, with limited and inelastic local revenue sources, weak revenue collection systems and poor financial management. Some cities, such as Cebu, Recife and Kumasi, have benefited from substantial transfers of resources from the centre. Others, like Johannesburg and Ahmedabad, have potentially huge revenue bases but face many difficulties in securing the revenues due to them. Some cities have made progress in improving their financial situation (for example, Ahmedabad), while others, such as Mombasa and Kumasi, remain in a financial mire, unable to improve services to anyone, let alone the poor. On the whole – and not surprisingly – richer cities are able to finance better services than poorer ones. For these cities, notably Santiago, Recife and Johannesburg, the critical issue is the equitable distribution of resources so as to ensure that disadvantaged sections of the population benefit. This is often hindered by outdated and perverse jurisidictional boundaries, as well as by inherited bureaucratic culture.

If cities are really to address poverty and exclusion, they require democratic and participatory processes that move beyond clientelistic arrangements in which benefits are distributed as favours, to a situation in which services are delivered as a matter of routine and right. This requires effective, participatory and accountable democratic systems in which the voice of the poor can be heard. It also requires an active civil society that can enable the poor to organize and articulate their needs. Furthermore, it requires city level government systems that are properly staffed, managed and financed, with transparent and accountable processes. And last but not least, it requires leadership, both political and managerial, which is responsive to the needs of the poor, has vision and has the capacity to overcome some of the constraints that city governments face. This is a tall order. Among the case cities, none matched up to these requirements. Nevertheless, there were some positive examples of movements in the right direction in several of the case study cities.

Some implications for policy and governance

A number of implications for policy and governance emerge from this study, and these are summarized below.

1 Information
Better information is needed on urban poverty: not just income data but also indicators which permit a better understanding of the multi-faceted and differentiated nature of poverty, vulnerability and exclusion at the city level, as well as of the livelihood strategies of poor urban dwellers.

2 Effects of interventions
The multi-dimensional nature of poverty means that there are multiple opportunities for intervention. However, interventions need to recognize the social, economic, and political processes – informal as well as formal – operating at the local level, and to value the delicate social and economic relationships that enable those in poverty to survive. They also need to recognize and build on social networks, altruism and mutuality among the urban poor, but without expecting these to bear the weight of social support in the absence of public provision. Furthermore, interventions need to ensure that the poorest and most vulnerable are not excluded from programmes addressed to the poor in general.

3 'Bad governance'
'Bad governance' undermines the position of the poor. In particular, oppressive regulation of the informal enterprises and settlements can destroy livelihood opportunities for the poor. Since it is easier to destroy jobs, livelihoods, networks and communities than it is to create them, it is important to address those aspects of 'bad governance' which undermine the position of the poor before, or at the same time as, seeking to adopt more demanding interventions designed to reduce poverty.

4 Civil Society
The various elements of civil society can play a vital part in relation to poverty reduction, and interventions should seek to work with and build on existing grassroots organizations within poor communities. But the limitations of such organizations, in terms of how far they are representative and inclusive, need to

be recognized. Formalizing such organizations may reinforce exclusion, especially of minorities and the poorest, and may obscure the competing and conflicting interests within low-income communities. Federating and networking GROs/CBOs at the city level enables them to work more effectively, and helps to prevent officials and politicians from manipulating community leaders, so long as these organizations maintain close links with the people they are supposed to represent. Trade unions, associations of small-scale producers and other civil society organizations can all play a valuable role in aggregating the interests of poor groups in order to lobby or bargain for improvements, or to provide common services; but they often do so in ways which exclude non-members and potentially disadvantage the poorest and most vulnerable.

5 NGOs
The local knowledge and experience that NGOs possess can make them important partners, but they have limitations in terms of scale and local accountability, and they should not be used as gatekeepers to the poor. While some NGOs have had a beneficial influence on policy at local and/or national level, many are poorly equipped for an advocacy role and may have weak links with the communities for whom they claim to speak.

6 Strategies for GROs/CBOs and NGOs
Moving beyond confrontation to the politics of engagement with city government may offer benefits for the urban poor. This may take the form of joint committees of community representatives, NGOs, councillors and local government officials, which offer the potential for developing inclusive and pro-poor policies and practices. But such strategies also carry the risk of co-option and disempowerment. In particular, adopting the role of contractor for government-initiated programmes may create dependence on the state and reduce NGOs' freedom of manoeuvre. On the other hand, it has the potential for high-profile advocacy and institutionalizing more participatory approaches to the delivery of such programmes.

7 Political relationships
Political relationships at city level are complex, informal as well as formal, and frequently opaque, but they can and often do deliver some benefits for the poor. This is more likely when electoral politics is combined with the practice of 'vote bargaining'. However, political relationships are often clientelistic, reinforcing the dependency of the poor. Interventions to address urban poverty need to recognize these complex political relationships and avoid imposing simplistic solutions that undermine those arrangements that currently deliver at least some benefits for the poor.

8 Democratization and claim-making
Democratization at the local level has widened the scope for the urban poor to make their claims, and for urban politics to move beyond clientelism towards more open political bargaining. While, almost by definition, the poor have less influence over the levers of power than the better off, by their sheer numbers

and by their persistence they can and do make their voice heard and thus achieve some gains.

9 The design of the city-level political system

The design of the city-level political system is important, including arrangements for electoral representation and executive control. While it is clear that no one model of urban government is necessarily superior to any other, some observations can be made. An elected mayor has to demonstrate a degree of responsiveness to the poor majority in order to get elected, whereas an indirectly elected or centrally-appointed mayor does not. However, conflict between a directly elected mayor and councillors (especially if the majority belong to a different party) can hinder decision-making. A centrally-appointed mayor can over-ride the wishes of locally elected representatives. Elected councillors representing poor wards can provide an avenue for influence for their poor constituents and must demonstrate a degree of responsiveness to them, whereas election by proportional representation (PR) on a party list basis gives power to the party machine. However, PR systems are likely to give a more balanced representation, especially to women and minority groups. Thus, it may be desirable to have a mixed system of ward councillors and councillors elected by PR, or some system of reserved seats for particular groups. Multi-partyism can offer opportunities which civil society groups, including the urban poor, can use to bargain for improvements. However, in many contexts, multi-partyism reduces local politics to factionalism, reinforcing ethnic or religious rivalries. The detailed design of the democratic system matters, including the spatial scales of representation, the checks and balances between executive and legislature, and the relationship with higher levels of government; but it also depends on the particular local context, so that specifying general rules is inappropriate.

10 Mechanisms of participation and accountability

Periodic elections alone are not a sufficient mechanism to ensure that decisions reflect the needs and priorities of local citizens. They need to be complemented by a range of mechanisms of direct, deliberative and participatory democracy that enable citizens to have a voice in the decisions that affect them. Participatory budgeting (PB) offers a valuable example, although not without its weaknesses. The design of these mechanisms needs to ensure that the poor are not excluded or drowned out by the better off and more articulate. Elections also need to be accompanied by effective and accessible mechanisms for holding elected representatives and officials accountable. In this, the availability of information, for example about the resources available and their use, together with the transparency of decision-making, are crucial for challenging patronage and dependency.

11 The media

The media can play a vital role in disseminating and interpreting information, and local radio can be particularly important in providing accessible information to a non-literate population. However, the lack of investigative reporting skills, combined with control by powerful interests, compromise its effectiveness.

12 Traditional authorities

Chiefs and other traditional authorities are still important in certain places. Although generally part of a system of hierarchical and patriarchal social relationships, and frequently resented as being not democratically accountable, they can provide a countervailing force and an alternative avenue of influence for the poor where local government performs badly. In certain cases, they may facilitate access to land for the poor.

13 Decentralization

Decentralization in many countries has focused attention on city government for addressing the needs of the poor. However, most city governments face severe constraints in terms of both capacity and vision about how to achieve this. Decentralization of responsibilities and resources, combined with democratization, can in the right circumstances result in greater efficiency and responsiveness of city government, bringing benefits for the urban poor. But there is nothing automatic about this, and cities need the right political and institutional arrangements, powers and resources if they are to achieve such improvements. National governments remain responsible for ensuring the right governmental structures and the macro-economic framework in which city economic development and poverty reduction can take place.

14 Functions and boundaries of city government

City governments should be strengthened, rather than assigning important functions to higher levels of government where accountability is more remote, or to separate agencies over which there is little or no democratic control. Where operational efficiency requires a separate agency, lines of accountability to democratically elected local representatives should be clear. The boundaries of city government should include the peripheral areas where the poor reside, so that city resources can be shared equitably (although there may need to be more than a single tier of city government, especially in large cities).

15 Sub-city levels of government

Sub-city levels of government can help to bring decision-making closer to citizens and be of benefit to poor neighbourhoods, providing that such units are at a sufficiently local level, are democratically elected, have an equitable share of resources, and have some constitutional protection from sudden changes in political favour.

16 Addressing the constraints on city government

If city governments are to be effective in addressing the needs of the poor, it will be necessary to tackle a number of constraints on their operations. Specific reforms include: better city-level information on poverty, environmental conditions and access to services; overcoming the institutional and legal obstacles, such as out-dated and inappropriate bylaws and regulations that inhibit informal sector businesses and livelihood opportunities for the poor and prevent services being provided in informal settlements; upgrading technical and managerial skills among staff, improving management systems, and encouraging more responsive and pro-poor attitudes and practices on the part of local officials; extending local revenue sources, improving systems of revenue collection and providing equitable inter-governmental transfers; establishing more transparent budgeting systems, expenditure management and monitoring, so as to make better use of available resources; and improving relationships with higher levels of government so that the latter can be supportive rather than undermining, and can enhance local level performance as well as ensuring local accountability.

17 Civic leadership

The personal qualities of civic leaders – both elected and appointed – can make a significant difference to achieving effective and pro-poor city governance. This requires an environment that encourages dynamic, responsible and responsive civic leadership to emerge, and an institutional framework that ensures that the poor benefit not just through favours but as a matter of routine. This in turn requires civic education for all those involved: officials, elected representatives and citizens.

18 Access to land, infrastructure and services

The ways in which city governments can have the greatest impact on poverty reduction are generally through ensuring access to land for housing and economic activities, and through the direct provision of infrastructure and services. This includes the maintenance of infrastructure – something too often neglected – as well as initial capital investment. Such interventions can increase income opportunities for the poor as well as reducing costs, time losses and risks to health. Even where municipal governments do not have direct control (for instance, in relation to land), they have levers of influence (eg willingness to legalize settlements and regularize tenure, as well as adopting realistic zoning, land development regulations and building codes). Since city governments have limited resources, they need to redirect those resources towards the infrastructure and service needs of the poor, while at the same time ensuring that the bulk capacity is there to support the services at the point of delivery.

19 Implications for funding agencies

A number of specific implications for funding agencies emerge from the study. These include: the need to engage with the institutions of city governance, not just with national governments, and to channel resources through local-level institutions not just national institutions; the need to build on whatever is already happening locally that is positive rather than bypassing existing institutions, processes and networks (while at the same time recognizing that community organizations may not be fully representative or inclusive); the importance of undertaking a 'political appraisal' as part of project design, in order to understand the complexity of local political processes and competing interests; the need to fund citywide infrastructure rather than just isolated projects, and to design such interventions in ways which take account of the interests and livelihood systems of the urban poor; and finally, the importance of long-term engagement in order to facilitate the transformation of city governance.

It must, of course, be acknowledged that changes such as those envisaged here are neither easy nor automatic, and are likely to take time to achieve. They may require radical changes in the local and national political climate. They will also require greater international resources to be directed at reducing urban poverty. For those operating in particular cities in the South at the present time, these changes and requirements may seem unrealistic. Nevertheless, as at least some of the city case studies show, progress is possible.

Directions for further research

This study has only scratched the surface of a vast and complex area of city governance and poverty in the South. We have only looked at a small selection of cities – most of them large. These issues also need investigation in the numerous smaller cities and towns of the developing world. We have looked at the ways in which urban economic change affects the incidence of poverty and the livelihoods of poor people, and how institutional and political processes affect decision-making. But we have not been in a position to test the impact of these changes, policies and decisions on poor people.

There is clearly a need for more research in this area, particularly on urban economic change and politics. The understanding of urban economies still relies on a patently unsatisfactory conceptualization that divides them into formal and informal sectors. Data collection is also often linked to the registered or unregistered status of enterprises, reinforcing this dichotomous view of urban economies and making it difficult to relate the study of economic development to labour markets or livelihoods. As a result, understanding of the dynamics of urban economic change is poorly developed. Analysis should include the impact of external forces, the effects of economic change on poverty and livelihoods, and the efficacy of alternative strategies open to city governments.

Research on political processes in developing countries has focused mainly on the national scene, in terms of both the conceptual underpinnings for political analysis and empirical work. More needs to be done to develop the framework for analysing political and institutional processes at the urban level adopted in this research, and to apply such a framework in the context of a range of urban areas within and across countries. For this to be successful, there is a need for more information to be available on a consistent basis so as to permit proper comparison. A priority concern for donor agencies should be to fund the collection and analysis of data on urban poverty using internationally agreed definitions and measures. Further research and analysis is also required to evaluate the conditions under which local democracy consolidates or atrophies in the medium to long term, to identify the circumstances and incentives that encourage responsiveness to the poor, and to assess alternative means of ensuring accountability.

Annex 1

Research Methodology

This research was carried out between the beginning of 1998 and early 2001. The research questions identified in the initial project document were wide-ranging:

- How can urban governance influence the conditions for urban economic growth?
- How do urban governance institutions seek to distribute the benefits of that growth, how this works in practice, and who benefits from these processes of distribution?
- How can and do the poor influence the agenda of the institutions of city governance in their interests?

Stage 1 of the research (1998 to mid-1999) involved:

- a review of the literature and international experience according to seven key themes identified as being critical to the research area (see the list of Theme Papers in Annex 2);
- a series of nine city case studies, carried out by local researchers in each of these cities, according to a research guide developed by the UK team; the research involved assembling and analysing available data, together with selected key-informant interviews, rather than substantial original research;

- an analysis of this material across the nine city case studies according to the key themes;
- a workshop with all the researchers at which the results were discussed.

In Stage 2 (late 1999 to early 2001), the research focused on a more specific question:

- What sorts of political and institutional processes, systems and mechanisms, both formal and informal, result in pro-poor and inclusive decisions (and outcomes)? (Outcomes were included in brackets since it is outcome, not just decisions, which are ultimately of interest, but recognizing that it would not be possible to demonstrate causal relationships in terms of outcomes.)

From this, a series of more detailed research questions were formulated.

Stage 2 included:

- identification of four of the original city cases (Bangalore, Cebu, Johannesburg and Kumasi) which appeared to offer the most interesting and fruitful insights for the research agenda; a further case was added (Recife), focusing on the participatory budgeting programme;
- a workshop with city researchers to discuss the research questions and methodology, and to identify key sectors and key groups for detailed study in each city;
- field research in the five cities, in each case involving the collection of aggregate data, analysis of city finances, interviews with key informants in various sectors, and focus group discussions, using techniques such as community profiling, oral histories, time lines, critical incident analysis and Venn diagrams. In each city, detailed case studies were carried out in two or three poor residential neighbourhoods and with two or three identified poor or excluded groups (eg street traders). Particular attention was paid to three sectors in each city: land and housing, water and sanitation, regulation of the informal sector;
- a concluding workshop at which the second round case studies were discussed and a cross-city analysis presented according to the main themes.

Some additional studies were also commissioned in Stage 2:

- on the AGETUR/AGETIP model of labour-intensive public works in Benin;
- an overview of participatory budgeting in Brazil, focusing on three cities, for comparison with the Recife case;
- a review of another series of case studies carried out by IIED of the experiences of innovatory urban poverty reduction programmes in eight municipalities in Africa, Asia and Latin America.

Annex 2 lists the theme papers, city case studies, cross-city analyses and additional cases published as Working Papers under this research.

Annex 2

Urban Governance, Partnerships and Poverty Research Working Papers

Theme papers

1 City Economic Growth – Elizabeth Vidler
2 Urban Economic Growth and Poverty Reduction – Philip Amis
3 Households, Livelihoods and Urban Poverty – Jo Beall and Nazneen Kanji
4 Who Runs Cities? The Relationship between Urban Governance, Service Delivery and Poverty – Nick Devas
5 Civil Society and Urban Poverty – Diana Mitlin
6 The Urban Environment – Fiona Nunan and David Satterthwaite
7 Rural–Urban Interactions – Cecilia Tacoli
8 Urban Governance, Partnerships and Poverty: A Preliminary Exploration of the Research Issues – Carole Rakodi

Stage 1 case studies

9 Urban Governance, Partnership and Poverty in Colombo – Austin Fernando, Steven Russell, Elizabeth Vidler and Anoushka Wilson
10 Urban Governance, Partnership and Poverty in Kumasi – David Korboe, Kofi Diaw with Nick Devas
11 Urban Governance, Partnership and Poverty in Mombasa – Rose Gatabaki-Kamau with Carole Rakodi
12 Urban Governance, Partnership and Poverty in Johannesburg – Jo Beall, Owen Crankshaw and Susan Parnell
13 Urban Governance, Partnership and Poverty in Cebu – Felisa Etemadi
14 Urban Governance, Partnership and Poverty in Santiago – Alfredo Rodríguez and Lucy Winchester with Ben Richards
15 Urban Governance, Partnership and Poverty in Bangalore – Solly Benjamin with R Bhuvaneswari
16 Urban Governance, Partnership and Poverty in Ahmedabad – Shyam Dutta with Richard Batley
17 Urban Governance, Partnership and Poverty in Visakhapatnam – Sashi Kumar with Philip Amis

Cross-city analyses from Stage 1

Stage 2 case studies

Additional studies

Policy Briefing Paper

Urban Governance and Poverty: Lessons from a Study of Ten Cities in the South.
Nick Devas, with Philip Amis, Jo Beall, Ursula Grant, Diana Mitlin, Carole Rakodi and David Satterthwaite, June 2001

These papers can be ordered from:

The Publications Office
School of Public Policy
University of Birmingham
Birmingham B15 2TT
United Kingdom
Tel: +44 (0)121 414 4986
Fax: +44 (0)121 414 4989
Email: C.A.Fowler@bham.ac.uk

Price: £5 for the theme papers (papers 1–8), £10 for all others.

Alternatively, the papers can be viewed on our website:

www.idd.bham.ac.uk/research/Projects/urban-governance/urbgov.htm

Articles based on the Stage 1 city case studies were also published in *Environment and Urbanization* **21** (1), April 2000.

Articles reviewing and comparing the results of Stage 1 studies were published in *International Planning Studies* **6** (1), 2001.

References

Abers, R (1998) 'Learning democratic practice: distributing government resources through popular participation in Porto Alegre, Brazil', in Douglass, M and Friedmann, J (eds) *Cities for Citizens*, John Wiley and Sons, Chichester

Abugre, C and Holland, J (1998) A Poverty Analysis in Support of Project Preparation in Kumasi. Ghana: Water Sector Improvement Project

Amis, P (1999) 'Urban economic growth and poverty reduction'. *Urban Governance, Partnership and Poverty Working Paper* 2, IDD, University of Birmingham, Birmingham

Amis, P (2001) 'Rethinking UK aid: lessons from an impact assessment study of DFID's Slum Improvement projects'. *Environment and Urbanization* **13**(1): 101–103

Amis, P (2002) 'Municipal government, urban economic growth and poverty reduction: identifying the transmission mechanisms between growth and poverty', in Rakodi, C with Lloyd-Jones, T (eds) *Urban Livelihoods: A People-centred Approach to Reducing Poverty*, Earthscan, London, pp97–111

Amis, P and Grant, U (2000) 'Urban economic growth, governance and poverty: a comparative city review'. *Urban Governance, Partnership and Poverty Working Paper* 18, IDD, University of Birmingham, Birmingham

Amis, P and Grant, U (2001) 'Urban economic growth, civic engagement and poverty reduction'. *Journal of International Development* **13**: 997–1002

Amis, P and Kumar, S (2000) 'Urban economic growth, infrastructure and poverty in India: lessons from Visakhapatnam'. *Environment and Urbanization* **12**(1): 185–196

Amis, P and Rakodi, C (1995) 'Urban poverty: concepts, characteristics and policies'. *Habitat International* **19**(4): 403–405

AMREF and OVP/MPND (African Medical Relief Fund and Office of the Vice-President/Ministry of National Planning and Development) (1997) *The Second Participatory Assessment Study: Kenya*, Nairobi, AMREF and OVP/MPND

Arrossi, S, Bombarolo F, Hardoy, J E, Mitlin, D, Coscio, L P and Satterthwaite, D (1994) *Funding Community Initiatives*, Earthscan, London

Bangura, Y (2000) 'Democratization, equity and stability: African politics and societies in the 1990s', in Ghai, D (ed) *Reviewing Economic and Social Progress in Africa: Essays in Memory of Philip Ndegwa*, Macmillan Press, Basingstoke

Barrera, M (1999) 'Political participation and social exclusion of the popular sectors in Chile', in Oxhorn, P and Starr, P K (eds) *Markets and Democracy in Latin America: Conflict or Convergence*, Lynne Rienner, Boulder CO, pp81–102

Beall, J (1995) 'Social security and social networks among the urban poor in Pakistan'. *Habitat International* **19**(4): 427–445

Beall, J (1997) 'Social capital in waste: a solid investment?' *Journal of International Development*, **9**(7): 951–961

Beall, J (2000a) 'Valuing social resources or capitalizing on them? Social assets and the limits to pro-poor urban governance'. *Urban Governance, Partnership and Poverty Working Paper* 19, IDD, University of Birmingham, Birmingham

Beall, J (2000b) 'Life in the cities' in Allen, T and Thomas, A (eds) *Poverty and Development* (2nd edn), Oxford University Press in Association with the Open University, Oxford and Milton Keynes, pp425–442

Beall, J (2001) 'Valuing social resources or capitalizing on them? Limits to pro-poor urban governance in nine cities of the South'. *International Planning Studies* **6**(4): 357–375

Beall, J (2002a) 'Living in the present, investing in the future: household livelihoods strategies of the urban poor' in Rakodi, C with Lloyd-Jones, T (eds) *Urban Livelihoods*, Earthscan, London, pp71–87

Beall, J (2002b) ' "A new branch can be strengthened by an old branch": livelihoods and challenges to inter-generational solidarity in South Africa', in Townsend, P and Gordon, D (eds) *World Poverty, New Policies to Defeat an Old Enemy*, The Policy Press, London, pp325–348

Beall, J and Kanji, N (1999) 'Households, livelihoods and urban poverty' *Urban Governance, Partnership and Poverty Working Paper* 3, IDD, University of Birmingham, Birmingham

Beall, J, Crankshaw, O and Parnell, S (1999) 'Urban governance, partnerships and poverty in Johannesburg'. *Urban Governance, and Poverty Working Paper* 12, IDD, University of Birmingham, Birmingham

Beall, J, Crankshaw, O and Parnell, S (2000) 'Local government, poverty reduction and inequality in Johannesburg', *Environment and Urbanization* 12(1): 107–122

Beall, J, Crankshaw, O and Parnell, S (2001) 'Towards inclusive urban governance in Johannesburg'. *Urban Governance, Partnership and Poverty Working Paper* 24, IDD, University of Birmingham, Birmingham

Beall, J, Crankshaw, O and Parnell, S (2002) *Uniting a Divided City: Governance and Social Exclusion in Johannesburg*, Earthscan, London

Bebbington, A (2002) 'Organization, inclusion and citizenship: policy and (some) economic gains of indigenous peoples' organizations in Ecuador'. Mimeo

Becker, C M, Hamer, A M, and Morrison, A R (1994) *Beyond Urban Bias in Africa: Urbanization in an Era of Structural Adjustment*, Heinemann/James Currey, London

Benjamin, S (1993) 'Urban productivity from the grassroots'. *Third World Planning Review* 15(2): 143–173

Benjamin, S (2000) 'Governance, economic setting and poverty in Bangalore'. *Environment and Urbanization* 12(1): 35–56

Benjamin, S and Bhuvaneswari, R (1999) 'Urban governance, partnerships and poverty in Bangalore'. *Urban Governance, Partnership and Poverty Working Paper* 15, IDD, University of Birmingham, Birmingham

Benjamin, S and Bhuvaneswari, R (2001) 'Democracy, inclusive government and poverty in Bangalore'. *Urban Governance, Partnership and Poverty Working Paper* 26, IDD, University of Birmingham, Birmingham

Bird, R and Rodríguez, E R (1999) 'Decentralization and poverty alleviation: international experience and the case of the Philippines'. *Public Administration and Development* 19: 299–319

Biswas, S (2003) 'Housing is a productive asset: housing finance for self-employed women in India'. *Small Enterprise Development* 14(1): 49–55

Blair, H (2000) 'Participation and accountability at the periphery: democratic local governance in six countries'. *World Development* 28(1): 21–39

Boonyabancha, S (1998) 'The urban community environmental activities project and its environment fund in Thailand'. *Environment and Urbanization* 11(1): 101–116

Bradley, C, Stephens, C, Harpham, T and Cairncross, S (1991) *A Review of Environmental Health Impacts in Developing Countries*, World Bank, Washington, DC

Bromley, R and Gerry, C (eds) (1973) *Casual Work and Poverty in Third World Cities*, John Wiley, Chichester

Brown, L D and Ashman, D (1996) 'Participation, social capital and intersectoral problem solving: African and Asian cases.' *World Development* 24(9): 1467–1479

Burgess, R, Carmona, M and Kolstee, T (eds) (1997) *The Challenge of Sustainable Cities:*

Neo-Liberalism and Urban Strategies in Developing Countries, Zed Books, London

Burgwal, G (1995) *Struggle of the Poor: Neighbourhood Organization and Clientelist Practice in a Quito Squatter Settlement*, Centre for Latin American Research and Documentation, Amsterdam

Carroll, T F (1992), *Intermediary NGOs: The Supporting Link in Grassroots Development*, Kumarian Press, West Hartford

Castells, M (1979) *The Urban Question: A Marxist Approach*, Edward Arnold, London

Castells, M (1983) *The City and the Grass Roots: A Cross-cultural Theory of Urban Social Movements*, Edward Arnold, London

Castells, M (2002) *Reader on Cities and Social Theory*, edited by I Susser, Blackwell, Oxford

Chalker, L (1991) 'Good government and the aid programme', Speech by the Rt Hon Lynda Chalker MP, Minister for Overseas Development, at the Royal Institute of International Affairs, 25 June

Chambers, R (1995) 'Poverty and livelihoods: whose reality counts?' *Environment and Urbanization* **7**(1): 173–204

Chambers, R and Conway, G (1992) *Sustainable Rural Livelihoods: Practical Concepts for the 21st Century*, IDS Discussion Paper No. 296, Institute of Development Studies, Brighton

Chant, S (1998) 'Households, gender and rural–urban migration: reflections on linkages and considerations for policy'. *Environment and Urbanization* **10**(1): 5–21

Chant, S (2002) 'The informal sector and employment' in Desai, V and Potter, R (eds) *The Companion to Development Studies*, Edward Arnold, London, pp206–213

Chazan, N, Mortimer, R, Ravenhill, J and Rothchild, D (1992) *Politics and Society in Contemporary Africa*, Lynne Rienner, Boulder CO

Choguill, C (1996) 'Ten steps to sustainable infrastructure'. *Habitat International* **20**(3): 389–404

Christian Aid (1993) 'A review report of Christian Aid/Joint Funding Scheme Urban Community Development Projects in Thailand, Chile and Bolivia'. Submitted to the ODA Joint Funding Scheme, November 1993, Christian Aid, London

Clark, J (1991) *Democratizing Development: The Role of Voluntary Agencies*, Earthscan, London

Craig, D and Porter, D (2003) 'Poverty reduction strategy papers: a new convergence'. *World Development* **31**(1): 53–69

Crankshaw, O (1997) 'Shifting sands: labour market trends and union organisation'. *South African Labour Bulletin* **21**: 28–35

Crook, R and Manor, J (1998) *Democracy and Decentralisation in South Asia and West Africa: Participation, Accountability and Performance*, Cambridge University Press, Cambridge

Crook, R and Sverrisson, A (2001) *Decentralization and Poverty Alleviation in Developing Countries: A Comparative Analysis, or is West Bengal Unique?*, IDS Working Paper 130, Institute of Development Studies, Brighton

Dahl, R A (1961) *Who Governs? Democracy and Power in an American City*, Yale University Press, New Haven CT

Das, V (1996) 'The spatialization of violence: case study of a "communal riot"', in Basu, K and Subrahmanyam, S (eds) *Unravelling the Nation*, Penguin, New Delhi, pp157–203

Davey, K (1996) 'The structure and functions of urban government' in Davey, K with Batley, R, Devas, N, Norris, M and Pasteur, D, *Urban Management: The Challenge of Growth*, Avebury, Aldershot, pp47–102

Davey, K, with Batley, R, Devas, N, Norris, M, and Pasteur, D (1996) *Urban Management: The Challenge of Growth*, Avebury, Aldershot de la Rocha, M and Grinspun, A (2001) 'Private adjustments: household responses to the erosion of work'. *UNDP/SEPED Conference Paper Series* Paper No. 6, United Nations Development Programme, New York

Desai, V (1995) 'Filling the gap: an assessment of the effectiveness of urban NGOs'. Final Report to the Overseas Development Administration (UK), Institute of Development Studies, University of Sussex, Brighton

Devas, N (2000) 'Connections between urban governance and poverty: analysing the stage 1 city case studies'. *Urban Governance, Partnership and Poverty Working Paper* 20, IDD, University of Birmingham, Birmingham

Devas, N and Grant, U (2003) 'Local government decision-making: citizen participation and local accountability: some evidence from Kenya and Uganda'. *Public Administration and Development* 23: 307–316

Devas, N and Korboe, D (2000) 'City governance and poverty: the case of Kumasi'. *Environment and Urbanization* 12(1): 123–136

Devas, N and Rakodi, C (eds) (1993) *Managing Fast Growing Cities: New Approaches to Urban Planning and Management in the Developing World*, Longman, Harlow

Devas, N with Amis, P, Beall, J, Grant, U, Mitlin, D, Rakodi, C and Satterthwaite, D (2001) 'Urban governance and poverty: lessons from a study of ten cities in the south'. Policy briefing paper, IDD, University of Birmingham, Birmingham

DFID (1997) *Eliminating World Poverty: A Challenge for the 21st Century*, Department for International Development, London

Dia, M (1996) *Africa's Management in the 1990s and Beyond: Reconciling Indigenous and Transplanted Institutions*, World Bank, Washington, DC

Dijkstra, A G and van Donge, J K (2001) 'What does the show-case show? *World Development* 29(5): 841–863

Dockemdorf, E, Rodríguez, A and Winchester, L (2000) 'Santiago de Chile: metropolization, globalization and inequality'. *Environment and Urbanization* 12(1): 171–183

Douglass, M and Friedmann, J (eds) (1998) *Cities for Citizens: Planning and the Rise of Civil Society in a Global Age*, John Wiley and Sons, Chichester

Drakakis-Smith, D (2000) *Third World Cities*, Routledge, London

Dreze, J and Sen, A (1989) *Hunger and Public Action*, Clarendon Press, Oxford

Dutta, S (2000) 'Partnerships in urban development: a review of Ahmedabad's experience'. *Environment and Urbanization* 12(1): 13–26

Dutta, S with Batley, R (1999) 'Urban governance, partnerships and poverty in Ahmedabad'. *Urban Governance, Partnership and Poverty Working Paper* 16, IDD, University of Birmingham, Birmingham

Edwards, M and Hulme, D (eds) (1992) *Making a Difference: NGOs and Development in a Changing World*, Earthscan, London

Edwards, M and Hulme, D (eds) (1995) *NGO Performance and Accountability: Beyond the Magic Bullet,* Earthscan, London

Enemuo, F C (2000) 'Problems and prospects of local governance', in Hyden, G, Olowu, D and Ogendo, H (eds) *African Perspectives on Governance*, Africa World Press, Trenton NJ, pp181–204

Environment and Urbanization (2001) Special issue on Civil Society in Action: Transforming Opportunities for the Urban Poor, 13(2)

Etemadi, F (1999) 'Urban governance, partnerships and poverty in Cebu'. *Urban Governance, Partnership and Poverty Working Paper* 13, IDD, University of Birmingham, Birmingham

Etemadi, F (2000) 'Civil society participation in city governance in Cebu city'. *Environment and Urbanization* 12(1): 57–72

Etemadi, F (2001) 'Towards inclusive urban governance'. *Urban Governance, Partnership and Poverty Working paper* 25, IDD, University of Birmingham, Birmingham

Evans, P (1996) 'Government action, social capital and development: reviewing the evidence on synergy'. *World Development* **24**(6): 1119–1132

Fainstein, S and Hirst, C (1995) 'Urban social movements', in Judge, D, Stoker, G and Wolman, H (eds) *Theories of Urban Politics*, Sage, London, pp181–204

Fanou, B and Grant, U, (2001) 'Poverty reduction and employment generation: the case of AGETUR, Benin'. *Urban Governance, Partnership and Poverty Working Paper* 29, IDD, University of Birmingham, Birmingham

Farvacque-Vitkovič, C and Godin, L (1998) *The Future of African Cities: Challenges and Priorities for Urban Development*, World Bank, Washington, DC

Fernando, A, Russell, S, Wilson, A and Vidler, E (1999) 'Urban governance, partnerships and poverty in Colombo'. *Urban Governance, Partnership and Poverty Working Paper* 9, IDD, University of Birmingham, Birmingham

Foley, M and Edwards, B (1999) 'Is it time to disinvest in social capital?' *Journal of Public Policy* **19**(2): 141–173

Fowler, A (1997) *Striking a Balance*, Earthscan, London

Freire, M and Stren, R (eds) (2001) *The Challenge of Urban Government: Policies and Practices*, World Bank Institute, Washington, DC

Friedmann, J (1998) 'The new political economy of planning: the rise and fall of civil society', in Douglass, M and Friedmann, J (eds) *Cities for Citizens: Planning and the Rise of Civil Society in a Global Age*, Wiley, Chichester, pp19–35

Frigenti, L et al, (1999) *Local Solutions to Regional Problems: The Growth of Social Funds and Public Works Employment Projects in Sub-Saharan Africa*, World Bank, Washington, DC

Gatabaki-Kamau, R with Rakodi, C and Devas N (1999), 'Urban governance, partnerships and poverty in Mombasa'. *Urban Governance, Partnership and Poverty Working Paper* 11, IDD, University of Birmingham, Birmingham

Gazzoli, R (1996) 'The political and institutional context of popular organizations in urban Argentina'. *Environment and Urbanization* **8**(1): 159–166

Gilbert, A (2000) 'Housing the Third World cities: the critical issues'. *Geography* **85**: 145–155

Gilbert, A and Gugler, J (1992) *Cities, Poverty and Development: Urbanization in the Third World*, Oxford University Press, Oxford

GJMC (1999) *iGoli 2002: Making the City Work*, Greater Johannesburg Metropolitan Council, Johannesburg

Goetz, A M and Gaventa, J (2001) *Bringing Citizen Voice and Client Focus into Service Delivery*, IDS Working Paper 128, Institute of Development Studies, Brighton

Gorman, R F (1984) *Private Voluntary Organizations as Agents of Development*, Westview Press, Boulder and London

Government of Ghana (1995) *Ghana Living Standard Surveys*, Accra

Grindle, M S (1980) *Politics and Policy Implementation in the Third World*, Princeton University Press, Princeton NJ

Grindle, M S and Thomas, J A (1990) 'After decision: Implementing policy reforms in developing countries'. *World Development* **18**(8): 1163–1181

Grootaert, C, Kanbur, R and Oh, G-T (1995) 'The dynamics of poverty: why some people escape from poverty and others don't. An African case study'. *World Bank Working Papers* No 1499, Washington, DC

Gupta, S, Davoodi, H and Alonso-Terme, R (1998) *Does Corruption Affect Income Inequality and Poverty?* Fiscal Affairs Department, International Monetary Fund, Washington, DC

Haddad, L, Ruel, M T, and Garrett, J l, (1999) 'Are urban poverty and undernutrition growing? Some newly assembled evidence'. *World Development* **27**(11): 1891–1904

Hagiopan, F (1994) 'Traditional politics against state transformation in Brazil', in Migdal J (ed) *State Power and Social Forces: Domination and Transformation in the Third World*, Cambridge University Press, Cambridge, pp36–64

Halfani, M (1996a) 'The challenge of urban governance in East Africa: responding to an unrelenting crisis', in McCarney, P (ed) *Cities and Governance: New Directions in Latin America, Asia and Africa*, Centre for Urban Community Studies, University of Toronto, pp183–204

Halfani, M (1996b) 'Marginality and dynamism: prospects for the Sub-Saharan African city' in Cohen, M, Ruble, B A, Tulchin, J S and Garland, A M (eds) *Preparing for the Urban Future, Global Pressures and Local Forces*, Woodrow Wilson Center Press, Washington, DC

Halfani, M (1997) 'Governance of urban development in East Africa', in Swilling, M (ed) *Governing Africa's Cities*, Witwatersrand University Press, Johannesburg, pp115–160

Hambleton, R (1990) 'Future directions for urban government in Britain and America', *Journal of Urban Affairs* **12**

Hardoy, A, Hardoy J E, and Schusterman, R (1991) 'Building community organization: the history of a squatter settlement and its own organizations in Buenos Aires'. *Environment and Urbanization* **3**(2): 104–120

Hardoy, J E, Mitlin, D and Satterthwaite, D (1992) *Environmental Problems in Third World Cities*, Earthscan, London

Hardoy, J E, Mitlin, D, Satterthwaite, D (2001) *Environmental Problems in an Urbanizing World: Finding Solutions for Cities in Africa, Asia and Latin America*, Earthscan, London

Harpham, T and Tanner, T (eds) (1995) *Urban Health in Developing Countries: Progress and Prospects*, Earthscan, London

Harris, N and Fabricius, I (eds) *Cities and Structural Adjustment*, UCL Press, London

Harrison, M E, and McVey, C E (1997) 'Conflict in the city: street trading in Mexico city'. *Third World Planning Review* **19**(3): 313–326

Harriss, J and de Renzio, P (1997) 'Missing link or analytically missing? The concept of social capital. An introductory bibliographic essay'. *Journal of International Development* **9**: 919–937

Hart, K (1973) 'Informal income opportunities and urban employment in Ghana', in Jolly, R, de Kadt, E, Singer, H and Wilson, F (eds) *Third World Employment*, Penguin, Harmondsworth, pp60–70

Held, D (1993) 'Democracy: from city-states to a cosmopolitan order?' in Held D (ed) *Prospects for Democracy: North, South, East, West*, Polity Press, Cambridge, pp13–51

Held, D (1996) *Models of Democracy*, Polity Press, Cambridge

Hirschmann, A (1984) *Getting Ahead Collectively*, Pergamon Press, Oxford

House, W, Ikiara, G and McCormick, D (1993) 'Urban self-employment in Kenya: Panacea or viable strategy?' *World Development* **21**(7): 1205–1223

Howes, M (1997) 'NGOs and the development of local institutions: a Ugandan case-study'. *Journal of Modern African Studies*, **35**(1): 17–35

Huchzermeyer, M (2001) 'Housing for the poor? Negotiated housing policy in South Africa'. *Habitat International* **25**: 303–331

Hulme, D and Edwards, M (eds) (1996) *Beyond the Magic Bullet: NGO Performance and Accountability in the Post-Cold War World*, Kumarian Press, West Hartford

Hulme, D and Edwards, M (eds) (1997) *NGOs, States and Donors: Too Close For Comfort?* Earthscan, London

Hurley, D (1990) *Income Generation Schemes for the Urban Poor*, Development Guidelines No. 4, Oxfam, Oxford

Hyden, G (1992) 'Governance and politics in Africa', in Hyden, G and Bratton, B (eds) *Governance and Politics in Africa*, Lynne Rienner, Boulder CO, pp1–26

Hyden, G and Bratton, B (eds) (1992) *Governance and Politics in Africa*, Lynne Rienner, Boulder CO

Hyden, G, Oluwu, D and Ogendo, H (eds) (2000) *African Perspectives on Governance*, Africa World Press, Trenton NJ

Imbroscio, D L (1997) *Reconstructing City Politics: Alternative Economic Development and Urban Regimes*, Sage, Thousand Oaks CA

International Labour Organization (1972) *Employment, Incomes and Equality in Kenya*, ILO, Geneva

Jacobs, J (1961) *Death and Life of Great American Cities*, Random House, New York

Jacobs, J (1984) *Cities and the Wealth of Nations*, Penguin, Harmondsworth

Jenkins, P (2001) 'Strengthening access to land for housing for the poor in Maputo, Mozambique'. *International Journal of Urban and Regional Research* 25(3): 629–648

Jerve, A M (2001) 'Rural–urban linkages and poverty analysis', in Grinspun, A (ed) *Choices for the Poor: Lessons from National Poverty Strategies*, United Nations Development Programme, New York, pp89–120

Johnson, C and Start, D (2001) 'Rights, claims and capture: understanding the politics of pro-poor policy', Working Paper 145, Overseas Development Institute, London

Jones, S (1999) 'Multi-layered responses to urban poverty: possible donor agency action', in Jones, S and Nelson, N (eds) *Urban Poverty in Africa: From Understanding to Alleviation*, Intermediate Technology Publications, London

Jones, S and Nelson, N (eds) (1999) *Urban Poverty in Africa: From Understanding to Alleviation*, Intermediate Technology Publications, London

Judge, D (1995) 'Pluralism', in Judge, D, Stoker, G and Wolman, H (eds) *Theories of Urban Politics*, Sage, London, pp13–34

Judge, D, Stoker, G and Wolman, H (eds) (1995) *Theories of Urban Politics*, Sage, London

Kanji, N (1995) 'Gender, poverty and economic adjustments in Harare, Zimbabwe'. *Environment and Urbanization* 7(1): 37–56

Kantor, P, Savitch, H V and Haddock S V (1997) 'The political economy of urban regimes: a comparative perspective'. *Urban Affairs Review* 32(2): 348–377

Karaos, A M A, Gatpatan, M V and Hotz, R V S J (1995) 'Making a difference: NGO and PO policy influence in urban land reform advocacy'. *PULSO (Pagsusuri Ukol Sa Lipunan At Simbahan), Monograph* No. 14, Institute on Church and Social Issues, Manila

Kasfir, N (1993) 'Designs and dilemmas of African decentralization' in Mawhood, P (ed) *Local Government in the Third World: Experience of Decentralization in Tropical Africa*, African Institute of South Africa, pp24–48

Kelly, R and Devas, N (2001) 'Revenue or revenues? An analysis of local business licences, with a case study of the Single Business Permit reform in Kenya'. *Public Administration and Development* 21: 381–391

Khan, A M (1997) *Shaping Policy: Do NGOs Matter? Lessons from India*, PRIA (Participatory Research in Asia), New Delhi

King, K (1996) *Jua Kali Kenya: Change and Development in an Informal Economy 1970–1995*, James Currey, London

King, R, Inkoom, D and Abrampah, K M (2001) 'Urban governance in Kumasi'. *Urban Governance, Partnership and Poverty Working Paper* 23, IDD, University of Birmingham, Birmingham

Klaarhamer, R (1989) 'The Chilean squatter movement and the state', in Schuurman, F and van Naerssen, T (eds) *Urban Social Movements in the Third World*, Routledge, London and New York, pp177–197

Korboe, D, Diaw, K and Devas, N (1999) 'Urban governance, partnerships and poverty in Kumasi'. *Urban Governance, Partnership and Poverty Working Paper* 10, IDD, University of Birmingham, Birmingham

Korten, D (1987) 'Third generation NGO strategies: a key to people-centred development'. *World Development* **15** (supplement): 145–160

Korten, D C (1990) *Getting into the 21st Century: Voluntary Action and the Global Agenda*, Kumarian Press, West Hartford

Kumar, S with Amis, P (1999) 'Urban governance, partnerships and poverty in Visakhapatnam'. *Urban Governance, Partnership and Poverty Working Paper* 17, IDD, University of Birmingham, Birmingham

Kyomuhendo, G B (1999) 'Decision-making in poor households: the case of Kampala, Uganda', in Jones, S and Nelson, N (eds) *Urban Poverty in Africa: From Understanding to Alleviation*, Intermediate Technology Publications, London

Leftwich, A (2000) *States of Development: On the Primacy of Politics in Development*, Polity Press, Cambridge

Lipton, M (1977) *Why Poor People Stay Poor: A Study of Urban Bias in World Development*, Temple Smith, London

Mabogunje, A (1995) 'Local institutions and an urban agenda for the 1990s', in Stren, R with Kjellberg Bell, J (eds) *Perspectives on the City: Volume 4 of Urban Research in the Developing World*, Centre for Urban Community Studies, University of Toronto, Toronto

Magutu, J (1997) 'An appraisal of Chaani low-income housing programme in Kenya'. *Environment and Urbanization* **9**(2): 307–320

Mais, P and Rakodi, C (1995) 'Urban poverty: concepts, characteristics and policies'. *Habitat International* **19**(4): 403–406

Malhotra, R (1997) 'Incidence of poverty in India: towards a consensus in estimating the poor'. *Indian Journal of Labour Economics* **40**(1)

Mamdani, M (1996) *Citizen and Subject: Contemporary Africa and the Legacy of Late Colonialism*, James Currey, London

Manor, J (1999) *The Political Economy of Democratic Decentralization*, World Bank, Washington, DC

Mawhood, P (1993) 'The search for participation in Tanzania', in Mawhood, P (ed), *Local Government in the Third World: Experience of Decentralization in Tropical Africa*, Africa Institute of South Africa, pp74–108

McCarney, P (ed) (1996): *Cities and Governance: New Directions in Latin America, Asia and Africa*, Centre for Urban Community Studies, University of Toronto, Toronto

McCarney, P, Halfani, M and Rodríguez, A, (1995) 'Towards an understanding of governance: the emergence of an idea and its implications for urban research in developing countries', in Stren, R with Kjellberg Bell, J (eds) *Perspectives on the City: Volume 4 of Urban Research in the Developing World*, Centre for Urban Community Studies, University of Toronto, Toronto, pp91–142

McGranahan, G and Satterthwaite, D (2002) The environmental dimensions of sustainable development for cities, *Geography* **87**: 213–226

Melo, M with Rezende, F and Lubambo, C (2001) 'Urban governance, accountability and poverty: the politics of participatory budgeting in Recife'. *Urban Governance, Partnerships and Poverty Research Working Paper* 27, IDD, University of Birmingham, Birmingham

Migdal, J (2001) *State and Society: Studying How States and Societies Transform and Constitute One Another*, Cambridge University Press, Cambridge

Miller, D (1993) 'Deliberative democracy and social choice', in Held, D (ed) *Prospects for Democracy: North, South, East, West*, Polity Press, Cambridge, pp74–92

Mills, A, Bennet, S and Russell, S (2001) *The Challenge of Health Sector Reform: What Must Governments Do?* Basingstoke, Palgrave

Mills, E S and Pernia, E M (1994) 'Introduction and overview', in Pernia, E M (ed) *Urban Poverty in Asia: A Survey of Critical Issues*, Oxford University Press, Oxford

Mitlin, D (1999) 'Civil society and urban poverty'. *Urban Governance, Partnership and Poverty Working Paper* 5, IDD, University of Birmingham, Birmingham

Mitlin, D (2000) 'Civil society and urban poverty: overview of stage 1 cases'. *Urban Governance, Partnership and Poverty Working Paper* 22, IDD, University of Birmingham, Birmingham

Mitlin, D (2001a) 'Addressing urban poverty: increasing incomes, reducing costs, securing representation'. *Development in Practice* 10(2): 204–216

Mitlin, D (2001b) 'Civil society and urban poverty: examining complexity'. *Environment and Urbanization* 13(2): 151–174

Moore M (1999) 'Politics against poverty: Global pessimism and national optimism'. *IDS Bulletin* 30(2): 33–46

Moser, C O N (1978) 'Informal sector or petty commodity production: Dualism or dependence in urban development?' *World Development* 6(9–10): 1041–1064

Moser, C O N (1996) 'Confronting crisis: a comparative study of household responses in four poor urban communities'. *Environmentally Sustainable Development Studies and Monograph Series* no.8, World Bank, Washington, DC

Moser, C O N (1998) 'The asset vulnerability framework: reassessing urban poverty reduction strategies'. *World Development* 26(1): 1–19

Moser, C O N and Holland, J (1995) *A Participatory Study of Urban Poverty and Violence in Jamaica*, Urban Development Division, World Bank, Washington, DC

Moser, C O N and Holland, J (1997) 'Household responses to poverty and vulnerability (Volume 4): confronting crisis in Chawama, Lusaka, Zambia'. *Urban Management Programme Policy Paper* No. 24, UMP, Nairobi

Moser, C O N and McIlwaine, C (1997) 'Household responses to poverty and vulnerability (Volume 3): confronting crisis in Commonwealth, Metro Manila, The Philipines'. *Urban Management Programme Policy Paper* No. 23, World Bank, Washington, DC

Moser, C O N and McIlwaine, C (2001) 'Violence and social capital in urban poor communities: perspectives from Colombia and Guatemala'. *Journal for International Development* 13: 965–984

Moser, C O N and Peake, L (eds) (1987) *Women, Human Settlements, and Housing*, Tavistock, London

Moser, C O N, Herbert, A J and Makonnen, R E (1993) 'Urban poverty in the context of structural adjustment: recent evidence and policy responses', *TWU Discussion Paper* DP4, Urban Development Division, World Bank, Washington, DC

Natrajan, I (1998) *Market Demographics*, National Council of Applied Economic Research, New Delhi

Nickson, A (1995) *Local Government in Latin America*, Lynne Rienner, Boulder CO

Nunan, F and Satterthwaite, D (1999) 'The urban environment'. *Urban Governance, Partnership and Poverty Working Paper* 6, IDD, University of Birmingham, Birmingham

Nunan, F and Satterthwaite, D (2000) 'Governance and the urban environment: a comparative analysis of nine city case studies'. *Urban Governance, Partnership and Poverty Working Paper* 21, IDD, University of Birmingham, Birmingham

Oates, W (1972) *Fiscal Federalism*, Harcourt Brace Jovanovitch Inc, New York

OECD (Organisation for Economic Co-operation and Development) (1988) *Voluntary Aid for Development: the Role of Nongovernmental Organizations*, OECD, Paris

OECD (2001) *Devolution and Globalisation: Implications for Local Decision-makers*, Organisation for Economic Co-operation and Development, Paris

Onibokun, P (1997) 'Governance and urban poverty in Anglophone West Africa', in Swilling, M (ed) *Governing Africa's Cities*, Witwatersrand University Press, Johannesburg, pp85–114

Osmani, S R (2001) 'Participatory governance and poverty reduction', in Grinspun, A (ed) *Choices for the Poor: Lessons from National Poverty Strategies*, United National Development Programme, New York, pp121–144

Parekh, B (1993) 'The cultural particularity of liberal democracy', in Held, D (ed) *Prospects for Democracy: North, South, East, West*, Polity Press, Cambridge, pp156–175

Peattie, L (1987) 'An idea in good currency and how it grew: the informal sector'. *World Development* **15**: 851–860

Peattie, L (1990) 'Participation: a case study of how invaders organize, negotiate and interact with government in Lima, Peru'. *Environment and Urbanization* **2**(1): 19–30

Perlman, J (1976) *The Myth of Marginality: Urban Politics and Poverty in Rio de Janiero*, University of California Press, London

Pernia, E M (ed) (1994) *Urban Poverty in Asia: A Survey of Critical Issues*, Oxford University Press, Hong Kong

Peters, G B (1998) ' "With a little help from our friends": Public–private partnerships as institutions and instruments', in Pierre, J (ed) *Partnerships in Urban Governance: European and American Experience*, Macmillan, Basingstoke

Pierre, J (ed) (1998) *Partnerships in Urban Governance: European and American Experience*, Macmillan, Basingstoke

Plummer, J (2000) *Municipalities and Community Participation: A Sourcebook for Capacity Building*, Earthscan, London

Plummer, J (2002) *Focusing Partnerships: A Sourcebook for Municipal Capacity Building in Public–Private Partnerships*, Earthscan, London

Polidano, C and Hulme, D (1997) 'No magic wands: Accountability and governance in developing countries'. *Regional Development Dialogue* **18**(2): 1–16

Pornchokchai, S (1992) *Bangkok Slums: Review and Recommendations*, School of Urban Community Research and Actions, Agency for Real Estate Affairs, Bangkok

Porrio, E (ed) (1997) 'Urban governance and poverty alleviation in Southeast Asia', in Porrio, E (ed) *Urban Governance and Poverty Alleviation in Southeast Asia*, Department of Sociology and Anthropology, Atteneo de Manila University, Quezon City, pp1–40

Portes, A, Castells, M and Benton, L A (eds) (1989) *The Informal Economy: Studies in Advanced and Less Developed Countries*, Johns Hopkins University Press, Baltimore, MD

Potter, R B and Lloyd-Evans, S (1998) *The City in the Developing World*, Longman, Harlow

Prud'homme, R (1995) 'The dangers of decentralization'. *The World Bank Research Observer* **10**(2): 201–220

Putman, R (1993) *Making Democracy Work: Civic Traditions in Modern Italy*, Princeton University Press, Princeton

Putzel, J (1997) 'Accounting for the "dark side" of social capital: reading Robert Putnam on democracy'. *Journal of International Development* **9**(7): 939–949

Quijano, N (1974) 'The marginal pole of the economy and the marginalized labor force'. *Economy and Society* **3**(4): 393–428

Raj, M (1993) 'Urbanization, infrastructure and besieged growth potential'. *Third World Planning Review* **15**(2): 159–174

Rakodi, C (1996) 'The opinions of health and water service users in Ghana'. Working Paper 10, *The Role of Government in Adjusting Economies Research*, IDD, University of Birmingham, Birmingham

Rakodi, C (1999a) 'A capital assets framework for analysing household livelihood strategies'. *Development Policy Review* **17**(3): 315–342

Rakodi, C (1999b) 'Urban governance and poverty: A preliminary exploration of the research issues'. *Urban Governance, Partnership and Poverty Working Paper* 8, IDD, University of Birmingham, Birmingham

Rakodi, C (2001) 'Urban politics and governance: a review of the literature'. *Urban Governance, Partnership and Poverty Working Paper* 30, IDD, University of Birmingham, Birmingham

Rakodi, C (2002) 'A livelihoods approach: conceptual issues and definitions', in Rakodi, C with Lloyd-Jones, T (eds) (2002) *Urban Livelihoods: A People-centred Approach to Reducing Poverty*, Earthscan, London

Rakodi, C with Lloyd-Jones, T (eds) (2002) *Sustainable Urban Livelihoods: A People-centred Approach to Reducing Poverty*, Earthscan, London, pp3–22

Rakodi, C, Gatabaki-Kamau, R and Devas, N (2000) 'Poverty and political conflict in Mombasa'. *Environment and Urbanization* **12**(1): 153–170

Rao, S L and Natrajan, I (1996) *Market Demographics*, National Council of Applied Economic Research, New Delhi

Rashid, A (1998) 'Ghaziabad, Orangi', in Arif Hasan (ed) *Community Initiatives: Four Case Studies from Karachi*, City Press, Karachi

Ravallion, M (2001) *On the Urbanization of Poverty*, Policy Research Working Paper 2586, World Bank, Washington, DC

Rhodes, R A W (1997) *Understanding Governance: Policy Networks, Governance, Reflexivity and Accountability*, Open University, Buckingham

Roberts, B (1995) *The Making of Citizens*, Edward Arnold, London

Robinson, M and White, G (1998) 'Civil society and social provision: the role of civic organisations', in Minogue, M, Polidano, C and Hulme, D (eds) *Beyond the New Public Management: New Directions in Latin America, Asia and Africa*, Edward Elgar, Cheltenham, pp228–245

Rodríguez, A and Winchester, L (1999) 'Urban governance, partnerships and poverty in Santiago'. *Urban Governance, Partnership and Poverty Working Paper* 14, IDD, University of Birmingham, Birmingham

Rodrik, D (2000) 'Institutions for high quality growth: What are they and how to get them?' *Comparative International Development* **33**(3): 2–31

Roy, A (2001) *The Algebra of Infinite Justice*, Penguin, New Delhi

Ruble, B A, Tulchin, J S and Garland, A M (1996) 'Introduction: globalism and local realities: five paths to the urban future', in Cohen, M, Ruble, B A, Tulchin, J S and Garland, A M (eds) *Preparing for the Urban Future, Global Pressures and Local Forces*, Woodrow Wilson Center Press, Washington, DC

Rüland, J (1992) *Urban Development in Southeast Asia: Regional Cities and Local Government*, Westview, Boulder CO

Rüland, J (ed) (1996) *The Dynamics of Metropolitan Management in Southeast Asia*, Institute of Southeast Asian Studies, Singapore

Russell, S (1999) 'Community Development Councils: grassroots testimony on Community Development Councils: local activists' experience and perspectives', in Fernando, A, Russell, S, Wilson, A and Vidler, E, 'Urban governance and poverty in partnerships. Colombo *Urban Governance, Partnership and Poverty Working Paper* 9, IDD, University of Birmingham, Birmingham

Russell, S and Vidler, E (2000) 'The rise and fall of government–community partnerships in urban development: grassroots testimony from Colombo'. *Environment and Urbanization* **12**(1): 307–316

Rutherford, S (2000) *The Poor and their Money*, Oxford University Press, New Delhi

Sahley, C and Pratt, B (2003) 'NGO responses to urban poverty: service providers or partners in planning?' *INTRAC NGO Management and Policy Series* No. 9, Oxford

Sahn, D E, Dorosh, P A and Younger, S D (1997) *Structural Adjustment Reconsidered: Economic Policy and Poverty in Africa*, Cambridge University Press, Cambridge

Salamon, L M and Anheier, H K (1992) 'In search of the non-profit sector 1: the question of definitions'. *Johns Hopkins Comparative Nonprofit Sector Project Working Paper 2*, Johns Hopkins University, Institute for Policy Studies

Sassen, S (1994) *Cities in a World Economy*, Pine Forge Press, Thousand Oaks CA

Satterthwaite, D (1995) 'The underestimation and misrepresentation of urban poverty'. *Environment and Urbanization*, **7**(1): 3–10

Satterthwaite, D (1997) *Urban Poverty: Reconsidering Its Scale and Nature*, International Institute for Environment and Development, London

Satterthwaite, D (2001) 'Reducing urban poverty: drawing lessons from recent urban programmes'. *Urban Governance, Partnership and Poverty Working Paper* 31, IDD, University of Birmingham, Birmingham

Savitch, H V and Thomas, J C (eds) (1991) *Big City Politics in Transition*, Urban Affairs Annual Review 38/Sage, Newbury Park CA

Scheper-Hughes, N (1992) *Death Without Weeping: the Violence of Everyday Life in Brazil*, University of California Press, Berkeley

Schneider, A (2002) 'Decentralization and the poor', paper presented to the American Political Science Association, Boston, MA

Sen, A (2000) *Development as Freedom*, Oxford University Press, New Delhi

Sepeheri, A and Chernomas, R (2001) 'Are user charges efficiency and equity-enhancing?' *Journal of International Development* **13**: 183–210

Sharpe, L J (ed) (1995) *The Government of World Cities: The Future of the Metro Model*, John Wiley & Son, Chichester

Shepherd, A (2000) 'Governance, good governance and poverty reduction'. *International Review of Administrative Science* **22**(2): 269–284

Shirk, S L (1993) *The Political Logic of Economic Reform in China*, University of California Press, Berkeley

Simon, D (1992) *Cities, Capital and Development: African Cities in the World Economy*, Belhaven Press and Halsted Press, London and New York

Sivaramakrishnan, K C and Green, L (1986) *Metropolitan Management: The Asian Experience*, Economic Development Institute of the World Bank, Washington, DC

Smit, W (1998) 'The rural linkages of urban households in Durban, South Africa'. *Environment and Urbanization* **10**(1): 77–87

Smith, D A (1996) *Third World Cities in a Global Perspective*, Westview, Boulder CO

South Africa: Department of Water Affairs and Forestry (1994) Water Supply and Sanitation White Paper, Pretoria, Department of Water Affairs and Forestry

Souza, C (2001) 'Participatory budgeting in Brazilian Cities: Limits and Possibilities in Building Democratic Institutions'. *Urban Governance, Partnership and Poverty Research Working Paper* 28, IDD, University of Birmingham, Birmingham

Standing, G, Sender, J and Weeks, J (1996) *Restructuring the Labour Market: The South African Challenge*, International Labour Office, Geneva

Stoker, G (1995) 'Regime theory and urban politics', in Judge, D, Stoker, G and Wolman, H (eds) *Theories of Urban Politics*, Sage, London

Stoker, G (1998) 'Public private partnerships and urban governance', in Pierre, J (ed) *Partnerships in Urban Governance: European and American Experience*, Macmillan, Basingstoke, pp34–51

Stren, R E (1978) *Housing the Urban Poor in Africa: Policy, Politics, and Bureaucracy in Mombasa*, Institute of International Studies, University of California, Berkeley

Stren, R E and White, R R (eds) (1989) *African Cities in Crisis: Managing Rapid Urban Growth*, Westview, Boulder CO

Stren, R with Kjellberg Bell, J (eds) (1995) *Perspectives on the City: Volume 4 of Urban Research in the Developing World*, Centre for Urban Community Studies, University of Toronto, Toronto, pp19–46

Swilling, M (ed) (1997) *Governing Africa's Cities*, Witwatersrand University Press, Johannesburg

Tacoli, C (1998) 'Rural–urban interactions: a guide to the literature'. *Environment and Urbanization* **10**(1): 147–166

Tacoli, C (1999) 'Rural–urban interactions'. *Urban Governance, Partnership and Poverty Working Paper* 7 IDD, University of Birmingham, Birmingham

Tanzi, V (1995) 'Fiscal federalism and decentralization: a review of some efficiency and macroeconomic aspects'. *Annual World Bank Conference on Development Economics 1995*, World Bank, Washington, DC

Tendler, J (1997) *Good Government in the Tropics*, Johns Hopkins University Press, Baltimore and London

Thomas, J (1992) *Informal Economic Activity*, Harvester, Wheatsheaf, London and New York

Thorbek, S (1991) 'Gender in two slum cultures'. *Environment and Urbanization* **3**(2): 71–81

Thurman, S (1994) 'Community development in Kenya: a review of the issues and proposals for action', Mimeo, Ford Foundation, Nairobi

Tokman, V (1991) 'The informal sector in Latin America: from underground to legality' in G. Standing and V. Tokman (eds) *Toward Social Adjustment: Labour Market Issues in Structural Adjustment*, International Labour Office (ILO), Geneva, pp141–157

Tomlinson, R (1996) 'The changing nature of Johannesburg's economy' in Harris, N and Fabricius, I (eds) *Cities and Structural Adjustment*, University College Press, London

Tovey, K (2002) The institutional responses to the water needs of the urban poor: A study of collective action in Delhi slums, India, Dissertation submitted to the University of Cambridge

Turner, B (ed) (1988) *Building Community: A Third World Case Book from Habitat International Coalition*, Habitat International Coalition, London

UNCHS (1996) *An Urbanizing World: Global Report on Human Settlements 1996*, United Nations Centre for Human Settlements (Habitat)/Oxford University Press, Oxford

UN-Habitat (2001a) *Cities in a Globalizing World: Global Report on Human Settlements 2001*, United Nations Centre for Human Settlements (Habitat)/Earthscan, London

UN-Habitat (2001b) *Good Urban Governance: A Normative Framework*, Summary for the Preparatory Committee for the Special Session of the General Assembly for an Overall Review and Appraisal of the Implementation of the Habitat Agenda, Nairobi, February

UNDP (1996) *Human Development Report, 1996*, United Nations Development Programme, New York

UNDP (1997a) *Corruption and Good Governance*, Management Development and Governance Division, Bureau for Policy and Programme Support, United Nations Development Programme, New York

UNDP (1997b) *Reconceptualising Governance*, Discussion Paper 2, Management Development and Governance Division, Bureau for Policy and Programme Support, United Nations Development Programme, New York

UNDP (2000a) *Overcoming Human Poverty: UNDP Poverty Report 2000*, United Nations Development Programme, New York

UNDP (2000b) *The Urban Governance Initiative*, United Nations Development Programme, Kuala Lumpur

van der Hoff, R and Steinberg, F (eds) (1992) *Innovative Approaches to Urban Development*, Avebury, Aldershot

van der Linden, J (1997) 'On popular participation in a culture of patronage: patrons and grass roots organizations in a sites and services project in Hyderabad, Pakistan'. *Environment and Urbanization* **9**(1): 81–90

Vanderschueren, F, Wegelin, E and Wekwete, K (1999) *Policy Programme Options for Urban Poverty Reduction: A Framework for Action at Municipal Level*, Urban Management Programme, World Bank, Washington, DC

Van Naerssen, T (2001) 'Cities and the globalization of urban development policy', in Schuurman, F J (ed) *Globalization and Development Studies*, Sage, London

Verhagen, K (1987) *Self-help Promotion: A Challenge to the NGO Community*, Cebemo/Royal Tropical Institute, Amsterdam

Vidler, E (1999) 'City economic growth'. *Urban Governance, Partnership and Poverty Working paper* 1, IDD, University of Birmingham, Birmingham

Volbeda, S (2002) 'Economic networks and the importance of rural–urban linkages, with the focus on Sub-Saharan Africa', in Baud, I S A and Post, J (eds) *Realigning Actors in an Urbanizing World: Governance and Institutions from a Development Perspective*, Ashgate, Aldershot, pp287–312

Von Braun, J and Grote, U (2000) 'Does decentralization serve the poor?' Paper for IMF Conference on Fiscal Decentralization, International Monetary Fund, Washington, DC

Walton, J (1998) 'Urban conflict and social movements in poor countries: theory and evidence of collective action'. *International Journal of Urban and Regional Research* **22**(3): 460–481

Wanyande, P (2000) 'Structural adjustment and governance', in Hyden, G, Olowu, D and Ogendo, H (eds) *African Perspectives on Governance*, Africa World Press, Trenton NJ, pp237–267

Watkins, K (1998) *Economic Growth with Equity: Lessons from East Asia*, Oxfam Publications, Oxford

Werna, E (2000) *Combating Urban Inequalities: Challenges for Managing Cities in the Developing World*, Edward Elgar, Cheltenham

Wolman, H and Goldsmith, M (1992) *Urban Politics and Policy: A Comparative Approach*, Blackwell, Oxford

Wood, G (2003) 'Staying secure, staying poor: the Faustian bargain'. *World Development* **31**(3): 455–471

World Bank (1990) *World Development Report: Poverty*, World Bank, Washington, DC

World Bank (1992) *Governance and Development*, World Bank, Washington, DC

World Bank (1995) *Sri Lanka Poverty Assessment*, World Bank, Washington, DC

World Bank (1997) *The State in a Changing World: World Development Report 1997*, World Bank, Washington, DC

World Bank (2000) *Entering the 21st Century: World Development Report 1999/2000*, World Bank, Washington, DC

World Bank (2001a) *Attacking Poverty: World Development Report 2000/01*, World Bank, Washington, DC

World Bank (2001b) *World Development Indicators 2001*, World Bank, Washington, DC

World Bank (2002a) *World Development Indicators*, World Bank, Washington, DC

World Bank/IMF (2002b) *Poverty Reduction Strategies and PRSPs*, PovertyNet, World Bank, www.worldbank.org/poverty/strategies/overview.htm

Wratten, E (1995) 'Conceptualizing urban poverty'. *Environment and Urbanization* **7**(1): 11–36

Index

absolute poverty 16, 17
access
  city comparisons 188
  employment 57
  financial accounts 118
  informal politics 77, 78
  land 55, 151, 164–185, 198
  opportunities 46
  services 2, 51, 54, 164–185, 198
  well-being 3
accountability
  decision-making 163
  democratization 33–34
  elections 176–177
  mechanisms of 117–118
  policy 196
  public 24, 81, 121
advocacy 86, 137–139
Ahmedabad, India
  city overviews 6–7, 20, 188
  civil society 128, 180–182
  contracted-out services 179
  informal sector 50, 66, 155
  labour markets 59, 147
  legitimacy 73–74
  peripheral settlements 97
  spending patterns 108
  see also India
alliances 88–89
apartheid 71, 101
assets 22, 149–152
attitudes 188
authority aspects 28, 33, 70–71, 118, 171,
  196–197

bad governance 190, 194
Bangalore, India
  access 151, 168, 169–170
  accountability 177
  city overviews 7–8, 20, 188
  civil society 128, 182
  decentralization 74, 77–78, 79
  economy 46–47, 48, 105, 108
  high-tech industry 44, 47

  informal sector 63, 156–157
  labour markets 57, 147
  responsibilities 98
  see also India
barangays 8, 84, 86, 108, 119, 120, 141,
  163, 167, 192
basic needs 16
  see also services
Benin 45
boundaries 80, 97, 193, 197
Brazil 19, 31, 70–71, 74–76, 114
  see also Recife, Brazil
budgetary processes 34, 110–112
  see also expenditure; participatory
  budgeting

capacity 4, 100, 176, 188, 190
capital 4, 22, 46, 64–66, 149, 150
care economy 60–61
casual labour 44–46, 59
Cebu City, Philippines
  access 167–168, 173, 174, 175–176,
  177
  city overviews 7, 8, 18, 20, 188
  conflicts 114
  decentralization 74, 75–76, 119, 120
  financial resources 105, 108
  informal sector 47, 128, 138, 154,
  155–156
  labour markets 43, 147
  NGOs 180
  participation 141–142
  political context 89, 161, 163
  societal representation 83
chief executives 81–82
Chile 71–72, 73, 76, 81, 173–174
  see also Santiago, Chile
citizenship 73
civil society
  advocacy 86
  city overviews 6, 182, 188
  defining 26
  democratization 33, 71–72, 93
  financial resources 112–113